The Long Horizon

THE LONG HORIZON

Iain R. Thomson

Illustrations by the author

Birlinn

This edition published in 2002 by
Birlinn Limited
West Newington House
10 Newington Road
Edinburgh
EH9 1QS

www.birlinn.co.uk

First published in 1999 by
Strathglass Books

ISBN 1 84158 180 1

British Library Cataloguing-in-Publication Data
A catalogue record for this book is available from the British Library

Printed and bound by Cox & Wyman Ltd, Reading

To Hector

Contents

Acknowledgments

Appreciations for the completion of this book are due to many, but in particular to Betty for proof reading and dealing with my bizar, sorry, my bizaar spelling. To Alison and John Ross for helpful comment and supplying the electricity. To Oliver Griffin for providing me with a very good, but tricky, printing machine. Iain MacKay and Ewen MacRae who jogged my memory and supplied some of the stories. Giles Foster, Malcolm Fraser and the staff at the Lovat Estate office for help and obligement. For the safe deliverance of a lost manuscript from the innards of my treacherous computer praise goes to Julia Russell. But by no means least, gratitude must go to the friends who persisted in asking me when I would finish writing, and to Jane for much encouragement and a bottle of Rare Malt which ensured that I did. Thank you all.

The books from which I have drawn factual material for some of the background are:-

Lovat of the '45, W.MacKenzie.

Lord Lovat, 1871-1933, The Rt. Hon. Sir Francis Lindley.

The papers of the Commissioners for the Forfeited Estates.

The Highland Floods, Sir Thomas Dick Lauder.

Particular recognition for the inspiration felt in writing certain parts of The Long Horizon is due to my regard for the late Lord Lovat's memoir, March Past.

Grateful acknowledgments for use of photos go to :-

Giles Foster and Malcolm Fraser, Lovat Estate office, Beauly

Bill, Ann and Willie Fraser, The Lovat Arms Hotel, Beauly,

Duncan Chisholm and Sons, Kiltmakers, Castle St. Inverness,

City of Aberdeen Art Gallery and Museums Collection,

Farmers Weekly,

Iain MacKay, Kilmorack, Beauly,

Biddy MacLeod, Kilmorack, Beauly,

Ewan MacRae, Farley, Beauly,

Archie Chisholm, Kirkhill, Inverness,

Robbie Fraser, Tornagrain, Cawdor, Nairn,

Alex and Lil Murray, Lurgan, Aberfeldy, Perthshire.

Cruinassie, June 1999

FOREWORD BY LORD LOVAT

It is my pleasure to add comment to a book in which the name of Fraser is one of the threads in a tapestry of Highland life long past and not so distant. Iain Thomson understands, and indeed, is part of it's subtleties, weaknesses and strengths.

The pace of today's change is so rapid and complete that a work in which the author can illustrate at first hand the ways of life and attitudes of a vanished generation is a welcome contribution for all those of us who revere our ancestry and inheritance.

Of the Frasers of yore, there is no attempt to 'gild the lily', they are shown with foibles and sometimes folly, yet the author manages to convey the sneaking regard and affection the Highlanders must have felt even for the old rascal Simon of the '45.' Nearer at hand Thomson clearly shows his admiration for my grandfather and his role during the second World War and this I much appreciate. For the Frasers of today there is much to savour of the bonds of clanship. For all, there is enjoyment and an insight on the workings of a rural parish with it's heart in the land of the Lovat Estates.

Many families, however successful, can suffer tragedies, and I am grateful to him that those of recent years which have befallen my family are treated with sympathy and respect. In turn I extend to him my feelings of regret for his own loss.

It is perhaps at the croft door or on the hill that Thomson's love of the land of his forebears is best felt, and for today's rushing world there lies quietly behind story and laughter the poetry of a communion with the Great Unknown, which for many readers will be his book's lasting strength.

Lovat.

Lovat Estate Office,
Beauly,
Inverness-shire.

June 1999.

Long Horizons, lost

There's many a mile,
O'er many's a stile,
But there's aye a hintward glance,
To the lang syne days,
And the old folk's ways,
And the hills of the heart's romance.

Prelude

EYE TO THE HILLS

Two figures, one black, one white, stood on the spreading African plain where human life took form. Ahead, the buffalo grazed step by step towards a thicket. Under the acacia tree he would lie up and cud, for rare is the chance of shade on the plains. The sun is master.

The buffalo paused, raised its head, swelling the arch of his proud black neck. Motionless, it stared. An animal known to attack and kill without warning, the rifleman stepped the pathway of danger and knew the utter thrill of dicing with life. The oxpecker birds fled twittering to the thicket. Man and beast drew breath, slowly, steadily, deeply.

A light touch on the white man's shoulder, "Now Massa." Andrew Fraser, fourth and youngest son of Lord Lovat stood square. He fired from the shoulder as his forebears had done amongst the stag roaring hills of Strathfarrar in the days of the great stalk.

The bullet sliced the mane. The beast whirled, hind legs dug, a crescendo bellow split the plains, it flew upon its assailant demented in the rage of pain.

Fraser stood, fired, a second, a third, the battering head came low, a rifle length, the last shot. The mammoth beast crashed with a lunging curve of horn that sliced the hunter through the thigh.

The black man looked down into pleading eyes, then gradually away to gaze on the western hills. They shimmered with doubt in the blaze of the day. Yet by the cool of the evening he knew would emerge, in all clearness, the long horizon at the edge of the world. And in the night, the solace of the stars.

Two widening red pools seeped onto the gently winnowing savannah. Slowly, on the baked earth, the blood mingled, man and beast. And, in the unblemished blue of the African sky, the black man with ancient wisdom, believed their spirits joined.

Amongst the spring birch on a bracken knoll Kim Fraser tuned the pipes. His sombre tartan, the Hunting Fraser, dark with the natural dyes of bog and oak, is the kilt of heather moorland and the silent corrie of a stealthy stalk. It fitted the day. He would lament, through the great music of the Gael, the corpse of Andrew, his dead brother. On the shoulders of kinsmen it would be borne from the porch of the church to its place of rest on a sheep grazed mound beside the plain granite slabs of the Barons of Lovat.

I walked the little way to the Church of Saint Mary's of Eskadale. White, hidden and private, upon an oak and pine sheltered rise it glimpsed in the soft running river the snow peaked reflections of the far hills of Strathfarrar and carried their hope of salvation to the heart of a Sacred place in the quiet of Strathglass.

Many bonded by blood, the congregation bowed, clan and loyalty strong. Rarely in today's diverse world could there be such a gathering of shared name and origin. Simon Fraser, Master of Lovat represented his aged and infirm father, the 17th Chief of Clan Fraser at the funeral, and with his sisters escorted Lady Lovat, crumpled with grief, to her pew beside the coffin.

Foxhounds bristled about the lawns of Beaufort Castle. A trail had been laid. All was ready for the drag hunt. Milling and chattering, a colourful concourse gathered under the spring sun of promise. Eager side stepping horses gleamed in its inviting light, heads tossing to be away. Riders took refreshment. Neil MacKay the piper struck a lively march and the hunt, watched by Lady Lovat from the Castle, moved off at a smart trot, led by Simon Fraser, the Master of Lovat.

At the foot of a sloping field known as the Lurigs, the riders paused and grouped together, jolly and chaffing. The piper played, the hounds circled, the Master of Lovat sat his horse and looked about the field. He leant and spoke to Donald Fraser, "Are the hounds alright?" His eyes glazed. A searing pain. Fraser caught him as he slumped from the horse's neck. The Master of Lovat lay on the field of the Lurigs, ashen white face against the blood red of his jacket. Hamish the Vet ran swiftly across and looked down. "He's dead." he said calmly, and walked away.

But three days had passed since the funeral of Andrew Fraser. On March 26th 1994, he too, Simon Fraser, the Master of Lovat, oldest of the brothers and heir to the title, was dead.

Balblair House stands on a ridge looking down on the ancient fording place of the river Beauly. Simon Fraser, 17th Lord Lovat, ill and infirm sat bowed. The centuries of history drifted through his mind. Across the river the Beauly Priory lay in his sight, symbol of the religion to which his family had clung. It was twelve months to the day since the death of his youngest and closest son, Andrew. Twelve months less a week since the death of his heir, the Master.

Lord Lovat, brave amidst brave, lifted the eye of his soul to the great breadth of hills, distant as youth, and in spirit set out, beyond the long horizon.

Lady Lovat hurried home from the Eskadale Church and the Memorial Mass for her sons. Simon Fraser, 'Shimi Lovat', roused himself, looked to her, and asked for the boys. She cradled his head and closed his eyes.

THE GREATEST
LORD LOVAT EVER

Norman in origin, the Frasers were in all probability henchmen to William the Conqueror, Duke of Normandy, and would have rampaged across the channel on a day ticket in 1066 to help win the Battle of Hastings. By the twelfth century and heading north, things were going even better. Sir Alexander Fraser married Mary, a sister of Robert the Bruce, became Chamberlain of Scotland and the Frasers had learnt that campaigning below the bedsheets was as useful as swinging the broadsword above them.

Many of the Norman aristocracy were of Viking blood and fighting apart, it is said these seafaring adventurers had three passionate loves, their ships, their cattle, and comely women. The early Frasers were merely land based pirates and their followers would have been local to the north west of France. Many true Frasers today are not unlike the Bretons, thick set hirsute people with brown eyes and dark hair.

The Lovat Frasers claim their descent from Sir Simon Fraser, brother of Sir Alexander the Chamberlain. This is the first recorded use of the name Simon which for seven hundred years has been the christian name of the Lovat's eldest son. The style in the Gaelic, MacShimidh, Son of Simon, refers to the Chief in general conversation but he is simply Shimi to all familiar with him. Throughout Clan Fraser, Simon was widely favoured as a first name but now after six centuries it's wearing thin, today's nuclear family needs novelty if not film star fantasy. Craig, Clint and Liams are creeping in.

The patriarchal Sir Simon during the War of Succession appeared no slouch with a sword. As recognition for treating the English invaders to stinging defeats three times in a day, he was awarded the honour of bearing three crowns on his Coat of Arms. There the motif remains. Splendid 'Boy's Own' stuff. Sadly upon capture, his efforts were further recognised by Edward the 1st, 'Hammer of the Scots' who had him executed.

Byron penned 'England thy beauties are tame and domestic', and who would contradict him?. By the end of the twelfth century, having reached the Borders, the Frasers were understandably bored with life in Tweeddale. Given Viking blood it should be no surprise these Norse venturers felt the pull of northern skies and abandoned their southern airts for the wider horizons of the Highlands.

The date of the Fraser 'flitting' is not recorded accurately but around the end of the twelve hundreds the Bisset family owned most of the fertile ground west of Inverness at the head of the Beauly Firth. On arrival in the area the Frasers, never backward where self interest featured, remedied any short comings in their status, due to a lack of real estate, by well considered marriages. The title Lovat was taken through a marriage of a Simon Fraser to Margaret, daughter of Graham of Lovat who must have held some of the clay marshland on the south side of the Firth and Beaufort was added by similar arrangement. Sound bed chamber policy, ever the tool of progress, and thus, with the acquisition of these desirable lands, swelled both Fraser pride and heritage.

During the early centuries of their history the Lovats openly boasted Norman origins, setting their civilised manners and superiority against the crude behaviour and brutish existence of the locals. There is no record of violence as they pushed north but resentment there must have been, except perhaps where their strong hand afforded a measure of protection. Either way they were the 'white settlers' of their day.

Lying a little south of the mouth of the Beauly river the present site of the Wester Lovat farmhouse and steading occupied a strategic position in olden days. From a slight eminence it overlooked the only fordable point of the river in its first twenty miles. On the wide lands north of this ford, flood free and fertile the Beauly Priory had been founded by John Bisset, another Norman, in 1230 A.D. For three centuries the Order of Valliscaulian monks kept alight 'the lamp of learning in the north' and during these years the great lairds of the district dispatched their boys to this 'local' school. The roll call included Kintail MacKenzies, Balnagown Rosses, the Munros of Foulis and in 1375 the Master of Lovat dawdled across to his classes from Castle Dounie.

Packmen and prelates, drovers and dogs, armies with the flying colours of advance or in the rags of retreat, all must have passed under the eye of this ancient Fraser stronghold as flanked by the hills and hemmed by the tide they forded the shingled waters of the Beauly with lunging horse and glinting hoof.

Such romantic conjectures sometimes occupied the enquiring mind of Donald Evan Coghill who tenanted the farm of Wester Lovat in succession to his father Robert. Hardiest of Caithness stock, Robert Coghill had brought family and flitting on the long haul from the North under a tarpaulin sheet on a little grey 'Fergie' tractor and trailer. Don Evan, whose husbandry of this namely clay farm could not be bettered, none the less did not allow the glaur to clog mind or boots and maintained a lively interest in matters antiquarian.

Having discovered through marks in his corn crops an ancient stone causeway leading from the fordable point of the river up the fields towards his buildings, Coghill determined to investigate. Was the track prehistoric, had the monks toiled in penance? Or, perhaps after the battle of Mons Graupius, fought it is believed in the outback of Aberdeenshire, the victorious Romans tramped at least as far as the Wester Lovat ford and threw up a marching camp in the vicinity of the antiquarian's steading. The latter theory was engaging.

In the absence of such luminaries of the archeological profession as Sir Mortimer Wheeler and knowing my passing interest in such matters, Coghill invited me to front the 'dig'. I arrived one sunny Saturday afternoon with a hydraulic digger on the back of my four wheeled drive tractor. Practical, but hardly the tool of sensitive research, I dismissed such shortcomings and waited instructions.

Don Evan paced thoughtfully to and fro. Suddenly, at no distance from his steading, he drew a line with his walking stick at right angles to a slight depression in an otherwise flat area. "Here," Aaron like he struck the ground. Divine guidance, inspired guesswork or the ghostly voice of Agricola in his ear? I boldly stuck in the digger bucket, though dubious of Coghill's grip on Latin.

Our aid to archeological enlightenment uncovered in moments material which might occupy a team of professional 'sifters' for a month. Lo and behold after the first few bucketfuls the feel of the machine told me the ground had been moved at some time in the past. Above the roar I imparted this piece of research information. The antiquarian peered eagerly down the trench.

Pulling levers with the speed of a barman at closing time, I excavated a slit twenty feet long by ten feet deep and risking an unembalmed entombment we clambered down. Sure enough I had cut across a large moat like channel. Its profile showed clearly on the wall of the 'dig'. Was it the defence ditch of a Roman marching camp? We sat, and being working chaps thought of the sweat involved in its digging. Did the triumphant Ninth Legion really toil here? The evening sun hid its smile behind a cloud. I filled the hole and the mystery was left to deepen.

Some years later Don Evan retired from farming and built a fine house overlooking the Beauly Firth. It enjoys an extensive garden and on visiting my friend to see how the 'chez nous' was coming along I found him at the far corner of the ground directing a digger machine in the erecting of a standing stone of prehistoric proportions.

I enquired seriously about its alignment, "Does it tip the summer solstice from your bedroom window?" He shook his head. "Some planetary sighting?" I pressed him. "Not really," he replied innocently in his slow Northern accent. "but if the beggars four thousand years from now do as much head scratching over this one as I've done over the ones built four thousand years ago, I'll be quite pleased." I admired his Caithness wit.

When the Scots buried their dead after the slaughter of Flodden in 1513, counted amongst the 'Flowers of the Forest' was the Master of Lovat. Only a generation was to pass before, in 1544, the heir and pride of Clan Fraser would again stain the turf of his homeland with his blood.

Amidst the far reaches of the Great Glen which divide the Highlands of the north from Scotland, the day dawdled in dreams, lulled by the fragrance of buttercup meadows. The waters of Loch Lochy lay without breath in the heat of high summer, and on its surface the blue tailed dragonflies danced in the simple happiness of a yellow world of sun and flowers.

Beside the shore the Clansmen fought, stripped to the waist, slipping, panting. Fraser against MacDonald, claymore cleaving bare flesh, screaming, dying in the scent of rich red blood. Brave blood, spilt amongst white garlands of daisies left only sadness in the homes. Blar na Leine, the Battle of the Shirts it was called. Few survived.

Hugh the third Lord Lovat together with his eldest son, the Master of Lovat, were cut down. This promising boy, just nineteen and only weeks home from an education at the University of Paris was bidden by his father to remain safe at Castle Dounie but taunted by his stepmother hurried over the hills and took the field, eager for the honour of his Clan.

Lovat saw his son butchered and lost heart. Of the three hundred Frasers who fought, scarce a half dozen left the field. The MacDonalds fared little better though their leader the doughty John of Moidart survived. For Clan Fraser the loss of manhood was devastating. Story has it that eighty gentlemen of the House of Fraser perished but had wisely left their wives pregnant, and in due course, each bore a son. Records claim, perhaps more realistically, at a marshalling of the clan's fighting men in July 1574 before the succeeding Lord

Lovat 'he had eighty young gentlemen with him whose fathers proudly fell on the Field of Lochy thirty years before.'

Blood of the Viking. Courage that led from the front, not your modern General safe at the back sending men to their slaughter. Not the watered down version of men that pass for leaders in today's aftershave world, but men that lead by strength of arm, force of personality, and sometimes, as we shall see, a vulpine streak of sheer cunning.

'The greatest Lord Lovat that ever was.' Not the claim of hindsight but an avowed statement of intent by Simon Fraser of Beaufort. His attainments transcended even the fertile imagination of this incorrigible braggart and romancer. For sheer style, plausibility and ingratiating charm, few can have been his equal. Behind this facade however lay a totally ruthless, mendacious self-seeker who confused the concepts of greatness and notoriety and proceeded to achieve the latter with conspicuous success. Already in 1696 by the age of twenty, Simon of Beaufort had sought to secure the Lovat title through an abduction, a forced marriage and rape.

Hugh, the 11th Lord Lovat, in the sixteen hundreds was married to a daughter of the all powerful Marquis of Atholl, Chief of Clan Murray who from his vast estates south of the Grampians controlled the route to the Highlands. An irksome fact for the Frasers who now possessed some of the finest and most extensive estates in the north of Scotland. Hugh's brood of children lacked a son and his will as a consequence ascribed these coveted lands throughout the Highlands to Amelia the eldest of his four girls. The prestigious Lovat title however must go to any 'true' Fraser she should marry.

Strange to relate during the year of his death, Hugh, the 11th laird, travelled to London accompanied by none other than his unctuous cousin, Simon Fraser, and whilst there executed a deed annulling the previous will to his daughter Amelia and conveying the prestigious properties to Simon's elderly father Thomas of Beaufort. For good measure there was a bond for fifty thousand merks left in favour of his attentive cousin, young Simon.

Hugh the 11th was barely cold when Thomas of Beaufort assumed the Lovat title and its possessions, which naturally made his son Simon the lawful successor. Mortified, the Murrays silently ground teeth and sword. A contemporary assertion had it that Hugh's final will was a fabrication, the view being taken that forgery came well within the scope of Simon's nefarious accomplishments but the signed will existed and that was good enough for a Fraser.

The immensely powerful Murrays whose fingers helped bake the pie of Scottish affairs were not a tribe to trifle with, least of all where honour and self interest coincided. Understandably they refused to recognise the validity of Beaufort's claims and were outraged at Simon's cool notion of marrying Amelia, heiress in their eyes, to the very estates of which Simon had defrauded them. Though only a girl of ten they promptly betrothed her to the Master of Saltoun, heir to Lord Fraser of Saltoun, head of the Aberdeenshire branch of the clan, thereby neatly meeting the condition in the original will that the innocent Amelia must marry a 'true' Fraser.

Pompously, and not a little presumptuously, Lord Saltoun accompanied by Lord Mungo Murray, a son of the Marquis of Atholl, visited the Dowager Lady Lovat. She remained in mourning at her home, Castle Dounie, the time honoured seat of the Lovat branch of Clan Fraser above the Beauly river. A mutually satisfactory visit saw their Lordship's gracious farewells rise to exultations as, once out of ear shot, Saltoun crowed to Murray, "I am in great hope that soon my son will be Lord Lovat." Before arriving home he was to be a great deal less confident.

Simon, well informed of the Saltoun visit and its objective, conceived an amusing idea, amusing from his standpoint that was, for deflating the delegations triumphant return to Aberdeenshire. Gathering an armed band of his clansmen he intercepted their jovial Lordships, forced them to surrender and confined them in a strong tower.

Saltoun had a troubled night and awakened at first light to the sound of workmen and much hammering. On looking out of the bedroom window his bleary eyes widened in alarm to see the men were busily erecting a gallows. Charming as ever, Simon arrived with his Lordships breakfast, and gently informed the prisoner, "Sir you have but two days to live." As a gesture however, one of Lord Saltoun's retainers, chosen by the throw of a dice, would bear him company on the big drop into the hereafter.

Not relishing the prospect of swinging, Saltoun had a sudden loss of appetite, declined his breakfast and as a contemporary chronicler quaintly wrote of the incident, 'The poor gentleman finding this a hard pill to digest contracted a bloody flux of which he almost dyed.'

Leaving Lord Saltoun with such purgative thoughts on his mind, Simon arrived next day with quill pen and paper. The much weakened Lord hastily signed a disclaimer to any pretensions he might have recently entertained as to the Lovat Estates and its glorious title.

By comparison with Simon of Beaufort's next exploit the Saltoun escapade seems a mere schoolboy wheeze, and the further humiliation of the Murrays of Atholl was to prove a truly dangerous ploy which shadowed Fraser for the rest of his life. Atholl was quickly to be furnished with grounds for obtaining the full weight of legal authority to deal with this insolent character.

Consumed beyond reason in his desperate passion for the Lovat title,

Fraser's next expedient was to forcibly marry Lord Hugh's widow, the Dowager Lady Lovat and daughter of the Marquis of Atholl whom he had already outwitted in the 'gallows prank'. The Lady was abducted from Castle Dounie, though Simon had the shameless temerity to assert she 'lo'ed him', and carried to a secret place. A parson was procured, doubtless at the point of a sword, the wedding solemnised and the sordid marriage consummated with the shrill notes of the pipes drowning the shrieks of the struggling bride.

A hiding place rather than a nuptial bower rapidly proved a necessity for the bridegroom as the Privy Council, on the initiative of the Murrays, had Simon and his father 'put to the horn'. This eloquent Scottish phrase empowered any person with the right to bring in either one or both of the Beauforts, dead or alive for a suitable reward. Simon lost no time in rowing his bride across to Eilean Aigas, the tiny wooded island at the mouth of the Kilmorack gorge on the Beauly river.

Negotiations through mutual friends succeeded in getting the bride back to her father though by then it appears, such were Simon's charms on both sides of the blanket, she left, not without some reluctance. Once the bemused bride was safely back amongst the Murrays they took armed action against the Beaufort pair who understandably gathered a body of fighting Frasers about themselves as a wise precaution.

In the manner of a grand deer drive the Marquis of Atholl and his two sons Lords James and Mungo Murray personally conducted the pursuit and with a posse of three hundred men planned a night surprise. The slippery Simon however was not to be caught napping. So successful were the Frasers in turning the tables the surprisers were neatly surprised and captured.

The frequently ridiculed Murrays were dragged between two jeering ranks of Simon's men. The point of a sword made for a snap decision, the Marquis and his sons hurriedly renounced any pretensions they might have entertained to land or title and the whole bedraggled bunch were driven out of Lovat territory like a covey of frightened partridge.

Such a gross indignity did nothing to improve Atholl's humour. The report of Lovat's unlawful gathering of armed men quickly reached Edinburgh and via a smirking Privy Council, to the case of rape, Murray easily added that of high treason. Father and son, condemned to death, fled to Skye where at Dunvegan, worn down by the antics of his ignoble heir, Thomas took a short cut out of his travails and promptly died. Simon, his beloved title forfeited, a price on his head and the wrath of Clan Murray at his heels, was deep in thought.

As a child before the Second World War, I happened to be coming north with my Mother on the overnight Inverness Sleeper and always excited, if not hyperactive when returning to the Highlands, as the clack clack of wheel on rail slowed I let the blind zip up, flooding the sleeper with intense light and wakening mother.

A frost bright morning whitened the strath which stretched below our embankment. Amongst the clumps of purple birch stood lines of horses, rugged and tethered. Khaki soldiers hurried between crinkled brown tents, the smoke of their breakfast fires in blue curls against the snow dappled corries of spring hungry hills. My mother rose on an elbow, "It's the Lovat Scouts at camp," I was told. At a sudden explosive chuff the horses heads jerked their tethers. Steam and smoke, the engine put its pistons to the climb. I craned my neck against the glass as a bend of the line took away the glimpse of an era.

Inter-clan feuding, Frasers versus Murray did not end with Thomas of Beaufort's death at Dunvegan in 1699, it lived and throve into this century. The Lovat Scouts of South African Boer War fame were raised in 1899 by the 16th Lord Lovat from the glens and crofts of his estates, and a body of fit hardy men they proved to be. Their great rivals in a clan sense were the Perthshire regiment of Scottish Horse commanded by Tullibardine, the Duke of Atholl and Chief of all Murrays.

Army manoeuvres between the Scouts and the Scottish Horse took place in the Grampians during the summer of 1909. In typically playful Army jargon the participants, North and South Land were to advance from Perth and Inverness respectively and give battle somewhere in darkest Badenoch. On the evening of the second day, Lord Lovat's cavalry patrols contacted Tullibardine's mounted sentinels at Kingussie and he formed a plan which suggested Fraser cunning had not been watered down by the centuries.

Swimming the regiments' ponies across the Spey below Kinrara, 'where ford there was none', he set about a clever outflanking movement which took men and horses through Glen Tromie, into Gaiack and up a tough climb to the high hill country of Forest Pass. Here the ponies were abandoned and Lovat led a fast night march on twenty miles of rugged track south over the Grampians to look down by dawn on the waters of Loch Ordie near Blair Atholl and the sweet sight of a sleeping camp of Scottish Horse.

Not since the Battle of Killiecrankie had the Braes of Atholl thrilled to the heart stopping scream of a Highland charge. Bonnie Dundee stirred in his grave. The exultant Frasers fell on the scrambling Murrays. Only Army games, instead of cutting throats, the cook house was seized for breakfast.

The prize however was not sizzling 'bangers' but a captured rival Commanding Officer, the Duke of Atholl, asleep in his tent. A great day for Highland patriotism.

Nor was that quite the last defeat. The following autumn Lovat, together with two brothers, all men who had fought in the Boer War, journeyed south to his wedding. The train pulled into Blair Atholl. Who should be on the platform seeing off some friends but the very Duke. 'A taunting enquiry as to his health and what time he got up that morning drew his Grace to the carriage door. He was instantly seized and pulled bodily, like a cork from a bottle, through the window. As the train started to puff away, Bardie, so called by his cronies, reappeared through the steam on the platform, but without his kilt.'

Simon of Beaufort's Dunvegan reverie rapidly resulted in action. Within months he had sneaked from Skye to Edinburgh, allied himself with the Duke of Argyll, irreconcilable foe of the House of Atholl and wisely side stepped his trial for rape and treason. "If he is found to-morrow in Edinburgh," said the Lord Advocate, "I would not give sixpence for his head." An outlaw without resources he headed for London, there to survive by his persuasive tongue and artful wits.

Campbell of Argyll, the patronymic MacCailean Mor, was the very man to salvage Simon's faltering fortunes. Ardent Anglo-phile as suited his ends, Campbell, an influential Whig, was in high favour with King William, the Dutch import to the English throne. Lovat's funds were low. Back home his tenantry had been squeezed dry, opportunities were ripening for 'fishing in drumly waters.' Simon found his vocation. He gave a suitably vague assurance to the Whigs to "keep them posted" and set out for France to ingratiate himself with the Jacobites.

Sailing aboard a Dutch vessel, under the name John Seaton, Lovat along with two companions, his younger brother John and a Major Fraser, landed in Rotterdam and made for Paris freshly disguised as a carter and a couple of local peasants. This unlikely ruse led them into several skirmishes where only the speed of their heels saved their skins. Eventually Fraser found himself at the French Court plotting revolution with the Jacobites and passing the details back to the English Government's agents in Edinburgh.

Though self interest remained paramount throughout his life, there is little doubt that such sympathies as Simon could divert from himself, lay with the Stewart cause. Yet in spite of abject protestations of loyalty, the plotting Jacobites in Paris suspected Fraser's duplicity. A boast that he could bring ten thousand fighting men to the field, and an offer to lodge his young brother John as a hostage, were to no avail. Simon was confined to house arrest in the village of Bourges.

His extravagance when spending other people's money, remained unrestrained. At a fête to celebrate the birthday of the Duke of Bretagne, he arranged fountains to be set up in the streets which spouted free wine. The effect upon the inhabitants of Bourges rendered them largely indifferent to his grand finale, an elaborate firework display.

By 1714 the Jacobites plan for putting James Stewart on the English throne was well advanced, but they suspected a 'leak.' Louis King of France, backer of the scheme was not amused. The shadow of the Bastille fell across Simon the spy. Knowing release from the fortress would be courtesy of Madame La Guillotine, Lovat, his brother, and the resourceful Major Fraser made a bold escape. Grabbing horses in the street they galloped to the coast with little molestation other than an exchange of pistol shots with two highwaymen.

At Rouen escape faltered, their flight was discovered, all seaports were watched. Lives at stake, desperate to cross the Channel they fled up the coast to Boulogne. Pistol persuasion hired an open boat. The November passage was sickeningly rough. Less so than the discomfort of staying in France, Simon cheerfully observed. The trio landed at Dover en route for London where, by virtue of his previous indiscretions, Lovat was still unfortunately an outlaw.

Archenemy Atholl with old scores to settle, soon winded the new arrivals. For Simon, dossing in an obscure lodging house in Soho Square was distasteful but safe. Until the June of 1715 that was, when a 'four o'clock knock', gleefully arranged by Murray, saw the adventurers flung into a downtown jail.

Hatred between the Scots and English was ever mutual. The Scots, abhorring English superiority, envied their wealth and style, whilst the English saw these northern natives as crude interlopers with a misjudged pride in their pedigree. Tyburn gallows, in regular service until 1783, was the popular London stance for hanging criminals, and should the victim be a Scotsman, so much the better.

The prospect of providing both entertainment and gratification for little old ladies sitting with their knitting to watch a Thursday afternoon's 'swingings' sprang easily to Simon's agile mind as he peered through the prison grating.

WE ARE RESOLVED TO MAKE OUR GRAVES IN THE STREETS

Fortunately for the length of Simon Lovat's neck, Jacobite affairs in the North by 1715 were moving apace. Lounging in a slum London prison, an early meeting with his Maker pencilled in his appointment book, found this 'Scots Pimpernel' requiring pardons from both opposing sides. From Jacobite James Stewart, prospective King, for supplying plans of his intended rebellion to the English Government, but more urgently from the fat hand of that repulsive import to the English throne, German George, for treason, rape, and numerous nods and winks traded to the Jacobites.

Lovat lost no time in contacting the Duke of Argyll, previous saviour of Simon's neck from the Murrays' wrath and his sponsor in the espionage business. Campbell well recognised the hypnotic power which the 'Old Fox' held over the Highlanders. It could be vital in suppressing the rebellion if he let Simon head for home, on a tight string of course. As one dissembler to another he didn't trust Fraser the length of his chameleon kilt. A pass to the north must suffice in the meantime. Royal pardon was only pending. Lovat's loyalty was on appro.

Several Gaelic speaking Highland soldiers made up the prison guard who kept an eye on Fraser and the insinuating Simon soon had an escape plan drawn up. Only the prompt arrival of Argyll's pass prevented him adding jail breaking to his list of criminal accomplishments. The docket covered a Major

Fraser and two servants. Thinly disguising Simon and his brother as menials, the trio hurried north.

Marching south were Jacobites of the '15' Rebellion, and scurrying before them a Mr. Murray. At a Dumfries inn he saw through Lovat's unlikely disguise and breathlessly informed the Provost, "The villain Beaufort is in town, certain to join the rebels." For the moment, given the circumstances, it was the last thing on Simon's mind. With a body swerve worthy of a rugger three quarter he headed for Lanark and a secret night meeting with Argyll.

Ushered surreptitiously into the Ducal bed chamber, Lovat mustered all the impressive gravity at his command. "I am headed North to create a diversion in favour of the Government," he assured his chief. Having hooked the Duke, he pocketed a hundred guineas towards running expenses and galloped on to Edinburgh.

Barely had Simon pulled off his riding boots and settled into the inglenook of his Grassmarket lodgings when a knock on the door heralded yet another arrest. The Edinburgh magistrates had not forgotten that on Lovat's last fleeting stop over in the capital, sixteen years previously, his contempt of court had deprived them of a juicy case of abduction and rape.

But contacts ever came readily to Simon's hand. The Provost of Edinburgh happened to be a Campbell, who, when shown Argyll's signature soon found the means to free them and see the travellers safely down to Leith.

The party sailed homeward under a bright summer moon, accompanied for sound reason by John Forbes of Culloden, a brother of Duncan the famous Whig supporter of the English Government. The Bass rock lay far to starboard when the skipper of their sailing ship, a Banffshire man from Portsoy unmasked himself as a Jacobite.

The Major as a precaution against their being handed to the rebels and with a gentlemanly hint of force, took command of the vessel. The captain was barely down below when a suspicious looking boat hauled alongside. The Major silently practised his Jacobite rhetoric but only a company of Highland drovers were on board returning from England after selling their cattle. They were mostly MacKays from Caithness and being Whigs needed little coaxing to assist the Major in keeping the skipper calm.

Heading up the Moray Firth the hills of home hove in view. Clear of the confinements of Lowland and Border, the skyline heralded the freedom and space of the Highlands. Political space was another matter. A contrary wind forced the vessel to anchor in Fraserburgh bay and there she lay to a stomach churning roll. John Forbes of Culloden, not nautically inclined, vowed seasickness would be his death. "We must attempt to avoid your burial at sea," Simon seldom lavished sympathy except on himself. Although knowing it to be extremely risky for Whigs to land in Jacobite territory, Lovat demanded a crew man row them ashore and the trio plus the vomiting Forbes put up at the local inn.

Barely had head touched pillow late that night when the Landlord announced the arrival of a visitor to check on their identity. A sleepy grunt from Lovat enquired as to whom it might be. "Lord Saltoun," the Landlord replied. Simon shot up, Lord Saltoun! Son of the very man for whom in his wilful youth he had playfully erected the gallows.

Saltoun waited at the foot of the stair, impatient and not a little suspicious. Lovat eyeing the window and using the Gaelic in a loud querulous tone to convey the effect of angry annoyance to his Lordship's listening ear, was in fact telling his companions to make the best they could of a potentially lethal situation.

The Major possessing a practiced gift for invention second only to that of his master, informed Lord Saltoun they were cattle drovers, Sutherlands and MacKays returning home from the English markets. "But I'm a MacRae myself," he confided with a knowing look. "Indeed," rejoined Saltoun, "I have news for you. Your Chief, Lord Seaforth passed Fraserburgh yesterday with thirteen hundred men on his way to join the Earl of Mar at Perth." "A toast," cried the Major, affecting tears of joy, "Health to my Chief and success to our noble Cause." The cause so laudably acclaimed being the Rebellion Lovat and the Major were hurrying home intent on undermining. But as one good toast deserves another Major Fraser and his Lordship were soon boon companions.

Numerous other worthy causes of similar sentiment were gustily acknowledged and as dawn filtered through the cobwebs, Saltoun happily provided the party with horses to see them on the road.

Not a moment too soon did the trio take to the saddle. The Jacobite skipper of their Leith vessel had managed to slip ashore and inform a befuddled Saltoun that one of the men galloping west on his Lordship's horse was Simon Lovat. Worse for the apoplectic Laird, a Simon Fraser in Whig clothing. Ah my, guile and gullibility, ever the twain shall meet.

For generations the Inverness-sians were noted throughout the Highlands for their correctness of grammar, purity of accent and good manners. The old Inverness twang is little heard today and indeed it once varied from one part of the town to another. A contemporary, writing of MacKintosh of Borlum in the early seventeen hundreds, states, 'he spoke with ane affected Inverness English accent', which might indicate the phenomenon was widely recognised and perhaps even a little disparaged in those days. Certainly the term, 'an Inverness gentleman', a phrase once used well outwith the town, implied if nothing more derogatory, a certain stylishness of dress and bearing beyond that of the mundane Highlander.

My grandfather had a draper's shop on Church Street in Inverness at a time during the 'twenties' when a small group flourished in the town called the Highland Dress Society. Not large in membership, what it lacked numerically was made up in quality and refinement. Much attention centred on such vital dress etiquette as length of kilt, angle of Glengarry bonnet and level of sporran. Correctness of tartan, with attached pedigree if possible, was a distinct asset. Anything less than a modified Inverness accent and one might soon feel ill at ease.

Summer outings were arranged to suitably decorous locations and the fastidious troop would mount a charabanc for a leisurely drive to the honoured location. On this occasion it happened that Beaufort Castle was deemed a suitable venue. An alfresco luncheon below the shading oaks was followed by a gentle perambulation of the gardens before the party gathered on the castle steps for the customary 'memorable' photograph.

The photographer vanished below his black sheet. Last moment preenings adjusted a cuff length here, a silk ruff there. Holes in grandfather's kilt had already been passed off casually as bullets encountered during the Charge of the Light Brigade. Generally however it meant a skirmish with moths.

Chins up, chests out, a hand to the lapel. The medals of the brave and sometimes not so brave glinted in the sun. A united pose was struck.

Behind the assemblage, unbeknown by the swell of vanity, young Simon Fraser, the Laird to be, with a large pair of scissors, was busily snipping fresh holes in their kilts.

Inverness, as in these days, so in those, controlled the north. Its urbane citizens even by 1715 well knew the value of southern trading connections and were little disposed to the antics of an aspiring Monarch. It came as no surprise to MacKenzie, Earl of Seaforth, marching south in a flush of Jacobite fervour with his men from the Western Highlands, to find the town defended.

The Earl of Sutherland opposed the rebels with a small body of men equipped mostly with cudgels and sharpened poles, the standard kit of Saturday night out town loiterers. Seaforth soon scattered the band to their accustomed haunts and leaving Sir John MacKenzie of Coul as Governor of Inverness, tramped away to help the Earl of Mar fight the dismal battle of Sheriffmuir on behalf of James Edward Stuart, styled with Jacobite pride as the Chevalier but known with Whiggish disrespect and a certain justification as the Old Pretender.

Meantime nearing Inverness, courtesy of Saltoun's transport, Lovat learned that three hundred Frasers from Stratherrick were under arms. However though Jacobite to a man, such was the troops' opinion of the self

styled MacKenzie of Fraserdale, encumbent Laird of the Fraser lands during
Simon's enforced absence, the men were refusing to 'come out' for the
Chevalier under MacKenzie's leadership.

Magic, the disingenuous Major was dispatched to bring the Highlanders
to Culloden House and meet their 'rightful Chief', by giving them a broad
hint of Simon's secret Jacobite leanings. The fighting Frasers came faithfully
and stood before Lord Lovat in 1715, not four miles from Drumossie Moor.
Could they have but foreseen the barbaric slaughter to be the Highlanders' lot
before the play was ended.

Twenty years had passed since Simon Lovat had stood before his men.
Always a master of the theatrical occasion, he harangued his cheering Frasers.
The blood bond of clanship rang in his voice, the tears of reunion filled his
eyes. Victory would be theirs, follow him. A heady mix of promises and thinly
veiled threats, and Lord Lovat once again had fighting men at his back.

In bold array, pipes skirling, Lovat and his Frasers advanced to capture
Inverness, Capital of the Highlands, for the Whigs and the English, much to
the mystery of the troops.

Not actually a difficult military undertaking, as it turned out. No shots
were exchanged and as attackers and defenders were friends and cousins they
warmly shook hands. More blood is spilt at a good going shinty match. Lovat
was Governor of Inverness. His pliable Frasers, now ostensibly Whigs, had
placed control of the north back in the hands of the English Government.

The Earl of Seaforth rallied and threatened him from the west, the
Marquis of Huntly, son of the Duke of Gordon, rumbled from the east and
vowed to lay the town in ashes.

Lovat sought and received help from the Governor of Fort William,
writing, 'Simon, Lord Lovat, commanding his Majesty's forces, near Inverness',
he continued, 'We are resolved to make our graves in the streets rather than
yield this place till it is in flames about our ears. But the wind of the Gordons
will not make us desert this place. We are resolved to shed our blood in it'.

Inverness was not attacked. The wind of Lovat's rhetoric cooled the
combined fighting ardour of Seafield and Huntly. Simon Fraser had finished
the '15' Rebellion.

Proud Governor of the Castle and Fort of Inverness in the name of
English King George, the rebellion throttled, Lovat had the Whigs fawning
about his feet. A pardon for his long standing treason was quickly prepared,
and the pending rape case overlooked. Simon hastened to London, knelt to
kiss the flabby hand of 'German George' and pulled off a £500 a year pension,
of which there would be doubtless much need.

Little did the Whigs know that only weeks before, on strength of a belated apology from James Stuart, the 'Old Chevalier' for his treatment of Simon in France, 'His Majesty's Governor', always a secret Catholic, almost marched his Frasers to the Jacobite Cause, and rather than genuflecting at King George's feet, he might well have knelt on the Royal neck.

What to do now with the rebellious Highlanders? Best keep an eye on these trouble makers by recruiting active young Highlanders, 'who wade ye rivers commonly better than any horse', from clans loyal to the Government to replace the inferior Dutch and Swiss mercenaries. Lovat's pragmatic advice for dealing with his fellow Highlanders naturally secured him Captaincy of one of the Independent Companies that were duly set up. Eventually in 1739, these soldiers formed the 42nd Regiment, the famous Black Watch.

Disarming of the Jacobite clans by the Government turned into the very sort of wheeze at which Simon was expert. Special importations of ancient Dutch weapons under plain wraps arrived at Beauly pier for general distribution throughout the Highlands before being handed into the Government by clansmen stuffing their serviceable firearms under the thatch.

Secure in title, lands, pension and a public position in the Whig administration, Lovat devoted the rest of his life to scheming behind their back for the Jacobite Cause. Effusive attention flowed from both factions. Lovat's swaggering vanity and self-glorification already in the hands of a master boaster spiralled to new heights of insufferabilty. He quarrelled incessantly with friend and foe alike. One violent exchange in a London coffee house with Sir William Gordon went to such extreme that only a duel to the death could satisfy honour.

Simon taking his old crony Rose of Kilravock as second, duly appeared the following morning on the Marylebone Fields. Fraser faced Gordon in a glare of hatred. Hands grasped swordhilts, poised for the signal, waiting to kill. A stranger sprang forward, levelled a loaded pistol and threatened to shoot the first man to draw sword. The opponents shouted and swore, six more men arrived and the duel was broken up.

The gunman made the point of stating he had been hired that morning by a person whose name he was not permitted to disclose. Days later, anything but a mock duel had fatal consequences for a Major Cathcart who had publicly accused Sir William Gordon of fixing the intervention. Sir William neatly dispatched the outspoken Cathcart, but why should the unfortunate Major precipitate his own demise unless put up to it? Certainly a lamentable oversight on his part. The 'who dun'it' hand behind the fiasco remains a mystery.

Simon Lovat's vainglorious struttings however received a sobering jolt in 1718 when, on a trip to London, he fell desperately ill. Envisaging a protracted negotiation with Saint Peter, he prepared his case in a rambling letter to 'the

Honourable the Gentlemen of the name of Fraser.' in which he disclosed what was probably as near to sincerity as he was capable of expressing.

'The greatest happiness I proposed to myself under Heaven was to make you all live happy, and make my poor commons flourish.' A dutiful opening, the antithesis of results so far achieved in that direction, he continued with instructions for the well being of his 'poor commons.' They 'should always be well clothed and well armed after the Highland fashion, and not suffer them to wear low-country clothes.'

Fearing the worst, he plunged into a lengthy confession, 'Should it be God's will that for the punishment of my great and many sins, and the sins of my kindred, I should now depart this life before I put these just and good resolutions in execution'. Thereafter followed a list of instructions which any failing to carry through will be cursed, 'even as most of the Scots people curse this day those who sold them and their country to the English by the fatal Union which I hope will not last long'.

Though a Nationalist at heart he was never averse to picking the English pockets, nor years later did he mind obliging his 'poor common' Frasers by hiring them out to King George's new Black Watch regiment at a profitable £3,10s per head. But by then, having put off his appearance at the Pearly Gates, he was back in form.

Final legal possession of The Lovat Estates and their title in Simon's favour was not in fact accomplished until 1734 after a prolonged litigation to evict MacKenzie of Fraserdale, the 'foul usurper.' The outcome could be in no doubt, opinioned Simon. Judgement was under Lord Grange who just happened to be a boon companion of Lovats in manys an Edinburgh debauch. Moreover Simon, some years previously had 'obliged' the judge in a matter which required a delicate but ruthless touch.

Grange, a model for Jekyll and Hyde, passed his days, when not presiding on the Bench, in expurgatory religious devotions and following this daily soul cleansing, spent his nights re-soiling it in libidinous orgies. Capricious as that may seem, it appears Lord Grange, an ardent Jacobite had been inflicted with a termagant of a wife whom he also suspected of being a Whig and passing to them the secrets she had learnt whilst hiding under his plotting couch. Simon, a noted authority on abduction and other affairs of a spurious nature, arranged her funeral, buried an empty coffin, had her carried from Edinburgh and shipped to a life of contemplation on his cousin MacLeod's isle of St. Kilda.

Not withstanding this novel 'obligement' for his legal friend, the settlement of the arbitration, though confirming the estates and title, announced the enormous payment to MacKenzie of Fraserdale of twelve thousand pounds sterling. Lovat flew into a boundless fury. The judgement was 'villainous', Lord Grange the judge, now very much his ex-friend, had 'betrayed and sold' him. Clearly Simon's view of human nature believed every man had his price and few would ever prove him wrong.

THE END OF ALL HUMAN GRANDEUR

Lovat at last achieved his ambition, all be it at a cost, and became the truly patriarchal Highland Chief. A sizable area of the north came under his rule, and certainly at local level, under his own view of justice. He regularly maintained a form of Court at Castle Dounie and saw himself father of the clan. An indulgent sympathiser with the sorrows of his people and magnanimous on occasion in ways that took his fancy, all provided of course the 'poor commons' did as they were told.

His Lordship's Musician, a David Fraser for example was dispatched to Skye to be 'perfected as a Highland Pyper' under the tutorship of the famous Malcolm M'Crimon and 'to sustain the boy for seven years, in Bed, Board, and washing, and to furnish and provide him in Clothes, shoes, and stockings, and likewise to satisfy and pay to him yearly and ilk year the sum of fifty merks Scots money in name of wages.' All such munificence lightly cloaked the stern despot who exacted unquestioning obedience from those within his domains.

The style of Castle Dounie is described by James Ferguson an astronomer of the time who stayed as Simon's guest for some months. 'A sort of tower that in England would be considered only an indifferent house for a private plain country gentleman'. There were only 'four apartments on a floor, and none large'. Sleeping accommodation for chief retainers, servants and guests of the common order was in fresh straw daily spread on the floor of the lower rooms. Ablution and latrine facilities were an adventure for even the unsqueamish.

Strict table etiquette or less politely, a peck order, applied at the dinner table. Lovat, principal quests, and local lairds took the head. Next the 'tacksmen', often relatives holding land on a lease entailing an obligation to produce men for military service. Below them sat the tenants or common husbandmen. The plentiful food and drink was also suitably graded, from claret or champagne, port or whisky-punch down to strong beer. Simon the genial host would say diplomatically to his tacksmen, "Cousins, I told my pantry lads to hand you claret, but they tell me ye like port and punch best." And turning to the commoners with an affable Hobson's Choice, "Gentlemen, there is what ye please at your service, but I send you ale because I understand ye like ale best."

Waiting at table were servants and dogs. No food was provided for either except the leftovers gleaned from diners' plates. Preyed upon by vulturous servants and drooling dogs, any guest laying down knife and fork and turning to speak would have his plate whisked from below his nose and licked clean before he'd uttered a sentence.

'Below the utmost extent of the table, at the door, and sometimes without the door of the hall', writes Ferguson, 'you might see a multitude of Frasers without shoes or bonnets, regaling themselves with bread and onions, with a little cheese perhaps and small beer'.

These were the days when Highland lords encouraged loyalty in their subjects by liberal use of 'pit and gallows.' The view from Simon's dining table looked out upon a few strongly branched trees. After dispensing a mornings jurisprudence the results of his Lordship's sentences could be seen swinging in the breeze, hung by their heels, for at least the duration of lunch. A novel aperitif, if only for the diners.

'Always tender of his carcass.' A description applied to 'Lovat of the 45' by his companion adventurer Major Fraser when recounting some of their escapades in France. Doubtless Lovat would always expect the softest bed and select what best catered for his personal comfort as befitted his station. Privilege apart, the accounts submitted to the Forfeited Estates Commissioners by the various surgeons and apothecaries for the treatment of 'His Lordship' and his family and servants make illuminating reading. They indicate something of the healthiness, or lack of it, amongst the upper classes of the 18th century. The apparent high cost of treatment might smack of soaking the 'rich' but the poor either enjoyed the blessing of good health or the cheapness of hedgerow herbs. Hypochondria would not have been common amongst the lower orders.

A Dr. Alex. Fraser, surgeon at Druimariach treated the Lovat household in the years prior to the '45' and, as a matter of principle it may seem, had not been paid. By Sept.1749 the surgeon, via an Edinburgh solicitor James Fraser, submitted his account. A gentlemanly pace in tendering bills not found today, and much in contrast to the developing approach of payment before treatment or die.

The surgeon's accounts indicate Lovat's fondness, amongst a variety of indulgences, for having his chest rubbed. 'Ane pectoral solution for your Lordship, 5s.6d. was supplied along with numerous doses of eye water at 1s.6d. a shot. Most frequent were entries for 'Ane Jugg full Sohosh, containing 24oz. £1,16s.0d', upon which one can only conjecture. 'Large Pots of White Ointment' at 10s. were liberally dispensed, Lovat's son, Mr. Archibald and a Mammy Meg being singled out for application. The latter may well have been a favourite nanny though servants didn't usually merit a name. They were nevertheless kept in tip-top form. 'Five Dozes purging powder for your servant, 3s.4d., and one 5s. box of Detergent Pills, would have enlivened the daily round of the household attendants.

Personal hygiene could not have been a social ritual when the Lovat family visited Edinburgh. Hand washing would not have been common and the preparation of food for the table meant a feast for bacteria. This is made quite plain in the accounts submitted by the family's attendant surgeons in the capital, John Rattray and Charles Congalton. The itemised debts ran from 1740 to 1745 before the final demand dropped through the letter box of the Forfeited Estates Commissioners in 1752.

Bluntly headed 'To Pains and Attendance.' it indicates that stomach complaints gripped 'His Lordship' with some regularity.'To yourself stomach bitter materials, 7s.4d. Vomits, 12s. To twenty-four dozes Emetic herbs, 12s.7d.' And moving to the bowels, 'To a doz. best rhubarb, 1s. Two dozes purging pills, gilded, 6d', and mysteriously, 'two gold leaves, 6d.'

Bleeding the patient as a fashionable method of curing headaches or drawing out poison seemed moderately priced by comparison to much medication of the time. The Master of Lovat was treated 'To a blooding, 10s,6d. Letting blood from a servant was half price, 'To your servant, a Bleeding, 5s. but possibly required less care and attention. Constipation featured in the young life of Lovat's daughter, 'To 8 dozes aperient pills for Miss Sibble,6s.1d.' and as a pick-me up for 13s.8d., perhaps to counteract the draining effect of the purgatives, 18 dozes of mercurial pills were dispensed.

His Lordship seemed no stranger to exotic potions. He dabbled from 'To half a pound of camphorated eye water, 2s.6d.' and '2oz. syrup of Violets with 9 wafers, 1s.3d.' to '3 dozes of Pacific Pills, 15s.' and the ultimately exclusive but puzzlingly cheap 'To three oz. Sacred Tincture, 1s.7d.'

Professional services are always expensive, never foolproof and neither Pacific Pills or Sacred Tincture nor Legal Council pleadings were to prevent the ultimate illness of Simon Fraser. In spite of the dramatic loss of case and client, Mr. Charles Hamilton Gordon, Edinburgh Advocate and Council for His Lordship whilst under trial for high treason, eventually collected £317,10s.0d. from the Estates Commissioners. George Ross, Gent. who handled Lovat's pleadings from the Tower presented a bill for £647,1s.0d. Even a Gentleman, so styled, saw no point in letting a shilling go past.

For ten years or more Lovat had posed as the great Whig champion of the Highlands, but the beliefs in his heart were truly those of the Catholic cause, and he became increasingly careless in concealing his double play from the Government. One by one the Authorities deprived him of his sinecures. Command of his Independent Company of soldiers, a dangerous toy in the wrong hands they considered, and to Simon's acute embarrassment the Sheriffship of Inverness, but worse for a resolute spendthrift, his State pension.

For a man of sufficient conceit to style a very modest dwelling as a castle, humiliation hurt. The mood of Simon the master flatterer was ripe to cast him the fated victim of his own vanity.

In 1740 James Stuart, the 'Chevalier' graced Simon with the Dukedom of Fraser and in 1743, the Lord-lieutenancy North of the Spey. Empty titles unless Stuart were to attain the English throne but sufficient to swell the head of a modest man, far less a person lacking in any pretensions to modesty. Betwixt Catholic faith and vain self-interest, Lovat was drawn into the '45' Rebellion, but not he planned, beyond his neck.

The two horses he rode were drawing uncomfortably apart.

Bonnie Prince Charlie with a handful of attendants beached on the island of Eriskay in the Outer Hebrides in July 1745. A romantic but amateur start to a rebellion. Lovat the Whig fulminated, "A mad unaccountable gentleman, no man should join him," but with a discreet ear to the ground, on the faintest vibrations of possible victory for the insurgents, Lovat the Jacobite dispatched his unwilling son, the Master of Lovat, a boy of sixteen, to join the Prince.

'An undutiful and unnatural son', who persisted in raising the Frasers for the Cause and 'flew in my face like a wild cat', when I remonstrated with him. Such were Simon's threadbare attempts to hoodwink Duncan

Forbes of Culloden, Whig supremo of the North, so threadbare in fact, they were soon to let in a fatal draught.

At this juncture Lovat, 'for the benefit of my health', wished to go to France. Naturally he reasoned, whilst sitting on a French fence he could calmly survey the campaign, issue dispassionate orders to his Frasers and, need it be said, with less discomfort. It had become difficult for Simon to account to the mistrusting Forbes for the several hundred clansmen he packed off to join the Prince at Derby and impossible to explain why he ignored a repeated order from Duncan Forbes to disarm the small private army he chose to maintain in his back garden at Castle Dounie.

The Earl of Loudoun had command of the Government troops in the north and when Whig patience ran out, Loudoun pounced. Lovat was carried to a house in Inverness preparatory to incarceration in the castle of which he had lately been Governor. But a town house held no bars for the wily Simon. He was quickly 'sprung' by a back exit and escaped to the safe and comfortable house of his kinsman, Fraser of Gortuleg.

Whilst in this congenial hiding place he received a letter in the Prince's own hand offering him command of the Jacobite army, still a substantial body of men. Dispirited but not beaten, the Prince and his commanders, toiling north through the winter, believed the hypnotic power that Lovat held over the Highlanders might yet turn the tide.

Lovat held back. Old and infirm he remained in comfort with Fraser of Gortuleg and offered prescient advice. The Jacobite leaders should not on any account meet the Duke of Cumberland in a pitched battle he warned. Retreat to the hills and adopt guerrilla tactics until the lie of the land could be used to their better advantage. Sage words are wasted on the foolish.

His foresight proved horribly accurate. At Gortuleg House after the carnage of Culloden, Lovat and Prince Charles were to meet for the first and only time. "Remember your great ancestor Robert Bruce, who lost eleven battles and won Scotland by the twelfth." Lovat spoke to a man dazed by the blood letting on Drumossie Moor, surrounded by tables from which his victory feast had been swept to make a brief place for binding the maimed and wounded.

Every man for himself, Prince or private, and the former led the scattering of the Clans.

That night Lovat, unable to walk, had himself carried west. Avoiding Castle Dounie he followed the hill tracks into Strathglass and crossed the Beauly river by Eskadale ferry, not a mile above Eilean Aigas and the memories of his youths lamentable folly. The hurrying Frasers skirted Erchless Castle, seat of The Chisholm, a fellow fugitive, and passed under the shoulder of Beinn a' Bha'ach Ard into the mighty Strathfarrar. Held in the glen's fastness is a tiny wooded island set in Loch Mhuilie, and here the 'old fox' went to ground.

Steep cairns of jagged grey rock overlook this forgotten island where green in the peace of trees and fragrant moss, hides a ruin. Favoured stones of a mason's hand, falling into memories, fragile as the shapely hills on the still waters of Loch Mhuilie.

A heavily armed body of men, green tweeds, deerstalker bonnets terriers and telescopes had been ferried across the head of Loch Mhuilie and rested on stick and rifle to survey the great scattered cairn on the slopes above them. Late March, before the April lambing, the cubs deep in a dry cairn would still be sucking, then was the month of the fox drives.

Glenstrathfarrar that April morning near fifty years ago, was still ringed by the snows of the high tops, but speckled ridges climbed free in a sunshine of promise as we made across to the Rough Wood. Remnant of the once great wood of Caledon, it covered the hillside beyond the rashy flats from Braulin Lodge. Each tree a dignified distance from its neighbour, an open wood where girth counted in a wrestle with winter gale.

Criss-crossed about us at the edge of the forest lay the peeling trunks of once proud trees, thrown in their prime and left to rot. In 1948 Aberdeenshire woodcutters set about this great stand of ancient timber but extraction proved too difficult and the felling was abandoned.

As I climbed about them, a heart warming sun coaxed the mossy scent of spring from its hiding amongst their wrinkled trunks. It came at each step in tantalising breath, shy, hesitant, elusive as the longing that trembled with the first call of a curlew far below on the homecoming flats.

We lined out through the wood, rifles covered the high ground, alert for the long shot, guns in the centre, crooked on the elbow and ready. Shouting, whistling men, yapping frantic terriers, happy to fight amongst themselves if nothing more challenging crossed their paths, our advance thought nothing beyond the lust of killing.

Shots rang out, roe deer went down, we tramped the miles of blaeberry and heather tussock, but the fox had slipped us and subdued men and dogs gathered down on the shore of Loch Mhuilie. The Lovat ghillies rowed us over. I looked to the island, untouched. Nobody spoke of it.

For the afternoon's drive I left shepherds and keepers at their piece, and circled high above the cairns to find a vantage point. Rifle across my knee I set my back to a large split boulder. A sprig of rowan sheltered in the crack. Had it survived the winter frosts? I scratched a twig, pale green and moist, it lived, I was pleased.

Men with guns angled on their backs or carried loose and ready climbed in slow line below. My eye focused beyond them in distance and time. Scratched fields of survival living lay beside the loch, stone heaps of childhood gathering still bare, and in the homestead ruins on the flood free hillocks only the Ring-ouzel sang, where once the smooring peat dawdled in laughter.

Two hundred years lay below me since Simon Lovat, 'the Red Fox', was rowed to the island, evil, proud, and crippled, his life in ruins. A fatal romance with the Jacobite Cause. And what of the men from the stones of a village I looked down on, and a thousand other such, they had nothing but their lives to give to a Cause not of their making.

A fugitive denying his identity, dragged before a Minister who lied, "I don't know this man," then to his croft house door and his wife feigning any knowledge of her husband, but the children ran out, "Oh Daddy, oh Daddy," and the soldiers led the Highlander a little distance, and shot him.

My eye returned. Excited men bounded up the cairn, agile, stone to stone, terriers yelping at fever pitch. A fox made a bid for life. Killing blood pounded my throat, the rifle cocked. At the top stones of the cairn a man leapt into view. The crash of his shotgun came sharp in the thin April air. I ran down to find Iain Mackay and his terrier standing over a dead vixen.

I rowed the stretch of water to Eilean Mhuilie. The same sun of spring promise which brought death to the cairn above the loch side on an April day forty and more years ago, now gave me the reassurance of life through its early warmth about that hidden place, where ageing pines, gaunt and peeling, still stand over the ruin.

Simple clean cut stones of mason care make two linteled fireplaces. Back to back, they draw into one square lum. Without trace of stone wall or gable, the tiny rooms that gave shelter to 'Lovat of the 45' would have been of timber and thatch. The stones are without moss and I rubbed their rough surface and stood where an old man, hunted like a fox, must have sat two hundred and fifty years ago looking out across the loch to a sun that set below the unending grace of Sgur na Lapaich.

On the shoulder of a great pine above me, a mistle thrush, deep in its throat, sang the first hushed notes of spring.

Sunlight fell on the empty hearth, I touched it, and knew then the stone came from the cairn where we killed the fox.

The Duke of Cumberland wiping his hands after the butchery of Culloden prepared for fresh blood letting. He regarded Lovat as the covert lynch-pin of the rebellion and determined on his capture. Fraser country was raked over and Simon hurriedly abandoned Eilean Mhuilie for another islet in Loch Morar on his West Inverness-shire estate.

Relentless pursuit by Redcoats from Fort William ultimately cornered him on the island, allegedly hiding in a hollow oak tree. 'I imagine that the taking of Lord Lovat is a greater humiliation and vexation to the Highlanders than anything that could have happened', wrote a gleeful Cumberland, exhibiting a shortcoming not uncommon in the aristocracy, of misinterpreting or ignoring the attitudes and dilemmas of the common man.

Out of the Highlands, down the deep hill passes, Simon Fraser, borne by litter to London, left devastated estates, saw his home, Castle Dounie, in flames and the loyal clansmen who had followed him, willingly or otherwise, in jeopardy of their lives. All that he sought to secure in life, land, title, Regal recognition, now awaited a palpable eclipse on the scaffold.

Whatever contrite thoughts may also have crossed his mind, he now earnestly bent his quill to supplicatory letters. Of little avail, the litter proceeded on the road to the Tower amidst taunting and abusive crowds. "You evil old Scotch dog," a woman catcalled, "You ugly old English bitch," Lovat shouted back.

Fame, or its reverse, spread before him, and during a stopover at the White Hart tavern in St Albans, time was found for the prisoner to sit for his portrait. Hogarth the painter of characters from Royalty to 'The Rake's Progress, 'depicts him as a sinister-eyed old man and no doubt got it about right.

The charge of high treason was brought against Lovat who conducted his own defence with skill and dignity. He had not actively taken up arms against the Crown, but his numerous connivances at rebellion were easily proved from the evidence of two Jacobites who saved their own lives by informing. One John Murray of Broughton, secretary to Bonnie Prince Charlie, the other, Lovat's own secretary, and a Fraser.

Lovat was sentenced to the revolting obscenity of a traitors doom, hung by the neck, cut down whilst alive to witness his own disembowelling and then hacked into quarters. His peerage mercifully secured him immunity from a practice generally reserved for the lower orders and death by beheading was ordered.

Once the importuning letters proved fruitless and all hope of reprieve was abandoned, Lovat showed that below a lifelong character of outright duplicity, vanity and greed, their lay a bedrock of calm courage and that intangible quality, 'Highland pride'. A restless man, nimble of mind, all his life an incurable romantic at the expense of reality, it brought about his end, and that of many others whom his charisma ensnared.

Simon Fraser of the '45' sat with his warders. The smoke of his pipe drifted before eyes which focused on the only horizon left to him. He spoke with humbleness, "The end of all human grandeur is like the snuff of this tobacco."

The last person in the Kingdom to be executed by the axe was led from the Tower. Two men lifted him up the three steps onto the scaffold. The large crowd fell silent. He tested the sharpness of the axe without fear and calmly examined his coffin. "I hope to be in heaven by one o'clock." and took leave of the clansmen who attended him, secure in his faith.

The rough hand of a brutish man bent Fraser forward and placed his neck on the block. In one axe blow he severed the head of Lord Lovat.

The executioner lifted the dripping head aloft by scrawny hair and paraded round the platform to an exultant crowd. It was the 9th April 1747. Instead of the grisly spectacle of his head rotting on a spike outside some prominent gateway, the authorities allowed Lovat's request to have it placed back on his shoulders in the coffin. Simon shared the morbid superstitions of the day and dreaded the possibility of rising headless at the Resurrection. The arrangements made by his friends to have the remains taken to Inveness by a ship called the Pledger were firmly refused. There was to be no chance of a returning martyr to refuel the Cause. Lovat was buried in the Tower.

In the way of people with time to contemplate their death, Lovat took comfort and satisfaction in anticipating his interment in the family vault at Kirkhill amidst the finest lands on his estates. All the pipers from John o' Groat's to Edinburgh would gather to honour him in the Ceol Mhor, the great music of Gaeldom. The old women of the Highlands singing a coronach would go before his coffin, 'And then there will be odd crying and clapping of hands, for I am one of the greatest chiefs in the Highlands'.

At one stroke of his axe an unknown executioner ended the great romantic period of the Highlands, ended an era. Simon Fraser's death signalled a change in the hearts and minds of the people, rich or poor. Lovat epitomised the life and breath of the clan system in all its good and evil as it had existed for almost five hundred years. The strengths of kinship in a subsistence existence, the misery and hardship of feudal service on the battlefield, the benefit of wise patriarchal leadership. A complex amalgam of common beliefs, customs, and shared suffering wrought a people of resilience and stature.

For Lovat, as for every Highlander of the day, pride of ancestry was paramount. A pride in his country and its history led Fraser and the independent minds of the time to a hatred of the English. His ancestors fought and died in the War of Independence and he saw Scotland under vassalage. It was his stated resolve that his eldest son be educated after his own manner, 'that is, as a true Scotch-man and a Highlander, for I had rather him buried as see him bred a thorough Englishman.' A watershed indeed.

EVEN A KING CAN SMELL
LIKE A HORSE

The Aberdeen-shire orraloon once represented the humblest human form found within that penal farming colony, excepting perhaps the 'gowk.' An innocent sixteen I stepped onto this lowly rung off a bus from Aberdeen which stopped at Gartly Station one Sunday evening as the leaning harvest beckoned to binder, stook and stack. I was soon to see plenty of all three and climbed the ladder into the loft above the farmhouse kitchen that night without foresight, but possessed by a deep longing to be part of the great cycle of a natural world.

A hefty six o'clock thump from the kitchen below had me out of youthful idealism and into a bowl of oatmeal brose. The yawning skivvy, a girl of seventeen with a tendency to keep irregular hours at night but fearful of being late in the morning, handed me tea without a word and barely a glance. Too young for a lassie of her ample requirements I guessed.

Out in the yard, Sandy Beattie the farmer of Whitelums had threatened the weather, planned the day accordingly, and by evening I had worked both tractor and binder. Small, red haired and wiry, irascible and kindly by turn, Beattie, hard but fair, broad in Doric accent and sayings, epitomised all the guts and sweat it had taken to break the harsh Northeast of Scotland out of stones into fields. Driving himself from dawn to dusk and others likewise, he ran about his work. The average 'loon' lasted a fortnight.

The sheaves at Whitelums rapidly grew into stacks. Sandy built, circle after circle, "Ye mun aye keep her up in the hairt, John," he always called me John, his mind racing on to more important things as he threw sheaves to the centre pole before kneeling to the outside round. Childhood flesh hardened into muscle. Hugh, his oldest son and myself did all the 'leading' from the fields, two sheaves to each forkful and if you valued your life, don't jab the man on the cart. Gordon the cattleman 'bigged' the loads. Mrs. Beattie baked. Placid and motherly, she saw to it that the scones, pancakes and tea arrived in a wicker basket covered by a laundered cloth prompt at each 'half yokin', and carried to the harvest scene by the knowing hand of the skivvy.

Whitelums soon sweated out a braw stackyard to boast to the neighbours. With tugs, pulls and pats of a spade, Sandy preened each stack to a handsome watertight shape, and after the last 'Lums' sheaf topped a stack that morning, he promptly hired Hugh and myself, doubtless at a profitable rate, to 'lead the hairst' three miles down the Huntly road on the wide acres of Culethie. Not a moment to waste. We gobbled our mutton and tatties and pedalled off to start at one o'clock sharp, "dinna be late noo," followed us out of the close. Sandy's daughter Margaret lent me her bike otherwise I was expected to run.

To me, after the homeliness of the Beatties, Culethie seemed a grand affair. Teams of men, horses, several tractors, a grieve and a steady trek of loads across the crackling stubbles to a stackyard where the carts were 'teemed' to stacks on either hand. Old Davidson, farmer, master, and polished brown 'tackits', tootled about on a wee grey Fergie with little understanding of its clutch.

In fields as wide as an empire, Hugh and I forked load after load, lifting a stook between us in a 'one'er' if we could, two men building the loads, place the sheaf to their hand, head in. The rustle of the straw, the oatmeal freshness, shirt off, sun on sweat, swing and toss, the flow of young strength and the belly flat. Even the 'gowk' caught harvest fever and insisted on building a load, but nervous of heights he piled the sheaves about him, disappeared into a 'crows nest' and wouldn't come down. The load wobbled its way to the stackyard and one blast from the grieve sent him scurrying back to his stick shed.

No work interfered with the midday dinner, eaten in the stone flagged farmhouse kitchen by all the single workers, the helpers, anybody who happened to call and the Davidson family. 'Old Culethie' sat at the head of a long scrub top table, collar and stud, portly and prosperous, Hughie and I, lowly and poor, sat at the bottom. Conversation did not feature, hungry bellies kept mouths full. Plates of broth, cold mutton and dry Golden Wonder tatties were enlivened by a pudding of rice and prunes. It could not be said our diet lacked fibre.

The Olympian heap of steaming tatties arrived on the table before me in a huge willow patterned tureen to be dished out by the skivvy onto the emptied soup plates in a conveyer belt system. As the week passed I became aware that the dark haired skivvy lent pleasantly against me as she served our plebeian diet of tatties.

'Corn rigs and barley rigs, and corn rigs are bonnie o', I'll ne'er forget that wonderful night amang'st the rigs wi' Annie o'. Sentiments in tune with the great Bard's weakness were surging. By the Friday as she stood close beside me, a trembling hand slid under her skirt, up slightly parted thighs and stroked a deliciously smooth, bare bottom.

The back break of the 'tattie hairst' drew mercifully to an end, pits were well 'happit' with straw and soil, and the feeding beasts were tied for the winter. The night brought stars to my skylight when I blew out the candle, the steady tread of winter to the step each morning. The Tap o' North, a hill above the farm felt the sting of sleet. Even at 'Lums' the pace of work slowed. There was energy to spare and more.

Long evenings and the young could slip out after supper, meet by the bridge, endless talk and sometimes a cuddle. Dances in the school hall, soap flakes on the floor, 'Brylcream' on your hair, and the rush for the last waltz might ensure a walk to an outlying farm with the 'quine' of your heart, if you were lucky.

Sandy was not all work. In company his lined face could crack with the best of laughs and stories. He sometimes took us youngsters out visiting of an evening. The green and black bull-nosed Morris, its brass temperature gauge perched on the bonnet, would back out of its special shed under high revs and a plume of white vapour. One night of prickling stars and keen excitement it took Hughie, Margaret and me to the badlands of Aberdeen-shire and a Tattie Shed Ball.

The sweep of our headlights exposed a pack of cars and bicycles, back seat heads ducked, tilting half bottles glinted, revellers relieving themselves turned their backs, the ball was well under way. Self-consciously we made across the yard. The strains of an Eightsome squeezed out between the stacks, amorous couples squeezed in. The roar of a generator fighting the band provided a string of flickering lights which hung from the rafters and revealed a cavorting mass of shining faces, but left the bottom end of the dance shed dark, dangerous, and for some, gropingly romantic.

At the sound of a slow waltz I shyly asked Margaret to dance. Only then did I find that half the sloping dance floor consisted of wooden sections laid side by side, whilst the remainder was plain earth. We glided off uphill to find the ballroom steps, of which I was so proud, were reduced to a series of trips and jerks with a step down half way round. A Dashing White Sergeant brought the action we needed and the night danced away without a thought of tatties.

Sandy drove us home. I sat beside Margaret in the back, gently our legs touched and little by little our heads. I longed for a kiss to seal the night, but I was only the orraloon.

Many years later when farming on my own account I went to see Sandy in hospital in Inverness. He sat upright in bed learning to eat with one hand. Two days before, a potato dressing machine had claimed his right arm. The little sharp eyes filled with welcome, and I saw I took him back to a Whitelums when their numerous family were about the farm and the harvests full of sun. We talked, remembered, and as we parted he paid me the only compliment I've ever valued, "Well Iain, you were the easiest learnt loon that was ever about the place." No loon could have been taught by a better farmer.

The influences upon youth are vital and lasting. Few months were to pass before, along with my auctioneering namesake and friend, I stood at his grave side and thanked him.

Two hundred years had passed. Accommodation and sanitation for the orraloon in the heartland of Aberdeenshire, when I was 'fee'd' for half a crown to an outlying farm at the 'Back of Bennachie', would have made one feel at home in Castle Dounie. Never the less on leaving Whitelums my weekly wage rose by five shillings to £2,10s, and as entry to a dance in Rhynie or Kennethmont was 1s,6p, it did allow scope for 'high jinks'on a Friday night.

I flitted, bus and one small suit case, started work as an experienced orraloon and moved into the free, find your own fuel, on-farm accommodation. Life in a North East 'chaumer' prepared any youth for the comparative ease of a corrective training establishment. A stone built wood lined bothy, it conveniently backed onto the dung midden, provided an unsprung iron bed, horse hair mattress, ex-army blankets and drafty rat holes. What tempted the rats to use them was not obvious.

Heating involved keeping warm gathering wood, cooling down whilst burning it, and crouching over a grate of which Scrooge would have approved. We got clean sheets when it suited the Skivvy, and working clothes made a good pillow with the added advantage of keeping them from freezing. Anything more fashionable, dancing suit and off white shirt, hung on six inch nails. The wonder of electricity? I suspected the news of its invention had yet to reach 'orraland'. An oil lamp, of a frugal size, sat on the corner of the mantel piece shedding enough light to read the large print of the Press and Journal.

In the matter of washing, life became primitive. Use of a cold tap in the stone scullery of the farmhouse was permitted, and sometimes a kettle of hot water materialised if the Skivvy was in tune. Mostly the cattleman, with whom I shared the bothy, and myself, went night about in the warm water from the radiator of the Fordson tractor.

Sanitation was simple and haemorrhoid free. Straw, a shovel and a quiet moment at the end of the byre or between the horses. Even the Skivvy, who milked the house cow at seven in the morning and four in the afternoon, was known to have a pee behind the byre door, but then she also had a fag, against orders, in her attic bedroom and blew the smoke out of the skylight.

Meals in the farmhouse could not be termed epicurean but were definitely wholesome, and tasty too, for devotees of an oatmeal diet. The kettle sat boiling on the open range each morning at a quarter past six and greed alone governed the amount of brose you could consume before oatcakes and two boiled eggs, burnished by the candlelight, were set before you. Dinner came as an oatmeal free interlude, apart from a choice of oatcakes served with the broth.

At supper came the full holy oatmeal ritual, tended on the open range by a hand maiden of the sacred oat. In our case the Skivvy, not thought to be quite of vestal virgin standard, but sufficient to stir the volcanic pan of porridge which popped aromatic curls of steam into the lamp lit rafters, and gurgled graciously at us famished worshippers as a lava flow of oatmeal poured onto winking plates.

'Food for horses and Scotsmen.' is the sarcastic definition of 'oats' given in the monumental English dictionary written by Dr. Johnson. Little did he know, we lusty orraloons left for the dances, our carbolic faces shiny with health and red with rampant expectation. The horses didn't look bad either.

Tied by the neck, side by side, a byre full of fattening bullocks each night also got a pail of bruised oats from the kist, and straw to fill their hakes. My storm lantern swung shadows onto frost blinking walls. Rats scuttled deliberately over the cobbles, slithering thick tails along the ground. The cattle, hoary coated, rose from cudding to stretch and belch. Neck chains jingled. Broad black Aberdeen-Angus faces looked round, a speck of yellow lantern light caught in dark round eyes. Calling low and throaty, their turnip breath came sweet as I pushed between them. The plop, plop of dung, firm and steaming, pungent as the scent of a fresh turned furrow on a day of spring showers. I would linger in the warm smell and scratch the thick mossy coat of a favourite.

In late November the overnight blizzard drifted halfway up the bothy windows. Out of a rat hole below my bed it blew a jet stream of snow across the floor which showed no inclination to melt. New light poured in, exposing dust on the cobwebs, embarrassing the spiders but certainly not the Skivvy who frisked a brush across our floor once a week. The prospect of a day clipping and carting turnips contrasted with that of Bing Crosby who was 'Dreaming of a White Christmas' from the battery radio as I rubbed cows udder cream into my gaping hacks.

Bent under an old army gas cape I worked on the drills of swedes blown clear of snow. Hook in the one hand, clipper the other, both hands frozen to the handles, the secret was to stay back bent and stop thinking. Each swede was tug, clip, throw. Sleet rattled on my ancient cape, minus buttons it draped to the ground either side of me. I resembled a slowly advancing tent which ejected swedes from under its flap at regular intervals. Raising frost caked eyebrows I watched for the Skivvy, bearer of my 'half yoking.'

In the hollow November sunshine the neat lines of bright purple swedes I had clipped shone in glory with a robe like richness. I spied the Skivvy. For a moment I remained bent. A pair of well filled ankle wellies lumbered up beside me. Her bare legs met me at eye level. I marvelled. Stunningly bright purple, they were exactly the same shade as the swedes.

Not too dissimilar in shape either, though I never did check the consistency. To warm my hands as she trudged away I put up a barrage of snowballs. The purple legs fled. A lucky snowball hit the empty cocoa kettle with a ding. My days were numbered, she had the ear of the farmer's wife.

The pair of Clydesdales put willing shoulders to collars that afternoon. Sleet clung to their coats and faces, every so often they threw it off with a harness jangling shudder. Snow built under their shoes until it kicked off in great white scallops, and yet they pulled on. Up the rows of swedes the iron bound wheels of the wooden 'cowp carts' cut deeply, heavy going, I turned the horses on the headland to load down the slope between the morning's clipped rows. Swinging graip prongs soon filled each cart, one behind the other, down to the turnip shed, cowped with a rumble and back up. The three of us made a team.

As the eastern sky began to purple with frost, we hauled down the last loads. It was getting dark and slippery. A welcome lantern threw light at the back of the turnip shed as I backed the young horse with the last load close to the wall in behind the door.

Standing between wheel and door post I pulled the wedge which let the cart tip. Swedes thudded out. Without warning the horse leapt forward. A splintering crash, the wheel smashed into the door post. In the second it took, I sprang, onto the cart shaft. If not, I was crushed, sure as the door post was cracked. The horse flung to its knees, squealed and kicked on the slippery snow. It could bolt no further. Grabbing the head collar I got the trembling horse on its feet. The Skivvy's cat flew from the shadows. For a while I let the horse stand and then without fuss manoeuvred out of the shed and put the poor beast in the stable.

After supper that night in the stable I hung the lantern above the corn kist and gave the hardy brutes an extra feed. As I brushed down the young horses legs he nibbled about my jacket pocket, I stood up and pulled his ear. We were still friends.

The crunch of boots on frost reached the door, a finger poked up the latch and in from the neighbouring farm came mufflers, caps, and old khaki greatcoats. " Man, man, ye hev it fine warm in here." And so it was, tight and cosy in the warmth of the hay with the boys on the kist and me at the 'moothy' tunes perched in the stall 'atween twa' happy munching heads. Even a king can smell like a horse.

Baron Nicholas Stackelberg in elegant posture rested his hand on the lid of a laboriously waxed grand piano of elephantine proportions. A white enamelled basin sat with the efficacy of a spittoon on the further corner of the instrument and at minute intervals, in suitably musical tone, a well aimed plop was to punctuate our conversation. The 17th century roof of Erchless Castle, one time seat of The Chisholm of Chisholm was leaking.

A man of singular appearance, the Baron's imperiously tilted head, set off a predacious nose and expansive brown eyes. Six foot two of solid manhood topped by a bald dome which vied with the piano for depth of shine. A wide check open neck shirt was tucked loosely into a voluminous pair of tweedie plus-four trousers, which would have been cheerfully donned by any Cossack dancer, and could certainly be considered admirable dress for a late night visit to the pheasant roosts. Hooded eyelids shielded cold pin points of frank appraisal. I soon learnt that the Baron talked by eye in an arresting variety of expressions, but for some moments he neither spoke or moved.

Gazing at me off the wall in full length portrait was a second version of the Baron. His hand this time rested with equal poise on the hilt of a sword rather than on the piano. He stood, blue tunic and white breeches in the gold braided splendour of a Cavalry Officer serving with a regiment of the ill fated Czar, Nicholas the 2nd. Along with many of the White Russian aristocracy after the murder of the Czar in 1917, Baron Stackelberg fled to Paris in little more than smouldering socks. 'Paree' and poverty are miserable stable mates. The Baron soon put foot to stirrup and with all the dash of a charging cavalryman, swung up behind him, on the saddle of love, a petite English woman, Phyllis Roscoe, who also happened to be surprisingly wealthy.

The Baron watched my eyes swivel from portrait to basin. He ignored the dripping ceiling with the aplomb of a born aristocrat. "You were cavalryman, in what, ah umm, regiment you were?" He glanced down at my application to be a cattleman with his herd of pedigreed Jersey cattle. "Yes, I served with the Household Cavalry, in the Royal Horse Guards." His eyes flicked from sombre slits to shining circles, hands lifted in Parisian delight, "Oh, la la," he exclaimed with more than a hint of flamboyance, and proceeded to question me closely on the form of my old regiment's ceremonial duties.

The gulf between a trooper in 'The Blues' and an officer in the Czar's crack cavalry he ignored as completely as anything I might or might not know about dairy cattle. Happy to have met a fellow cavalryman I was engaged on the instant, and soon discovered why, down in the byres, they called him 'Lala.'

Chisholm is the Saxon name of a Border property and in all probability the name came north towards the end of the eleven hundreds at a time when assorted troupes of land grabbing Normans were pushing into the Highlands and generally giving the local Celts a hard time.

Around the year twelve hundred Guthred Chisholm, Thane of Caithness married a daughter of the Earl of Atholl to become one of the most powerful chiefs beyond the Moray Firth. A fact which he continually underlined by fomenting disturbance throughout the Highlands in a most professional manner. Unimpressed by this form of self expression, King of the day, William the 1st of Scotland, known as The Lion, sallied north defeated the Thane, and cured his high spirits in pre-emptory style by putting him to death.

Disconcerted at the loss of their leader and shorn of their lands, Guthred's men made a run for the safety of Strathglass and lay low for a generation or two. Over the hill from this Chisholm retreat, at the foot of Glen Urquhart lay an arrogant fortress with a masterful sweep over the black waters of Loch Ness. Castle Urquhart, built by 'The Hammer of the Scots', Edward the 1st of England, was not a 'monster' spotting venue but the control centre for traffic on the loch and the web of glens which thread north from Glen Mhor. Its Constable was a man of some consequence.

In 1334 this honour fell to Sir Robert Lauder who gave his daughter and heiress in marriage to the Chisholm chief. The clan were back in business. The offspring of this union, Robert Chisholm, duly became Keeper of Urquhart Castle, pulled off a knighthood from King David the 2nd, and fought alongside this son of The Bruce in 1346 at the lamentable defeat of Neville's Cross. In this horrific pitched battle near Durham, fifteen thousand Scots were slain and many captured. King David and many nobles, including Chisholm, were amongst the prisoners. It cost the Scottish people an astronomical ransom of 100,000 merks to buy back from the English a King they were better without.

Sir Robert Chisholm eventually returned home from his jail spell in the South, a man of piety. To prove it, out of his extensive possessions he granted six acres of arable ground within the bounds of the old castle of Inverness for the relief of the poor. Called 'Tir na Bochd' in the Gaelic, or 'Land of the Poor' it's now corrupted to Diriebught. The Charter attests this gift to have been 'for the salvation of my soul', suggesting perhaps a pious insurance policy.

During the fourteen hundreds much of the clan's property was dissipated due to the lack of a male heir. Ultimately only the original bolt hole of Strathglass remained Chisholm country, but for old times sake, in 1513 peace and piety were put aside, and Uilan Chisholm of Comar, together with his pal Alistair MacRanald of Glengarry, passed a happy weekend, much as the society of today's society might throw a barbecue, in storming the Castle of Urquhart. Of which frowning fortification, the Chisholm forbears had once been honourable custodians. The two gentlemen were not at home when the police called.

Before the days of bus parties and pipers my sister and I as children ran about the Castle's sprawling ruins, rolled on its sheep cropped mound and balanced along the tumbling red stone walls. Our parents climbed the tower and made grown up talk to a man who showed them swords. The day shone on us, the castle was ours. Secretly we made down to the water's edge, "Lets wash our faces in the loch," my sister laughed, "for luck." The water splashed crystal cold. We ran up at my father's shout, our faces glowing, the fortune of happy childhood in glistening eyes.

Years passed. Tickets, tourists and turnstiles arrived. Neglected walls donned plaster, 'flymos' ate the grass and uniformed guides kept an eye on scampering children. But late on a summer's evening as the watching moon rose through silhouetted trees on a far ridge, and tremulous light set an orange flame on the lochs last ripples, I rowed under the shadow of the old tower and scaled its walls. The great castle lived in the whispering moonlight. I felt its power.

Killiecrankie, the '15', the calamity of Culloden. Two hundred fighting men marched out of Strathglass for Prince Charlie and the last throw of the old faith. Roderick, Chief of Clan Chisholm, Jacobite but realist, sent his sons to fight on opposing sides. Chisholm fought Chisholm across the body strewn heather of Drumossie Moor. An empty ploy, only forfeited estates, a broken clan and misery at the hearthstone resulted. Alexander succeeded Roderick to the family honours and in 1785, whilst enjoying the esteem of restored estates, he left an only child Mary who married James Gooden, Esq., of London, and perhaps under his influence, she turned her back on the Highlands.

So to the degradation of patriarchal bonds and the clearing of the clan lands of Strathglass for the grazing of Cheviot sheep. Homeless Chisholm families were to find shelter over the high ridges above Glen Cannich in the Fraser lands of Strathfarrar. The loins of a chiefdom which once styled itself 'The Chisholm' faltered in faith and fecundity.

On a verdant burial mound overlooking the ancestral Erchless Castle can be read of premature death and unstated sadness. A turbulent family of great antiquity had run its course.

Coal mine owner, Lancashire cotton spinner and proof of the saying, 'Where there's muck there's brass', George Roscoe amassed a sizeable fortune amidst the satanic squalor of English mill towns. His daughter Phyllis bore no evidence of contact with shawl or curlers, was a good pianist, keen French linguist and, when her father 'popped his clogs', found herself heir to a fortune of several million. However Daddy, not totally blinded by the idle conceit of an aristocratic title, and upholder of the belief that money was for making in preference to spending, had, with an eye on the squandering skills of his daughter's expansive Russian husband, thoughtfully salted the bulk of his 'brass' under trustees.

None the less for the sum of twenty-six thousand pounds the Baron and Baroness in 1946 bought Erchless Estate. A namely property magnificently situated in a rippling bend of the Beauly river just down from its confluence with the Farrar, and the gateway to Glenstrathfarrar. Broad swathe of alluvial fields, few thousand acres of hill, furnished castle, stately avenues, oak and larch, numerous cottages and a sprinkling of tenant farmers. Crofters, stags, woodcock and salmon, what more could one ask to create the image of 'Highland gentry?'

Central heating? Hardly the thing. Rigours of life behind a tapestry draft screen. Good for one, cold shower too, humph. But the Baroness being a bloom of southern climes, for a figure not dissimilar to its purchase price, the castle succumbed to radiators and an oil tanker arrived once a fortnight to keep the home fires burning.

To maintain a polish on the black inlaid furniture, cook, mend and generally minister to the needs of the couple was no mean undertaking. A staff of six busied themselves to that end. Control of the menage lay in the no-nonsense hands of Miss Bell. During the war the castle had been requisitioned as a rest centre for entertainment artists from the Forces and the strictly Presbyterian Miss Bell saw to it that Colonel Hanky -panky did not appear on their recuperation programme. Her flare for discipline had not dimmed.

The Baron and Baroness were generous employers, paying top wages to the five of us working in the byres, another five men on the farm, a couple in the gardens and by no means least, Duncan Chisholm, the stalker. Together with the village folk it made for a thriving community. Lots of children, a busy school, hall, Post Office and shop. Weddings, funerals, whist drives and dances, all within walking distance. And, for those so inclined, the Struy pub boasted Ale and Porter.

Inclined one would have needed to be for the wayside howff consisted of a chairless wooden room little bigger than a coffin on its end, with a tiny scrub topped hatch opposite the lid. Strictly men only, into the gloom of this shrine you spoke and passed a votive offering. A hand slid out, your money slid away. Silence, then a faint clink of glass muffled by darkness. A pint slid out, the hand slipped away. Only a frothy trail remained.

Not being a regular worshipper in those days I never did glimpse what lay beyond the hand, but believed it belonged to a Mrs. MacDonald, known to the faithful as Auntie Mary.

With the construction work on the three major hydro-dams taking place in the '1950s', it was only fitting that the Struy pub should enjoy complementary treatment, it being the vital link between pouring concrete and consuming pints. This onerous responsibility fell to retired Police Inspector, Willie Boa, who with commendable energy raised the premises to the standard of 'spit and sawdust.'

Tables infringed drinking space, but as a compromise limited seating was installed. The simple ingenuity of nailing a broad plank along each wall afforded hitherto long standing drinkers something approaching the comfort of a church pew, plus a safety zone on the floor beneath the bench for parking their pints and sheltering collie dogs. A transverse bar now supported a gantry of mouth watering 'malts' whose glint of amber delight danced to a faintly weaving 40 watt bulb which hung in mournful temperance above the happy drinkers, spreading a sickly dappled light across their merry faces due to its heavy crust of fly dirt.

Much thought went into the matter of sanitation. Thanks to the advent of street lighting, no longer could a 'run off' in the garden be considered seemly nor even necessary. Herbicides were sweeping the country as a weed control policy and made the 70% proof 'pee' seem positively anti-diluvian. The Inspector sighed, further drinking space must be sacrificed.

A 'Gents', complete with sliding door, gave just cause for an opening celebration and the ensuing 'good nights takings' by happy chance covered the cost of installation. Chauvinistically the ladies were left to advertise that nature called by crawling under the bar counter and making a bashful exit to an upstairs 'loo.' Maidens of a less retiring temperament or perhaps 'in extremis' were known to use the Gents with a foot against the door. Only by degrees did the fair sex gain foot holds in a male domain.

In due course this hub of village life passed from the Police Inspector to the popular, if somewhat less circumspect hands of his son John Boa. Affectionately known as 'JB', ex banker and man of wise 'investments', he was generally to be found, when not singing Gaelic songs after hours, sheltering behind the pink pages of the Financial Times. He saw no reason to further debase the true Highland character of his establishment with floor coverings or chintzy curtains, and firmly believed that one sound drinking local, of which there were several fine examples to hand, was worth ten English tourists.

Lunch time would find 'JB' behind both counter and Financial Times, his agile mind calculating the percentage rise of the latest gushing oil share, oblivious to an opening door.

Enter a classic. Ruddy face, knee breeches, red socks and ever so slight a paunch. Boa's mind had just off loaded a thousand shares. Discreet pause, "Ah, ah humm, I say barman, d'you think," Without even a rustle of the 'FT' and only the merest glance over his half spectacles, "Half of Lager Shandy?" "I say barman how clever, you must be a mind reader."

It was only worth washing glasses that had graced a 'double', and 'JB's' tetchy treatment of the half pint tourist or the cavalry twilled 'toff', drew admiration from the distillery investing locals.

The door of the Struy pub stood listlessly ajar. The glen an open window of oppressive sun. The sheep lay in leaf drooping shade against the fence, heads outstretched, just the flick of an ear showed life. In low sweltering sighs, the gossip of river and stone, drifted across the churchyard field. Man and beast in the heat looked to the high cool corries of Beinn a' Bha'ach Ard where idling stags rolled the last of winter coats on dying snows and chattering ptarmigan, red tipped in summer glory, scraped and strutted amidst peaks of endless blue. Before the days of hurry the Highlands were beautiful.

"Three large gin and tonics please." Under the canopied Financial Times 'JB', who had been known to sleep through an order for a half of shandy, came instantly awake and arose with a smile. Into the relative cool of the bar had strolled a couple who, sporting southern English accents, talked excitedly and gulped their drinks. Bar counters are more revealing than any psychiatrist's couch and Boa, as a practiced observer of the human predicament, was highly curious. The third drink in the round was carried outside by the woman. Order followed order. The till clinked. Boa beamed.

Donnie Cameron, retired crofter, retired collie at heel, came over the road for a lunchtime pint, and mixing courtesy with curiosity, paused to pass the time of day with a benign looking elderly gentleman who sat in the rear of a Bentley saloon sipping gin and tonic. The glorious combination of weather and scenery had the old boy captivated, he had not been to the Highlands before, and above all "the peace of the place," he sighed. Cameron leant on his stick, snippets of conversation passed in moments. The butler and housekeeper were taking the gentleman a run to Glen Affric. He so looked forward to seeing its unrivalled splendour. "You'll not be disappointed," Donnie assured him, and turned in for his pint.

Three weeks later below deep fronds of bracken beside the graceful Plodda falls, midst the humbling serenity of Glen Affric, the police stumbled on the old chap's body. He had been hacked to death, with a garden spade.

LAZY, IGNORANT AND
ADDICTED TO DRINKING

Treason, a popular sport amongst aristocracy down the ages, always carried dire penalties. Being caught offside was generally jail, confiscation of all but your underpants, a squeeze of the thumb screws, a stretch on the rack, and a head job just to emphasise the point. Simply the rules of the game which the '15' and '45' rebels learnt a trifle too late.

In 1715 the English Crown annexed the extensive estates of Jacobites caught on the wrong foot and with a magnanimous gesture, not a common feature of Government policies, agreed to honour the legitimate debts of the dispossessed owners. 'Opening the books' of the 'baddies' however revealed spectacular liabilities. Cutting off a head or two, cheap, 'coughing up' for the excesses of aristocratic life styles, something else. Disconcerted politicians found their administration financially lumbered. A shortsighted takeover had been made. Reverting to type, profit eclipsed principle. Privatisation appeared the solution.

The hurriedly set up 'Commissioners of the Forfeited Estates' were promptly instructed to 'flog off' these enclaves of fiscal and cultural liability at public auction. Unhappily such was the dearth of 'bawbees' below Scottish beds at the time that heated bidding seemed about as improbable as blazing inflation. Assets might be for the picking. The sweet scent of lucre drifted south and set atwitching the sensitive nostrils of a certain London lawyer.

'The Governor and Company of Undertakers for Raising the Thames Water in York Buildings', was the inspired name of a highly respected London company, which had been established in 1691 to supply the citizens of the Strand with the refinement of untreated river water. Moreover the Charter of this 'York Buildings Company' (its name having been mercifully shortened), allowed for the purchase of land. A fact which, together with a whiff of the Government's dilemma, tickled the whiskers of our sniffing solicitor.

Enter Mr. Case Billingsley, a gymnastic lawyer performing on the trapeze wires of speculation whose name alone should have alerted all but the illiterate. But not so, and he busily devised an ingenious coup. For £7,000 Billingsley and five accomplices bought the entire share capital of the Yorks Buildings Company, wheeled in the Duke of Chandos as Governor, to give the operation a veneer of respectability, and the revamped team moved smartly from raising water to raising capital. Invest now 'For the purchasing of Forfeited and other estates in Great Britain' trumpeted the glossy broadsheet and floated a colossal stock issue of £1,200,000.

Cash poured in, one and a half million within months, shares flew from £10 to over £300. The greed stampede took off. Come October 1719 and the Commissioners for the Forfeited Estates began to auction a fair chunk of Scotland.

"I have £50,000, it's against you Sir, £50,000. £55,000, thank you, now you Sir, don't miss this desirable Panmure residential estate for a bid, £55,000, £55, £60,000, I have £60,000 on my left, make no mistake, £60,000 it's your last chance Sir, £60, £60,000, are you bidding sir? £60,400, thank you, £60,400, once twice." Smack, the hammer fell. "Sold to the York Buildings Company, thank you Sir." A token ripple of applause barely covered the - protesting sobs of Lady Panmure. "Next week we have the sale of the Kilsyth Estates, details can be had in the office." Attending the sale on behalf of this burgeoning Scottish landowner were two theatrically named gentlemen, Messers Wicker and Hacket.

Spats, cravats, and silver topped canes, twelve months of nodding and winking on the part of this pair spent £308,913 of Company funds. Such namely estates as Southesk and Linlithgow appeared on the Boardroom map. Even the estates of Rob Roy were coloured red for the modest sum of £820. But back at the ranch, as they say, all was not well.

Raising a copy of sale particulars for the last bid in the safety of the Sheriff Court was one thing, gaining control of these outback purchases by peaceful means, quite another. The natives, resenting strangers, proved ugly. Also each purchase included the debts of the dispossessed, and worse, some of the Edinburgh solicitors acting for the York Buildings Company were suspected of bribery to favour the rebels.

Nothing retreats faster than a frightened shareholder. Between August and November 1720 at the height of Wicker and Hacket's bidding spree the Company shares plummeted from £295 to £14 and were unsaleable. Mr.Case Billingsley, with a touch of contemporary imagination for his final fund raising throw, organised a shareholder's lottery. Sadly for Case, the sport of powdered gentlemen, gambling in Scottish land from the cosiness of a London coffee house, had lost its fun. For the York Buildings Company, briefly the biggest landowner North of the Border, there began the slow business of winding up the ramificatious affairs of an audacious gamble.

When in 1725 the whole tawdry charade was concluded, out of the £411,082 raised from the sale of fifty forfeited estates, the nett sum received by the Treasury was £1,107. Lessons were learnt. In the interests of common sense, leave as few affairs as possible to management by politicians. The next forfeitures came round after the '45' rebellion and this time control of the 'nationalised' land was placed firmly in the hands of a body of august Scots appointees. Speculation in Scottish land for a decade or two fell out of fashion.

Contrary to popular belief, apart from the unforgiven brutality of Cumberland after the '45', there was no intention on the part of the Government to ruin or lay waste the Highlands. Quite the reverse. Acts of Parliament relating to the Forfeited Estates are explicit. 'to raise money out of them severally for the use of the public.' To effect this deliberate policy, thirteen versions of the 'good and the great' were enrolled on an executive body known as the 'Commissioners of the Forfeited Estates', archetype of a form of administration still familiar in the Highlands, the 'Quango.'

Two tasks immediately faced this committee, a valuation of the properties involved, including their debts, and an overall survey of the estates' populations and possibilities.In 1746 the Commission's work began. Official paperwork took off, and has yet to slacken pace.

Subsequent reports clearly show that monies generated by the estates were expended on public works, and projects for the provision of work, made some attempt at the amelioration of hardship common amongst Scottish people of the day. Many progressive schemes attracted support, the Forth, Clyde and Crinan canals, the Scottish Records Office and the extending of Leith docks amongst them. In less obvious ways, £2,000 was granted to the Society for the Propagation of Christian Knowledge, £3,000 to the Highland Society in Scotland and, out of a more pressing need, £1,000 towards the building of Inverness Jail.

On the restoration of the estates in 1784 to many of their original owners, quite a number, including the Lovat Estates, were in a substantially improved condition. Road works, agricultural innovations and afforestation, were all undertaken to a degree unlikely to have been practiced by a Highland laird steeped in the society circles of Edinburgh or London and fomenting rebellion.

Amidst all the Commissions' reports and deliberations the Lovat Estate stands out. At a period when the total circulating capital of Scotland was merely £800,000, half of which sunk out of sight in the farcical Caribbean Darien scheme, the beheaded Simon Fraser of the '45' had accumulated personal debts of £24,673,18s.6d. and 5 farthings. For an individual to obtain credit on 3% of Scotland's cash will be viewed with awe or horror according one's business principles.

Having dealt with the Laird's debt the Commission's Reporter is disarmingly blunt and equally revealing in describing the denizens of the Lovat lands. His findings are prefaced with an account of the area and a zealous concern for the 'locals' spiritual welfare. The Barony of Bewley, he spells the name with less affectation than of today, lies in the parish of Kilmorack. A helpful enough beginning before the writer lifts the lid on the district stew pot and the smell of its people.

The parish Minister, we are informed, preaches each Sunday, once in English, once in Irish, for which his comfortable stipend amounts to £55,11s.3 1/2d. with a Chalder of meal and a Chalder of 'Bear' thrown in. As the word 'chalder' refers to the old measure of thirty-six bushels and 'bear' obviously to ale, the Minister, it might seem, had small need of a well on the Glebe, and slender grounds for preaching the evils of drink.

An itinerant preacher, presumably of less standing, netted £25 a year, no meal or booze and not a word of travelling expenses. There is a notable lack of churches and schools in the area the Reporter laments, there being but one Society School and no Parochial School. 'The English language gains very little ground', a major shortcoming. Two English schools and two spinning schools are recommended. In particular a new church is vital to Glen Strathfarrar in spite of the difficulty of access due to lack of road and bridge. His main concern reads, 'it lyes [the strath] at a great distance from the Parish Church. The people are grossly ignorant, and amongst them a great number of Papists, and scarce a person who can speak one word of English.'

Turning to the land he mellows and confidently opines, 'the Eastern side of the Barony is a most excellent soil and produces great plenty of Rye, Oats and Pease. The West is fitter for pasture and a good many black cattle are reared from forty to fifty shillings Value, a good deal of butter and Cheese made and brought to Inverness Market for sale.'

The first hint of the Reporter's assessment of the local problem creeps in. 'A pretty large Fir Wood in this Barony, but was much destroyed after the rebellion. There is still a considerable quantity of old trees fit for sale, which ought to be valued and sold as soon as possible, it being difficult to preserve them from being stolen.'

His enthusiasm for development will make familiar reading to those writers of glossy brochures for todays multitude of official bodies that flounce about the Highlands extolling it as a pollution free environment for industry and, moreover, offering 'state of the art' opportunities such as satellite communication from the back room of your croft house with bags of spare time to cut peats or gaze at the scenery.

Reference to the natives apart, a page from his report runs along remarkably similar lines, 'There is a little village called Bewley, where the ruins of the Old Priory still remains, and this I think, with great submission, is an extreme proper place for erecting a village, as nature seems to have intended it for such a thing. It is situated on the north side of the water of Bewley, and the tide comes a little further up than the Priory, and a convenient little harbour could be made at small expense. It lyes in the centre of a very populous fine country, of excellent soil, but where the inhabitants are strangers to the right method of Agriculture, Manufactures and Industry.'

'The very fine Salmon fishing', his survey becoming expansive, 'is capable of great improvement and would be of great support and encouragement to the trade and manufacture that might be established here.' All these commendable features, he points out, becoming inspired, are together with 'extremely commodious communication,' and the Report concludes with passion, 'in short a Village properly encouraged here could not miss to attract strangers of different professions from many corners, and would consequently soon diffuse a spirit of Trade and Industry, as well as promote Agriculture through all this extensive country.'

To the fulfilment of his dream, his entrepot of the North, his bustling Hong Kong of the Highlands, the Reporter concedes one lamentable snag. The 'natives.'

'Several yearly Fairs are already held about the place, a Mercat Cross, and a great collection of poor people, who live in huts and retail ale and spirituous liquors to the people who resort thither.' For the welfare of these idlers he dictates, 'the large flat fields of most excellent soil should be feued out for house and gardens,' and sensing the further critical needs of the people, 'there is already a court house and a prison, which might be fitted up at small expense.'

So to the crux of the problem, 'Manufacturers have made no progress here, and the people are for a great part of the year quite idle. The East part of this Barony is not well provided in firing as their moss is greatly destroyed by the Distillers.' Doubtless a man of upright and abstemious character as befits a public servant he elaborates upon this woeful detraction to the social and spiritual uplift of the 'locals'.

'There are fourteen or fifteen different stills in this Barony for the Distilling of Aqua Vitae or Whiskie, and as many public houses. And the owners of these stills, lett them out for hire, sometimes even to servants, so all the people of this Barony are concerned in the pernicious trade Distilling.'

A final righteous broadside sinks all hope of redemption for the natives, 'The prevailing name here is Fraser, and the common people are generally, lazy, ignorant, and addicted to drinking', but holding out a fig leaf of relief to the Beaulyites, he adds, 'tho not so poor as in some parts of the Estate of Cromarty.'

Having vilified a lifestyle many might consider idyllic, and perhaps failing to confine his comments to the pen, a rough handling amongst the 'papists' of Strathfarrar leads the Gentleman to a last bitter sentence, 'in the Western part of the Barony there are several poor creatures and many perverse, obstinate fellows of bad character.'

Nevertheless such was the civilising progress of the ecumenical movement in the Parish of Kilmorack by the turn of this century that the 'Papist' priest of Cannich and the Protestant Minister of Erchless would frequently betake themselves of an evening by pony and trap to savour the mellowing influences of a Beauly hostelry. The sight and sound of their late return up the strath by plodding pony as they stood swaying arm in arm on the backboard of the trap, singing Hymns of Praise at the tops of their voices, did much to inspire the 'locals' in the spirit of tolerance and forgiveness towards their fellow man.

'Me like the Scotch', Baron Stackelberg would say, referring at that time to the 'natives' rather than the product. He had much to learn of their propensities, particularly when faced by the challenge of free drink. On the Baron and Baroness's first New Year in residence at Erchless Castle they threw a party for the tenantry, staff, and some villagers. Behaviour and singing were muted. The reassured hosts basked in widespread approbation.

Next New Year rolled around, accompanied by much anticipatory licking of lips on the part of the 'locals' for in that era one bottle of whisky saw most households through the Festive Season, even a sip of ginger wine could set off a 'knees up.' The Baron, a dab hand with wood plane and fret saw had built a cocktail bar in one corner of the first floor 'Great Room' and welcomed the guests from behind its curly structure with a liberality normally reserved for the return of a prodigal.

Somewhat naively no filtering system operated at the Castle's stately portal. Amongst the throng there gained ingress certain characters whose drouth could only be equalled by that of a parched traveller crawling towards an oasis. Ritual toasts rapidly turned to futile attempts at thirst quenching.

The Baron poured drinks with the alacrity of a Cossack dancer performing with a nail in his boot. Warning signs took the form of sporadic snatches of Callin Mo Rhunsa and similar maudling ditties. Miss Bell frowned. The Baroness glanced apprehensively between the swaying figures and her precious antiques. Miss Bell snatched away glasses that formed rings on lovingly polished surfaces. The Baroness wrung her hands. Concerted singing developed into a free style Eightsome. Hand clapping, foot stamping, soon the Castle was rocking.

The Baron poured on, a fireman adding fuel to the flames. Who threw the first punch was not clear. Some said it was Miss Bell, but for certain the Baroness shrieked and retired. The large Turkish rug doubled as an arena. Foe punched foe and sometimes friend. Pacifists scored black eyes. An abuse screaming Miss Bell threw open the front door and swept the embroiling mass down the Castle steps.

The Baron poured himself a large dram and sat down. "Me like the Scotch," he sighed, downing a glass. From that night on he never again confused the two.

Setting up a pedigreed herd of Jersey dairy cattle and supplying Inverness with bottled milk bearing the Erchless Castle motif became the mutual obsession of the Baron and his wife once they settled into their Highland retreat.

The old Chisholm Estate had never scrimped on the quality of its houses and steadings. All were a tasteful blend of natural semi-dressed stone with lintels, corners and windows built in warm red sandstone. The commodious Erchless steading above the castle with its prominent clock tower and key stoned arches, lent itself ideally to the conversion needed for a dairy herd, without detracting from these handsome features.

Byres, milking parlour, calf pens and bull boxes, tubular steel neck ties and water bowls, everything for cattle comfort down to an elaborate dunging out system. This latter refinement, the pipe dream of a schizophrenic planner, involved a large tipping tub which swung along on an overhead track from the byres to the midden in the manner of an Alpine cable car. When slopping full and poised for emptying it provided us simple rustics with the prospect of being enveloped to the knees in the wellie pulling suction of a 'sea of shit.' A hazard 'not thought through' by the designer.

Everywhere shone, high gloss paint on marble smooth concrete, Royal blue and cream no less, a loyal colour scheme. Green or brown would have been more practical but, in short, no cattle in the country could have been more sumptuously accommodated and have a Baroness, in matching blue 'nightie' come round most evenings to plant a 'good night kiss' on the noses of her favourite cows. Less sentimentally we in the byres knew these 'pets' as vicious little thugs and were forever stitching up the gashes inflicted on those down the peck order by the brutishly horned attacks of some of "Mummies petsy wetsy darlings."

Many of the foundation cows came from a Strathconon Jersey herd west of Dingwall belonging to Major MacDonald-Buchanan and were plain Mayflowers and Margarets but their offspring born at Erchless bore such imperious names as Ludmilla and Natasha after the murdered daughters of Czar Nicohlas.

The stock bull swanked about his trendy pen rejoicing in the name, Chesham Sonata's Revelation. Bought by the Baron at the Reading pedigree Jersey cattle sale after frenzied bidding against nobody in particular, he cost 1,500 guineas. An unheard of price which held the breed record for many years.

A revelation he indeed proved. Highly temperamental, vicious, and for no obvious reason suffering long bouts of impotence. In concerned conversation about the bull's short coming, a worried Baron took streams of 'experts' to look over the bull pen wall and survey his crestfallen bauble.

Explanations varying from shyness to over feeding with draff, a whisky by-product, might have reflected personal experience. Solutions in similar vein, such as presenting Revelation with a nubile young heifer, had no visible effect. Stuart the vet tried everything a needle could offer to raise the bull's flaccid libido. Duncie Chisholm the keeper, one trusts displaying a sly humour rather than any painful experience, persuaded the Baron we should attempt a decidedly vulgar and certainly dangerous solution involving stinging nettles.

Revelation took his problem to the slaughterhouse. Such is the omnipotence of the cattle breeder.

Two Yankie limousines of a size to justify a speaking tube between the rear passenger and the chauffeur, stood patiently in the coach house at the corner of the Erchless farm steading. One a blue open topped swashbuckling Studebaker, the other, a morose black eight cylinder Buick which required to be shadowed by a petrol tanker when proceeding any distance beyond Hughie Gordon's village pump. Indeed Hugh claimed to be unable to wind the pump handle fast enough to refuel the vehicle unless its engine were switched off.

Each summer the Baron and Geordie Morrison, saw miller, handyman and estate comedian, trundled one of the 'automobiles" onto the yard and proceeded to rev it, pump it, oil it, and finally massage it with chamois leather and yellow duster to transform its bulk into the spriteliness of a gazelle. Chrome searchlights gleaming, green leather opulently fragrant, and 'Good Year' in white whizzing round on each tyre, it was suitably groomed to whisk the happy couple away to their vineyard in the south of France and the convivial festival of pressing their grapes.

A monster wicker hamper packed in the boot contained all the sorts of 'goodies' of which Mr.Toad would have thoroughly approved, plus of course the Baron's personal supplies, several cases of 'Ten year old Malt.' With the petite Baroness in the front, only able to see the tops of the hedges and her personal maid, the diminutive Miss Rickards in the back, only able to see the sky, the Baron in yellow driving gloves would roar away to a series of 'Le Mans' gear changes which left the staff on the castle steps, fog bound in blue fumes, waving hankies and shedding crocodile tears.

So to the leisured days. Miss Bell, always the business woman, had coffee brought to her desk at eleven whilst she considered the days allocation of duties, Petro the Russian chef felt free to communicate his inspired judgement of the days 'racing form to the 'bookie' in Inverness, whilst Colin the butler in the 'sacred pantry', lay on his couch considering the silver cutlery and surveying the ravages of gout. The demands of the Baron's two ill-tempered gun dogs kept the castle on its toes.

For us in the byre nothing changed. The herd continued to be milked in the middle of the night, a somnabulant five in the morning and again at four in the afternoon. Two hour's break at middle day and one long weekend off in three. A regimental routine dedicated to doorstep pints.

No freedom roam to wood or hill, nor space to spread the mind, no loiter in another world, which other beings find.

But summer's morn, down thrush sung dawn, on the road to work, twixt tree and dyke a shivering light, lit my hidden way, for engine's cough had yet to foul, the haunts of owl, before the edge of day.

Faint lingering shadows knelt, soft moss on tombstone dyke, a hymn through vaulted beech, to the leaf of autumn's fall. Grey pillared doorway wide I stepped, down an echoed aisle. I breathed a holy incense. Communion once held all.

Gentle on the sweet grass, below the tree lined hay, a roe and bob-tailed twins so deft, that every web was left. High amongst the branches, hide and seek and play, squirrels fluffed their tails, swung a schoolboy day. And lifted heart, I laughed aloud, and wished their simple way.

Often on the castle fields, an ocean mist would drift, and trunkless trees would float, upon a yellow sea. And under wondering pigeons coo, each track tell tailed the dew, a meander here, a hurry there, in a world they told to few.

The cows in coats of silver, would rise and tend my call, the ground was warm, a scent of milk, perhaps the wee folk knew. For many once had seen, the little men in green, and for an inst, a blink of eye, ere sunrise slipped away, my mind grew wide, and I stepped inside, to the place its secrets hide.

Byres at five a.m. Wellies slip on green 'skitters' of spring grass shot at random over concrete floor and wall as the Baroness's doe-eyed darlings hustle into neck tie and stall to munch a wisp of hay in the hope of settling their stomachs. It's the first step towards putting milk on your corn flakes.

Swinging pendulous tits, the shameless cows follow their bellies into the tubular steel house of pleasure, otherwise known as the milking parlour. Here, in troughs, a breakfast of cattle cake awaits them. Do the gluttons care that Pavlovian greed, gobbling scoopfuls of addictive 'Happy Day's Dairy cake' is liable to explode their distended udders? I doubt it. The more they eat the greater the swelling. At least some well endowed beauties will produce milk records which qualify them for the Cattle Society's 'Order of Merit', and the honour of having '0.M.'after their name, stencilled by the Baron in red paint on a plate above their stall.

The first maiden of the morning skips into the parlour. In moments her nose in a trough, clank clank, her neck in a yolk and a chain holds her hips. Gobble, gobble, along with breakfast she savours the pleasures of the seductive handed cattleman. Pail of warm water, cloth in hand, he advances, no by your leave, to massage her full and shapely mammaries. They swell, firm and beautiful. Ss-ll-up, on the slide pulsating teat cups. Does a gentle moan emerge? No, except perhaps from the seducer as disinfectant bites his hacks. Soon thick yellow jets of butter rich milk ejaculate with regular beat into the glass jar suspended on a spring above the ecstatic maidens munching head. Ecstatic? A rough tongue rasps the trough and she turns her nose and moo's for more. Cake?

Fiss tu, fiss tu, fiss tu, goes the vacuum milking machine, staccato, mindless, mechanical. Plop plip, plop plop, plip, goes the cow, splitter, splatter, mindless, mechanical. "Stand still, damn you bitch, will you bloody well stand?" swears the cattleman, moody, mindless, mechanical. A sudden splodge of warmth on the back of his off white milking coat as he bends to remove this bovine breast pump tells him she objects to the language. Her counter attack is none too subtle and it sticks.

Five minutes, it's all over, her shapely udder, flat, wrinkled and very much an empty bag. Its bubbly contents transferred to the milk jar boasts a head to shame a pint. The cattleman, a glance at the weight, a flick of a switch, a pull of a handle, and away goes her milk, 'swoosh' to the bottle. Away goes the cow, 'pppppp' to the field. Two and a half gallons off her mind, en route to your tea.

Now master planning is the Baron's forte and on the wall of the parlour, well behind the cows, hangs an expansive chart, the scope of which would draw admiration from even the most forward thinking medical practice. Every detail of each cow's private affairs is there for all to scan. Her age, when she calved, any stitches required, her daily milk yield and, dare I tell you, the date of her latest dalliance with the bull. An indiscreet pencil hangs on a string.

With each parlour departing matron, a lick of the pencil point scrawls her vital milk statistic in the relevant column. With a well timed cough and deadly aim a disdainful cow has been known to record her own comment on the board. The distance is approximately three yards. No mean feat.

Woe is me, the dangers of a cattle man's life and exposed twice a day, quite a merry-go-round. But sexy, don't you think?

Pride of the Erchless dairy herd was the home reared heifers. To this wealthy couple who lacked nothing save children, they became a surrogate family and a heifer's individual progress within the herd was watched with the cherished interest normally lavished upon a favourite daughter having her manners manicured at finishing school.

Between nine and nine-thirty each morning the Baron would call a conference before the all revealing chart. Whosoever had been responsible for the previous two milkings faced interrogation. As Lala's eye followed down the daily yields of the sixty odd cows, his mobile face rose or fell in direct proportion to the milk flow of his favourites.

A whoop of "Oh LaLa" at an extra half gallon might descend in seconds to a despairing Shakespearian clasp of the brow if the next maiden's milk supply had slumped. The bleary brained cattleman faced an angry note of censure. If his excuse for the cow's off day failed to convince, LaLa's contorted face would flush the colour of a Pre-Raphaelite palette. His displeasure was crushing.

Worse were the days when the Baron decided to help. Hugh Grant, Willie Farquharson and myself might intend to move a bunch of young cattle from the Laundry field near the Castle to the grazings at Struy, a task requiring both tact and strategy, for the bovine brain harbours no small degree of subtle cunning.

"You move heifers today Iain?" "Well Baron, er, er, I WAS thinking about it," He notes my change of tense, "Ah yes, um you must, look it, um, lovely day," wave of arm, "I come, ah um, what time you start?" "Ach we'll manage fine Baron." "Oh la, no no, I come, I help." Our hearts sank.

The doe eyed darlings could be coaxed gently towards the open gate. They would stand, lower their heads, sniff the ground and look round. Aah, those long dark, heart melting eyelashes, aah, the innocence. But behind that chaste flutter there formed a plot. We waited. Would they go? Not a word, wait, wait, not the slightest cough, they might, wait, don't move. The Baron, impatient, "Shoo, shoo." That's it. Action.

Tar-ta-rah, tar-ra-ra-tar-ta-rah, they're off. Tails up, hooves drumming, turf flying, bowels emptying. Epsom never had a more flying start. The Baron, arms flailing, a semaphore signaller protesting a false start, narrowly misses being trampled. He springs into the race, he slips, down at the first fence one might say, no, no, he's up, he's off.

Bawling Russian expletives, the Baron, lacking only helmet and sword, is at full gallop, cavalryman to the core, bit between his teeth. Heifers in the lead, three times round the field, twice past the gate, now it's the hurdles. The Baroness calls feebly from the spectators Land Rover, "Nicky, Nicky," and waves a white handkerchief.

Four heifers clear the top barb of the Castle fence, head for the daffodils. Oh dear, the fifth one falters, stuck on the barb. Panting Baron, "Oh la la, I get vet, it cut udder. Phyllis, Phyllis," he semaphores directions to the lamenting Baroness, "We cut fence, I get Geordie."

Tomorrow Calum the gardener will have returfed the Castle lawn, Geordie will have repaired the fence and the Baron will be having a day off. Then's our chance boys. It might be difficult to teach cattle semaphore. Russian, impossible.

Central to the dairying operation at Erchless, apart from the Baron and the cows, was the sterilisation by steam of all the equipment involved. Once a day the paraphernalia of rubber tubes, teat cups, glass jars and anything moveable was stowed into a sizeable steam chest and cooked for twenty minutes. To raise this head of steam required a substantial machine. One such sat in the middle of the dairy. A lengthy steel affair sporting several dials, a bulbous red light on top and, strangely rounded at both ends, it resembled a stranded submarine despite a coat of primrose yellow paint.

The enigma surrounding this machine's operation remains one of the great unsolved mysteries of my life. It ran on Epsom Salts. Whilst I appreciated the merciless purging properties of this chemical, its connection to producing steam from electricity strained my simple imagination. To ensure it functioned smoothly this apparently constipated machine was treated with five tablespoons full of the laxative once a week through a pop hole in its side. The duty of dosing the machine fell to the dairy woman, Mrs.Polson, a cheerful Caithness expat with a highly developed sense of humour.

Panic ensued one day. Mrs.Polson came running to the byre. The steamer had expired. I hurried to the dairy. It certainly didn't look well, no flashing red light, no gurgling from its innerds. Baron away, me in charge. I hesitated. Should I call a Doctor or an electrician? Neither, I ascertained from Mrs.Polson we had merely run out of medicine.

Just time to catch the chemist shop. I cycled down to Beauly, "Please may I have 5lbs. of Epsom Salts?" Stepping smartly back but restraining himself from ducking under the counter, Iain Campbell the Chemist, gazed at me in the manner of a sapper viewing an unexploded bomb. "5lbs?" he repeated softly, "Well I go through five tablespoons full a week, it soon mounts up." Horror registered on his prim face, "That I can believe."

A hastily wrapped parcel was thrust into my hands without further word. As I stepped onto the street, the lock clicked, I turned to look. He was staring through the window.

Ultimately Baron Stackelberg was placed firmly under the heel of a scrupulous exchequer, the trustees of his father in laws fortune. Sadly the terms of this deed appeared to be uncomfortably stringent for the scope of the Barons free spending spirit. Thus to produce 'pin money', the theme of hawking 'tatties' round the Inverness shops appealed and neither he nor the Baroness spared themselves. Also as many of the Castle staff who couldn't venture an excuse were drafted into the ranks of a 'tattie scrubbing brigade.'

Muster at ten, the team paraded smartly down to the spidery old greenhouse which stretched along one side of a spacious walled garden. There beneath the odd cracked pane, there amongst arthritic branches spread eagled on the back wall, whose bounty once plopped delicious nectarines onto the dining table of 'The Chisholm', there the 'volunteers' stood to their scrubbing sinks. Brave to a man, and Miss Bell as well.

Several bags of that famous dry tattie, the Golden Wonder, freshly lifted from the field, would have been positioned by Ian Cumming, the farm grieve, beside the washing troughs. Wearing rubber gloves and forced smiles the conscripts carefully subjected each bronze potato to an invigorating scrub in the freezing water.

At the head of the assembly line the Baron spread the shivering tatties on a table to dry. At the tail of the conveyer belt, due to a discrepancy in her height against that of the trough, the minuscule Miss Rickards fought to keep up. Used only to the finest needlework amidst the Baroness's silk costumes, for this coarser call of duty, she was kindly provided with a box to stand on.

Thursday morning and the Land Rover stacked with bags of clean smiling tatties, sped round its 'shop drops' and proud under their banner, the 'Erchless Castle Golden Wonder Potatoes' headed for the chip pans of the jolly housewives of Inverness. Tired but equally jolly, the Duffle coated Baron, mission complete, headed for the rear entrance of a certain House of Happy Beverages and rubbing his hands reloaded the Land Rover. At the namely home of these humble tatties the staff were also rubbing their hands, with healing lotion.

Only Colin the butler escaped potato scrubbing blight. By skillfully combining his care of the Baron's snarling black dogs with debilitating attacks of gout, his duties, beyond wielding a corkscrew and laying the family silver for dinner, were limited to walking his charges each day and collecting the newspapers.

Above Castle and steading a narrow stone bridge flanked by a sweep of mighty larch and spruce took a bend in the Cannich road across a gorge in the Erchless burn. Lively waters hurried below its hewnstone arch, at once powering the estate sawmill, run by the unhurrying Geordie Morrison, and removing deer's entrails from the back of the venison larder, operated by the stately stalker Duncie Chisholm.

Around late morning Robertson's bus trundled up from Beauly making for its home base at Cannich. Pausing at Erchless bridge , the conductress, bonnie dark haired Nan Ross, would hand out to the awaiting Colin a tightly rolled bundle of the world's hot news.

Colin the butler, by contrast, found the hottest news of consequence could be gleaned within a five mile radius, and he manifested an insatiable interest in the affairs of those in the locality whom, it might be said, transgressed. The speed with which the butler collated and disseminated information was a tribute to the system known as word of mouth, and stood in reverse proportion to his characteristic rate of locomotion. To describe Colin's daily walk to and from the mail bus as a loiter would be ascribing jet propulsion to the snail. His lack of progress, coupled with an endless gazing at the upper bathroom windows of the farm cottages he passed, did not escape the notice of their comely occupants.

On a bright summer morning made for mischief, before the days of polyunsaturates and cholesterol counts, we dairy team sat in the farm cottage kitchen enjoying the flavour of full cream coffee made from Jersey milk. The butler's barely perceptible shuffle and rapt upper window gaze drifted into view. Our achingly desirable dairymaid, seventeen and luscious, looked out. In a roguish leap of delight she rushed upstairs, balanced gracefully on the lavatory lid and with an adroit flip of her skirt, bent and pressed the most curvaceous of bottoms against the pane.

Colin blinked, once, twice, and in a mouth sagging stumble fell back. Eyes covered with trembling hand, papers and gout thrown to the wind, he raced for the Castle. Up the back stair, sanctuary door snibbed, he lay, safe on his favourite chaise longue, panting in the pantry. And, it was observed, did not come out for the best part of some time.

When farming meant people, before the days of cost effectiveness, efficiency, viable units and economic outlooks, it had fun.

HOMES FOR THE HEROES

People were plentiful throughout the Highlands three hundred years ago but was it a halcyon age? Pre-industrial, stress free and pure, a simple life of self sufficiency, ruddy health and no birth control, or just a pastoral idyll extolled in verse and lauded in song by romantics who never dug a peat in their lives. Even for those generations who knew of the realities, nostalgia for shieling and sunshine ran deep in their dreams. My grandmother used a long forgotten Highland phrase as she sat, old amongst the centuries, in a pokey Inverness flat, "well boy, a sad day we left the croft."

The extensive parish of Kilmorack in 1761 numbered about 2500 souls recorded the reporter for the Commissioners of the Forfeited Estates. Infant mortality rendered any children under puberty a dubious statistic and was ignored. Nor was religious tolerance his strong point, he counted inhabitants as those of 'a catechismal age.' Old enough that is to mouth the questions and answers of the Longer and Shorter Presbyterian Catechism.

Of this potential church going throng a regrettable 600 were Papists asserts the Reporter, mainly upon the Estate of Chisholm of Strathglass. But take heart, most of these idolaters were extremely anxious for a school, there being but one in the Barony, anxious even to the extent of agreeing to have their children 'bred Protestant.' The Reporter earnestly suggests sites for a number of these seats of inculcation, not least in the heathen remoteness of Glen Strathfarrar. A schoolmaster might easily be accommodated with 7 or 8 acres of land enclosed with a dry stone dyke for £15. As to the school and schoolmaster's house, the Reporter opines, £60 the pair, stone and lime, heather or bracken thatch and the tenants obliged to cart the material.

The first Presbyterian missionary minister in Strathglass around 1750, is a Mr. Alexr. Mackay, who apart from lamenting the smallness of his stipend at £30 a year, bewails the fact that more than half the inhabitants are 'bigoted papists and have always one, and sometimes two, Popish missionaries amongst them.' The fact that only one Society school exists at Balblair near Beauly, 'about an English mile from the church' to serve a parish forty miles long does not weigh heavily on his scales of redemption.

Eastwards along the shore of the Beauly Firth, still on the Lovat estates, more secular matters concern the parents in the Parish of Kirkhill. A petition, signed by eight Frasers, only one of whom writes his name, pleaded with the factor for a replacement schoolmaster. Dominie Donald Maclean has packed up. His school is neither wind nor water tight he complains, 'the poor people are thereby much discouraged to send their children to it.' Drafts and leaks do not prevent 60 and sometimes 80 children attending class. His curriculum covered not only Latin and Greek, but reading, writing, Church music, ciphering and book-keeping. For which effort he was paid £10 by the Society for the Propagation of Christian Knowledge.

If religion formed part of the prescription, so be it. A poor people of innate intelligence sought scholarship as the high road out of the clay hovel. Another path was soon to open.

Fraser acumen did not die on the block. Simon, son of the beheaded 'Red Fox' was quick to see the error of his ways. Though attainted for treason along with his father, he escaped the axe by pleading overbearing parental influence on his youthful sixteen years, and by 1750 a pardon arrived.

Lucky but landless his education at St. Andrews University prior to the '45' coupled with an inherited shrewdness, saw him called to the Scottish Bar at the tender age of twenty-three, but 'twas the call to the battlefield that restored Fraser fortunes.

The Seven Years war broke out, Simon Fraser was on the King's doorstep in minutes. Highlanders? mused German George, good thinking, send the Highlanders. Fighting? second nature, get them out of the country too, cannon fodder for Canada, and as General Wolfe coolly remarked, 'it matters little if they fall.' In less than a month Fraser had raised 1800 men, mainly from his father's forfeited estates and, as their Colonel, he led the 78th Fraser Highlanders to the glory of Quebec, to scaling the Height's of Abraham and the conquest of Canada.

Major General Simon Fraser, flushed with victory, petitioned the King for the return of his estates. By special Act this was granted in 1774 upon the payment of £20,983,0s.1d. Lovat was back on his lands and the bravery of the Highland Regiments became a byword down the centuries amidst a memorial of tears.

Victory for the Generals conferred Royal preferment, wealth, honours and public adulation. For the 'ranks' it brought discharge, hardship and poverty, the bonus being four intact limbs. 'Homes for the Heroes', a familiar cry after the Great War, was an echo of previous resettlement schemes upon land already under population pressure. The end of the Canadian campaign saw the return of many soldiers to the Lovat Estates in the 1760's, some of whom had enlisted on the promise of land by General Fraser.

The Forfeited Estates Commissioners, known as 'the Board' and harbinger of others to follow, did what it could to provide jobs and a roof as demobbed veterans walked home. At a cost of £591,14s.5p. the Lovat factor arranged the building of 58 houses on the estate and writes to 'the Board' in 1763, 'I have also contracted for many more houses which will come considerably cheaper than imagined, particularly at Barnyards near Beaulie. I have employed a man to make mud or clay houses, which will be very neat and answer the purpose abundantly well.' An account totalling £89,4s.4p. arrived on his desk for thatching them with straw. For little over £10 a time the proto Council house appeared.

Down in Edinburgh at the prestigious High Street address of the confiscated house of the late Lord Lovat, 'the Board' consulted the pre-eminent architect Robert 'fireplace' Adams as to its conversion to their office accommodation. At the very least £300 comes the reply, and further, 'We beg leave to observe that the accommodation would be very much confined, and indeed less than such an Office ought to have. We are very respectfully, Sir, your most Obedient Humble Servants, Robt., and Jas. Adams.' For an unpublicized figure an office to match the perceived status of its incumbents was put in hand. A worthy precedent which subsequent 'Boards' have happily emulated.

Up north the neatly housed tenants, known as the King's Cottagers, had loans of £9 authorised by 'the Board' to those married settlers with a patch of land. A free spade and a guinea of 'seed money' further encouraged their farming enterprises. Most importantly, mud houses apart, employment in land improvement and afforestation was provided.

Limestone quarried on the estate of Abertarff at the west end of Loch Ness and sailed down the loch, began the process of raising fertility on the coastal flats around the Beauly firth. Sea banks and drainage slowly brought into cultivation thousands of acres of alluvial clay. Highly productive land but stiff to work, it would half the life of a horse and bend the back of the strongest plough man.

Young trees arrived, 'To carriage of said Firs from Aberdeen to Lovat, being 77 miles, with 4 Cart loads of a double Cart at 1s. per Cart, £15,8s.' Planting costs were 15s. an acre with the disbanded soldiers on 7p. a day. Pittance of pay maybe but not the ignorance of today's blanket afforestation. Oak, elm and ash enhanced hawthorn hedge and roadside verge, and on the 22 Nov. 1768. one hundred and sixty standard apple trees at 8p. per tree were planted in the soldiers gardens at Barnyards of Beauly. Enlightenment indeed.

The tenants suffered from the loss to trees of outrun and moorland. It provided the grazing ground for their stock during the summer months of growth on vital arable fields. But the curtailing of their wilful cutting of wood and their devastating practice of running herds of goats, could only be right. The beauty and diversity of the present woodlands at Beaufort and in Strathglass owe much to the social necessities and foresight of that era. Today the ageing oaks topple one by one, and river banks, without binding roots, crumble in floods.

Runrigged lands on the Lovat estate were measured by a Mr. Peter May and his assistants at 13s. per day. The ancient system of subdividing the fields amongst the locals did not lend itself to the 'modern' methods being introduced, the improvement of the landlord's ground nor the payment of higher rents. It must go. Once laid out in enclosed plots a policy of granting longer leases to the land holder became desirable. The factor could decree a period he thought suitable to the circumstances and twenty-one years became popular. The tenant had a period of relative security provided he adhered to the nine principles of good husbandry laid down in his lease. Rules of crop rotation and dunging which ensured an improvement in the fertility of the farm.

In tandem with agrarian upheaval 'the Board' attempted to establish industries in which the women folk could partake. Margaret Philip the spouse of a returned soldier and a dab hand with the needles, at 5s. a head, taught 17 Lovat estate girls to spin and knit stockings. Attempts to establish lint and hemp factories where 'the guid wife' could work largely failed, as did the planting of 'Lintseed' to provide flax and encourage the linen trade. Forty 'hogs heads' of seed were sold on the estate at 75% of cost and each soldier given 'a half peck gratis.' Inverness struggled to develop the manufacture of cloth.

Returned sailors were not left to drift. Fish were for the taking, the firth sparkled with shoals, sated sea birds flecked the tide rips and rose to scream in the wind as the men made back to sea in open boats to work the long lines. A six oared boat, 25ft. on the keel, built in Inverness and fitted with sails, nets, hooks and lines cost £18,15s. whilst a 28ft boat with eight oars, brought up from Leith cost double. Fishermen from the Forth were engaged, they taught the sailors the skills of the 'catch', but wisdom in the ways of the sea lies in the genes.

Change there was, improvements there must have been, but at a price. Who payed, or was expected to pay? Arrears of rent on the Lovat estates from the beginning of the 'Boards' control in 1747 up to 1763 amounted to the colossal sum of £36,114,1s.3p. Most tiny patches of land with hovels attached hitherto had paid rent to the Laird in kind, so many 'bolls' of meal being the common measure with the obligation on the young men to take up arms when required. The 'Board' swept aside anachronism demanding cash rentals. Poverty struck.

An earthy Highland saying, 'I'll need to pay the factor', tells more than having been taken short with only moss to hand. Neither of the gentry, whom he aped, nor of the people, whom he browbeat, the factor standing on his dignity was hated the length and breadth of the north. The authority of the Forfeited Estates Commissioners on the ground lay with the factors, and Capt. John Forbes of Newe in 1752 became the appointee for the Cromarty and Lovat Estates. No time lost in making plain his requirements. Via the pulpit, he issued a dictate.

'Rents to be paid timeously, the populous to conduct themselves by obeying the law, apply themselves to agriculture, manufactures, the education of their children in the Protestant religion, to speak and read English and the women to knit stockings.' All this and more to be read from the pulpit of each parish church and, would the ministers please kindly explain it to the people in the 'Irish' language. The church colluded, never in doubt on which side its communion wafer was spread.

Hardship fell heaviest on widows and families. Food and warmth in the home meant unceasing manual labour, cas chroam and sowing, sickle and binding, and the empty heart of loss. Lieut. Simon Fraser of Col. Fraser's Regiment was one of a party who charged a French Canadian battery in the expedition against Louisbourgh. Wounded during the attack he died two days later leaving his widow and three infant children on a 'small possession of six bolls pay in very narrow circumstances.' She prays to the factor for the security of a Lease.

Elizabeth Thomson, a widow with three children whose husband, a marine aboard the man of war H.M.S. Marlborough, died after the taking of Martinico and Havannah, has been turned out of the farm of Croyard near Beauly without allowance for the 'biggings there on, built by him'. She is now in danger of being turned out of the small farm on which she has laboured for four years. The woman petitions the 'Board' and prays they may give her 'such relief as they shall think proper.'

Riding the back of poverty came starvation. The balance twix land and population was a primitive husbandry at the mercy of the elements. Forbes, the Lovat factor, to his credit struggled to feed his poorest tenantry. From Banffshire in 1763 came five hundred bolls of meal to relieve 'the distressed and calamitous situation of the poor.' Ten years on, four hundred bolls of meal given to the poor to prevent them starving, 'most of the Gentlemen of the estates in the Highlands finding themselves under the necessity of nursing their tenants upon this melancholy occasion when the crop turned out so ill, and so many of their cattle perished for want of fodder in the severe winter and spring.' The factor was moved, 'The other day a great body of the people assembled and begged with tears in their eyes to bring them more yet otherwise some would starve.' He wrote to the 'Board' requesting two to three hundred bolls to supply them and if possible brought to Beauly.

Under the pressures of subsistence living resentment against incomers ran high. Hugh Glass a Chelsea pensioner, and James Fraser quarrelled. Both lived on the Lovat estate and Glass attacking Fraser 'under the silence of night, beat him severely, dislocated his neck, and afterwards threw the body into the river Beaulie.' The factor knowing the relations of the murdered man to be poor, thought it incumbent to interfere, and had the criminal apprehended and committed to jail at Inverness.

Penal rent increases by 1773 brought about the boldness of a Petition to their Lordships of the 'Board' from one hundred and seventy-six small tenants of the Lovat lands. Only thirty-seven of whom could write their names and they protested their case with suitable humility. Most of the petitioners occupied tiny scraps of land, 'from three to eight bolls victual rent and from £2 to £4 where it is money rent. On the victual farms it is well if in years of scarcity the produce even in a starved way can support the farmers family', they wrote.

The document points out, 'we are tenants only from year to year, dismissable at the pleasure of your Lordships', By borrowing at very high rates of interest the tenants have endeavoured to pay their rents as promptly as possible. They woefully continue, 'We have lived on credit until it is no more, unless we are relieved we must follow the same steps which our unhappy neighbours have pointed out to us, of quitting our farms, transporting ourselves and families to new and distant lands to find the Bread which our native country denies us. We mean not to offend, we humbly beg leave, with great deference, to inform your Lordships.'

Testifying to the accuracy of the tenants straitened circumstances were ministers of the Gospel, Malcolm Nicolson of Kiltarlity and John Fraser for the Parish of Kilmorack.

Not all Ministers made so bold as to support the material needs of their flocks. The Rev. Donald Macleod of Gairloch in Wester Ross flattered the 'Board' 'The spirit shown by your Lordships for introducing religious knowledge and industry into the Highlands will be productive of the most happy effects.' but warns, 'Knoydart the southern part of our bounds is the most unmixed nest of Popery in all the Highlands, and will require that a particular regard be had to the manner of reforming and civilising it.'

The Ross-shire village of Conon lies on the edge of the Black Isle at the first crossing of the river from which it takes its name. Today's prosperous urbanity knows nothing of the straggle of thatched cottar houses, pigsties and scratching hens that would have been the scene when my great grandfather, Hector MacKenzie Fraser was born there in 1817. Part of the estates of the old MacKenzie family of Gairloch and Conon, the village was typical of the Highland clachan of its day. Destitution, earth floors, bare feet, sanitation in the garden and wash your clothes by the river. Fraser knew it all first hand. A man of capability and sympathy he became Poor Inspector for the Parish at a time when Potato Famine and Clearance stalked the Highlands and the hollow cough of consumption behind a curtain brought death to the box bed.

Without bitterness in old age my grandmother rocked gently, slowly twisting the thumbs of her clasped hands and telling me of her father's efforts to administer the few shillings it was in his power to grant under Poor Relief schemes to the tragedy of widowhood in a subsistence society. He walked to Edinburgh on a number of occasions to plead for additional funding. The journey taking five days and four nights would not have been uncommon. Her abiding memories were of the strength of neighbourliness. Practical help and understanding suffused to bind the Highlanders together under shared hardships, in the face of which, all the pious mouthings from pulpits were but chaff on the wind.

MacKenzie Fraser's son left Conon to sail the world's oceans before the mast. Slant decks awash, frozen canvas to the hands and the sleet of the Roaring Forties round the Horn. The Far East drew him, along with the first Scottish adventurers, into the forbidden Shogun Empire and, as Captain Hector Fraser he fought at sea for the Japanese through their wars with China and Russia at the turn of the century. For bravery in action a Conon boy was decorated with Japan's highest honour, the Order of the Rising Sun.

Japan entered the Great War on the side of the British, and Fraser though close to retiring stayed at sea, skippering the crack Japanese liner Hirosha Maru on her troop carrying duties. The 4th of Nov.1918, a week before Armistice Day. Fraser's last trip before 'coming ashore' to wife and family. The liner lay out from the Liverpool bar lightship awaiting the tide. Docking at Princess landing stage a few hours away. Heavy seas and driving rain on a sou'westerly gale swept the mouth of the Mersey, but a thousand troops from the trenches sang Tipperary. Unseen through the spray a German 'U' boat surfaced. It fired one torpedo. Three hundred men were drowned. Hector Fraser went down with his ship.

My father's ship the 'Brittany Coast' lay in Liverpool's Gladstone Dock loading mines and ammunition for another Malta convoy. That evening a few hours before sailing for the Mediterranean my father came home to say goodbye. They talked, I slept. Late, the siren hurried us into the open. Searchlight blades cut into a black night. German planes droned. Dull thud thuds. Outside on a village green with my mother bomb flashes made frightened shadows. Over Liverpool the crimson sky was alive, fairy lights to a child. Dockland was ablaze.

Only one bomb fell close. It destroyed the Blind Children's Home and spared thirty babies the curse of blindness.

Across the green my father hurried to find a means to return to his ship. Losing him in the dark amongst milling people my mother called his name, "Hector, Hector," a name unheard in England and known only as a cartoon Scottie Terrier on the front page of the News Chronicle newspaper. Villagers scurried to air raid shelters. A clerical collar glowed in the blackness. "I say Mrs. Thomson, have you lost your dog?" enquired the Vicar. "No, no, my husband," laughed my mother in spite of her concern. "Ah I see." he coughed lightly. My father arrived, "Good evening Captain Thomson, another dreadful night, not much chance of sleep with this little lot." Of all things, my father loathed being addressed by rank. A Highlander of long generations he believed in leadership by courage and example, not birth or title. They talked, bombs fell and stars shrank before the blaze of Liverpool homes.

The Vicar in high nasal twang lamented the privations of war on the home front and turned conversation to his maroon Ford 8 car, a familiar sight tootling about the village, "You know this petrol rationing, I can't possibly get round my parishioners on a measly two gallons a week," he whined. " Well Vicar," replied my father in softer tone, "a convoy doesn't stop, if you'd seen the boys leaping from blazing oil tankers, and steamed past their drowning waves, you'd go round the village on a bicycle." They parted.

My father, Hector Fraser Thomson, sailed with munitions for much of the Second World War. Mines for the Corfu channel, shells for Battle Cruisers, and in 1943, was made Port Commissioner for the naval base of Valetta on Malta. He died in 1946 of a heart attack, perhaps stress induced by long hours on the ship's bridge. My mother was refused a War widows pension. In 1947 the Vicar was left a handsome legacy by a spinster parishioner and retired from his Church to an island in the Caribbean.

Down the centuries few ministers of religion were ever wet, cold, or hungry.

HOW MANY SHEEP THE LANDS WILL CARRY?

Sheep droppings and cattle dung were once a feature of the Inverness High Street on market day and why not? Many of the townsfolk had crofting connections, knew the smell to be less toxic than car fumes and wore sensible shoes. The capital of the Highlands drew livestock 'frae a' the airts' and those animals that had travelled distances, perhaps from Skye or Kintail, would be driven from the station yard to 'parks' on the outskirts of the town to rest until 'droved' to the Marts for sale. Since the great Annual Wool Fair started in 1817, the town turned the hub of livestock trade in the north, cycling half a million pounds in a couple of days between Yorkshire wool merchants and Highland flock masters. Gathering the spin off had once made sheep smell quite sweet to shop keeping noses even if a little sweeping had to follow.

Tuesday's sale morning scamper of an endless flock of hill lambs over the Ness by the turreted old suspension bridge, up the car width confines of Bridge street, and past the front steps of our frumpish Town House, always contained the makings of a spot of fun. Jamming the High Street with an undulating carpet of bleating smell, controlled by tail waving barks and stick shouting men, forced office bound bankers to shelter in shop doorways shielding pin striped trousers, and 'modern' shopkeepers' to glare out and think of marks on their new 'lino.'

My uncle Tom MacKenzie was no exception. A man of some

importance, by his own judgement, he put the first spectacles on Highland noses and soothed their chests with patent cough cures from his dignified Chemist and Optician business opposite the Town House and beside 'The Bank.' MacKenzie mixed potions, peered into eyes and combined acumen and gravitas in proportions sufficiently suitable to ensure his progress from a humble abode in the Ross-shire village of Conon to a grand three storey mansion in 'the town.' He viewed the passage of sheep on the High Street with certain misgivings.

Grandmother's indigestion gave frequent concern. Early one Tuesday, an impressionable five year old, I was dispatched to Uncle Tom's for 'twopennerth of bi-carb', to 'ca the wind oot o' Granny.' The sound of distressed bleating drew me like a charm. I ran hard.

To my glee the Town Square swirled with lambs. Excitement galore, I dodged through a side door into the shop. The esteemed establishment lay shattered. Sheep raced round, cases crashed, spectacles flew, assistants shoo'ed. Surveying the demolition from the stairhead stood MacKenzie. A portly man blessed in normal circumstance by the shining red complexion of good living. For this occasion his countenance assumed the bright purple of apoplectic rage as lambs gambolled over broken glass, paddled in pools of sticky linctus and I'll swear one dashed out wearing a pair of newfangled bi-focals.

Anyway, something drew a bellow from the top of the stairs. I stood popeyed, the colour of his face impaled on my memory.

Two straining bullocks, tongues out and slobbering froth, were stuck side by side in the front doorway of the neighbouring Miss MacDonald's flat. The bellowing of cattle in the street brought my young legs two at a time down the stairs of Granny's flat to stand on the rails of the front garden gate and watch. Neither beast gave ground. Doorjambs splintered. An upstairs window shot open, hysteria looked out, screams followed. Below, a drover belaboured the bawling heads. One beast shot backwards, made for the landing, faced a brush whirling Miss MacDonald, turned about, repulsed on the stair you may say, and smashed the banister. A revolting smear was added to the wall's floral pattern. Rare indeed are cattle that enjoy the refinement of paper.

Regrouped on the street, the herd, shying at garden and gateway, louped off towards the mart. Slipping out I followed, trotting side to side collie style, breathing the smell of sweating cattle and their fresh dung, drawn by an instinct clear as the drum of hoof beats on the grassland of a thousand generations. I reached the old auction ring at Hamilton's Mart, it's green railings were just wide enough for my head. Now sheep danced a circle at childhood level. Odd ones paused to sniff my hands, their breath sour, acidic but intoxicating. I wanted to smell like them, roll amongst them, live with them. Frightened eyes, flicking ears, hypnotic eyes, bright eyes into bright eyes, I dreamed, lost for an hour. An uncle searching the town hauled me home by the 'lug', but too late, a roving, droving love of livestock had awakened.

"I have lived in woeful days," said an Argyllshire chieftain in 1788. "When I was young the only question asked concerning a man's rank was how many men lived on his estate, then it came to be how many black cattle it could keep, but now they only ask how many sheep the lands will carry?"

It wasn't always sheep, sheep, sheep, as the lament implies. Records of the King's Privy Council from the fifteen hundreds to the early seventeenth century, catalogue cattle reiving complaints from John o' Groats to Jedburgh with a regularity sufficient to rate it the paramount occupation of the Scottish people, and not surprisingly. In a lawless country short on cash, cattle were walking wealth.

Most raids would be local and under 'cloud and silence of nycht', but some were planned and executed with the skill and dash of a commando strike. Alastair Stuart of Ardvorlich above Loch Lomand 'lifted' 160 head of cattle from West Perthshire in 1592 and strode into the plaintives lands 'with twa bagpypis blawand befoir thame.' A paltrey excursion by comparison to the efforts of the men of Glen Garry who in 1602 'visited' the lush grazings of Glen Isla, Glen Shee and Strathardle. They coolly drove off 2,700 head of bawling 'bootie', only to lose a rearguard battle to the pursuing owners as the cattle struggled up the Cairnwell Pass.

Clan MacGregor were the specialists. A six hundred head 'lift' from the lands of Colquhoun of Luss ended with a fight in Glenfruin, eighty bodies in the heather and the name of MacGregor proscribed. Tale upon tale to stir young blood. Today the fashion of historical story telling has died, the art of enthralling a fireside ceilidh with stories to excite the imagination is lost.

But not so in 1947 beside the peat flames of a stalker's fire at Pait, the remote home of the MacKays beyond Loch Monar in the furthest reaches of Glen Strathfarrar. On a blustery autumn day the late Professor Renwick, sometime Moderator of the Free Church of Scotland, walked east from Kintail to the ruins of Maol Buidhe for a last look at the home of his childhood. It was late. Thoughts of bygone happenings were with him in the stumbling light as he picked out the path to Pait, and the welcome he knew would be given in the style of the old ways.

Supper past, the Mackays and their caller gathered to the hearth. After a long silence Renwick told a story which he heard as a small boy sitting at the foot of an old, old man from Kintail who called at his father's fireside in their Maol Buidhe home. Iain Mackay, just a youth, sat quietly at the fire and in its turn the tale lived again.

"It was a day in June when a gang of marauding Chisholms suddenly appeared in Glen Elichaig. For some reason, perhaps they were cutting peats, all the fit men were down in the Killilan area. The Chisholms quickly killed the two young boys who were herding the local cattle, and gathering a fair herd together made off out the head of the glen." Young Mackay, used himself to watching cattle, listened, silent in horror.

"Other boys fled down the glen and in less than an hour the able bodied men were alerted, but instead of trying to follow their enemies they quickly made up the river Ling. In those days, sixty or seventy years before Culloden, each fit man carried sword and dirk at all times, and no doubt the force would have gathered strength as they hurried up the river, for at this time quite a large number of people lived along its banks and on the west end of Ben Dronaig as well. Scouts ran along the high ridges to watch the Chisholm movements."

"Had the thieves, once they got out of the steep pass west of Iron Lodge, crossed into the head of Glen Cannich they were safe on their own ground. But the climb with cows and calves would take three or four hours, and as there was no sign of pursuit, they decided to carry on to the hundreds of acres of lush pastures at the head of Loch Monar where they might pick up a few more Kintail and Lochalsh cattle with as little opposition."

The story teller paused. Peat flame flickered on unblinking eyes. The clock ticked and waited . Mackay saw hurrying men force tongue lolling cattle down a path he well knew.

"The reivers reached the curving corner of An Cruachan, a large force lay in ambush. The battle was short and furious. No quarter asked or given. The Chisholm were killed to a man and their hacked bodies dragged off the track and dumped in a swamp. Several Kintail men fell and their clansmen, slowly driving weary cattle, carried the bodies homeward towards the tears and lament of burial amongst the ancient graves of Clachan Duich."

A dying peat crumbled silently to ash, a breath of cold wind tapped at the window, the curtain shivered. The oil lamp dimmed, shadows moved. The room seemed chill. No one spoke. Mackay watched the old man stir and with a sigh rub his hands. This swamp, known as Pol na' Siosal, Chisholm's Pool, never appeared on any map but lived secure in memory and recounted tale. Now I have told you, the spirits live on.

––––––––––

From cattle thief to honest drover, a mere stride in practice involved a quantum leap in status. Nothing less than a Commission, set up in 1680, encouraged the export of Scottish cattle to England and recognised the drover as being a key element in this vital sector of the country's economy. The Disarming Acts of 1716 and 1748 following on the heels of the Jacobite uprisings, specifically exempted the drover. The gun, sword and pistol allowed him under its clauses were far from ornamental on the lonely trail south from Lochaber.

Cattle rustling, still the free booting lifestyle of the seventeen hundreds, helpfully extended its services by diversifying into extortion. Professional reivers such as Rob Roy MacGregor, classed themselves as 'cattle protectors' and owners of stock were 'insured' by the thieves against theft. A comforting arrangement, but one which left the policy holder unlikely to default on premiums. As late as the first half of the eighteenth century the small black 'Skye doddies' when making across the hill for Glen Garry, drove uncomfortably close to the wilds of Knoydart and in the passing provided Colin MacDonell, 'cattle insurance agent' of Barrisdale beside Loch Hourn, with a comfortable £500 a year 'back pocket' cash. Black cattle into blackmail, a neat scheme.

By contrast, integrity marked out the drover. Currency of around £200,000 was reckoned to be circulating in Scotland at the time of the Union with England in 1707. Many drovers setting out from the Highlands with scant cash would possibly buy £10,000 worth of animals at croft door or tryst and pay in Bills of Exchange or Promissory Notes. These signed scraps of paper, made drawable after three months on perhaps an Edinburgh mercantile finance house or the infant Bank of Scotland, were the precursor of bank note and cheque book, an exchange system slow to catch on in the backwoods of Kilmorack.

Old Murdo Fraser, known as 'the Batten' crofted a lifetime on the 'Braes' and by way of recommending this bucolic theme, he scored a century of hardy, healthy years. Longevity! Old Murd's grandfather fought at Quebec, helped the Fraser Highlanders scale the Heights of Abraham and imbued 'The Batten's' father with a suspicion of paper money.

Well, well, one Inverness Wool Fair in the '20s' Murdo trotted out a fine pony which took the eye of a gentleman and his groom. "Is your horse suitable for a young lady?" enquired the gentleman of Fraser as the groom ran hand over loin and limb. "Suitable?" choked 'The Batten', no slouch at theatricals, "Is there a young lady in the Highlands suitable for my pony?" "I think so," replied the 'gent' in coolish tone and handed Fraser a cheque for £11. Old Murdo flew to the 'Braes', £11, half a year's wage to a plough man, three times what he'd expected.

Old Murd's father looked at the cheque, "You bloody blind stupid fool," he screamed, and more besides, "You swopped your pony for a scrap of paper?"

Fraser slept little, rose at dawn and walked hurriedly the twelve miles to Inverness. The door of MacLeay's Sporting Shop in Church Street opened promptly at nine. Old Murdo was in. "Is it possible please, Mr. MacLeay, could you, er?" the word cash remained unspecified. The Gunsmith glanced at the signature and looked up. "Though the cheque were for a thousand pounds I would honour it for you. This man is a Gentleman," and he gave 'The Batten' £11, minus a few pence for the obligement, naturally.

A leather pouch carried the rough oatmeal, mainstay of drover and dogs down the long walk to Falkirk or Crieff. A ram's horn slung on a thong across the shoulder contained the 'uisge beatha', enlivener of cold brose in the white breath of dawn. Ewe milk cheese and onions with a bannock balanced the diet on the open drove, whilst a night at inn or stance provided the hot water for a welcome change to porridge. And for sure, as the bleeding of cattle was common throughout the Highlands well into the nineteenth century, and congealed blood keeps fresh, there'd be, onions, oatmeal and ox blood, the guid auld Scots black pudd'n. Boy, boy, what better for the hard miles?

Little is known of the drovers hardy collies who made it feasible to herd a thousand unruly 'kye' out of Skye, swim the narrows at KyleRea, head tied to tail onto the mainland. Hill tracks, bare, midge ridden, stone stumbling, heather skirted trails. Glenmoriston, the Corrieyairack, in the footsteps of Montrose's great march. Aberfeldy, Crieff, the Border gullies, and on to the soft going of the low road to Lincoln. 'Dogged' miles indeed, barking hoarse, swinging on cattle tails, kicks, bleeding pads, frozen nights, and no word about it.

The Fair at Saint Faiths in the heart of East Anglia had existed since the twelfth century and here at the end of their herding the dogs were turned loose. Home by sea went the drovers, home by the hill went the dogs, fed at the stances they remembered from the way south. Home to a Highland doorstep, to a barking, tail wagging reunion, the bond of faith and affection.

The men? Bare-kneed and bare-headed, belted plaids of shaggy brown homespun, pistol and poniard, a reek of heather and peat smoke, a man whose clothing and physique equalled the rigours of droving. Lochaber to Lincoln and never under a roof to eat or sleep. Constant vigilance over the cattle, swollen rivers to swim, high passes and early snow, mist and driving rain on the open moorland, wild cattle trampling at their first bridge, stampeding at the crowds. Shoeing and surgery, taming and trading, ten miles a day and no aftershave. Whom of the present, passing as men, could match them?

"Trees, trees, nothing but damn trees, you couldn't see a thing for trees." Neil Sinclair, friend of the 'wee sma 'ours' on the Isle of Barra had visited a daughter down in the depths of rural England. For him, bred to the horizons of the Hebrides, any view that didn't stretch ten miles was a cage. I understood. Border syndrome, a similar sense of scenic oppression, also struck me on a trip to Langholm in Dumfries-shire during the couple of years that I managed Crossaig, a small estate on the east side of the Kintyre peninsula.

The bracken strangled slopes of this property were at least gifted with the grace of Arran Island peaks reaching across Kilbrennan Sound and lifting the daily toil, for the term 'managing' simply covered the fact that I did the bulk of the work. A million midges, a hundred horn waving Highland cows, eighteen hundred maggot prone ewes, a stone lighter, it was a considerable relief to learn after a year of sweat and scratch that the owners, Tony and Mary McCraith had decided to sell their ground into afforestation. The Economic Forestry Company, a body of 'progressive' London accountants, were the purchasers, and soon this 'far flung corner of the Empire' was being visited by strings of their tax crippled clients, who wished to cast off some of the wealthy man's burden by planting a few thousand acres of Sitka spruce on the wasteland of Scotlands barren hills.

A potential 'planter' suffering advanced 'Mal de Tax' arrived at Crossaig one afternoon by Rolls-Royce. His Harley Street practice and a penchant for salmon fishing pleasantly complimented each other and, trees apart, we became friends. The gentleman was under the spell, the long cast and the green waders were gripping his 'oxters' and his motives. A letter arrived, he'd heard of a property in the Borders, Georgian house, mile of salmon fishings, livestock farm, all in job, £25,000. Would I be interested? Take on the farm, tenant of course. He would buy, just for the fishing you understand.

A £12 a week 'Manager, 'I left Kintyre sporting our new Austin van, straight cash out of savings, straight door up the back, all of ten horse power. The peep,peep of a summer's dawn skidded into the sky, I flashed down Loch Lomond, all of forty, pausing seconds to collect Kilmorack 'ex-pat.' Alex Murray. By middle day we penetrated a narrow winding glen. Hills crowded closer and tighter. Some round, green and smooth to the top, many suffocating under tax avoidance trees. Along with the hills I struggled for breath, claustrophobia gripped my guts.

Before panic could follow we pulled into the farm. A panting man grasped our hands in greeting, blurted out a double barrelled name, choke barrel Douglas, and indicated a Galloway cow glowering from the corner of the yard. "Calving problem, mercifully rare in this breed thank God," he gasped. The beast turned to flee, two yellow hooves protruded from below her switching tail. Just another day at the rodeo for a couple of cowboys, Murray and I circled. She charged. Jackets flung, Murray, a matador pass to draw gasps in Madrid, and he deflected her into the byre. A flick of lasso over her neck, a secure post, a calculated touch of choking, we had her down and the calf out before Mr.Something-Douglas had time to peep over the barricade he'd hastily erected.

Gratitude and the cow were unleashed, "My word, splendid, splendid. Do come and clean up, you must meet Mother, afternoon tea sharp at three, she will be de-lighted to meet you." Mr.Double barrelled-Douglas edged us towards the outhouse sink and we washed off the blood.

At the head of a medieval refectory table, so long it narrowed into the distance, sat a frail silver haired lady surrounded by matching silverware. Her dark dress melted into the gloom. Hair and silver shone alike, altar pieces below the portrait of a knight in black armour who's withering eye reached the length of the hall. Her pale hand motioned. Mournful portraits hung from sombre oak panels. Swivelling eyes watched our approach. Introductions were bowed and murmured, we sat to either hand of the antique Lady on high backed chairs.

A light tea, artistically arranged, lay before us. Water biscuits, 'fromage', exotic by the smell, scanty lettuce and tomato sandwiches, precise little triangles without crusts, and slivers of plum cake. A hungry Murray, like myself, rather better acquainted with hunks of cold venison between the ends of a loaf, eyed the sandwiches with the lust of a glutton at a cake shop window.

"Yes," the full length portrait of the Knight was The Black Douglas. "Yes," it was an ancestor. A door creaked, I shot round, expecting the clank of armour. A Victorian print emerged on hollow footsteps. A long sleeved black dress decked with a high necked crochet collar hung on a contourless form. Starched cuffs and a white doily cap enlivened a cadaverous apparition carrying two tall silver tea pots. It hovered behind Murray's chair.

Making an impressive impact on the plate of dainty triangles Alex was, during and between mouthfuls, enchanting the Dowager with an elaborate story. He paused to swallow. "Would Sir care for Indian or China?" the spectre croaked. Murray glanced over his shoulder, "Ach I don't mind lassie, just as it comes." A sandwich halted half way to the Dowager's mouth, a grin cracked the paint on the face of Black Douglas. Set to succeed in life, Alex Murray never allowed trifling detail spoil a good story.

We turned for home. Slits of glens cut out the last flame of light. I felt trapped and threatened. The Border hills were not for me, for I've lived looking west, the rocks at my feet, the headlands long in the light, the death of the sun on the edge of the world, and the islands dipped in the sea.

But the Border hills were of sheep and shepherds. Of flock masters who counted their 'yowe' stock by the scores. Of farmers who were abreast of the far reaching agricultural innovations that paralled the industrial revolution in the latter half of the seventeen hundreds. Steam engine and 'Spinning Jenny' killed cottage craft. Reaper and threshing mill disbanded peasant labour. A rural populous shuffled onto the assembly line, dependent on the corner shop, not kailyard, sty and spinning wheel. Increased farming 'efficiency' fed the factory treadmills with plodding labour dispossessed of a supposed Arcadia. Displaced from a supposed pastoral simplicity drooled over by the great romantic artists and poets who portrayed a golden age where hirling shepherds canoodled with full bosomed damsels in sunny hayfields. Was it so ideal?

Which, by the by, reminds me of a day on the island hills of Rhum. I climbed the corrie of burrow nesting shear waters and in the hot sun lay basking on a summit. The happy twitter of female voices drifted into earshot, to be followed by three handsome girls bare to the waist. "Ah well," I remarked, surveying them with ill disguised pleasure, "shepherding was never as good as this in my day." I digress.

Was the farm to factory phenomenon just a neat circle of exploitation perpetrated on a population fed up with pulling turnip? Did they go willingly, thinking green grass grew in top flat window boxes. Are the pundits correct, had an early nineteenth century Highland population outstripped its food supply? Rustic bliss or just nostalgia, when fading memory forgets the icy draft up the dry loo?

The truth remains, factory fodder required feeding. Sheep were booming. Border farmers were on the make, they could pay higher rents than subsistence crofters. Highland lairds, penniless as always, capering in London with English affectation, cut ties of blood and kinship and took the cash. Sheep swept north, South Country Cheviots to the green ground of Sutherland, the Linton ewe, forerunner of today's Black face breed to the wetter hills of the west. And the long striding shepherds came.

Elliots, Renwicks, Moffits, Boas. Border men with generations of sheep husbandry in their blood, in their eye and step. Men of the open, wind or rain, winter storm, summer shine, an affinity with animals. Natural men without pretension, content with a lifetime in their calling. Of such were the Boa's. Foreign in origin, they possibly fought in the Borders during the 1540's as part of a contingent of Spanish mercenaries known to have helped Henry the Eighth's 'rough wooing' of the Lion Rampant Crown. Maybe, Lisbon is Lisboa after all.

Whatever the truth of their origins, the story of this family is 'the coming of the Great White sheep' of folk tale and history book.

Progenitor of this fecund line of people was an Ettrick shepherd, 'hired' at Hopehouse, one William Boa, who married a sound Border name Catherine Scott in the 1780's. In a tight knit farming community Boa would certainly have known the more famous Ettrick Shepherd, James Hogg, the man who saw himself, a dash immodestly and with little justification, as a second Robbie Burns.

The Boa's first child Peter, one of eight, went a shepherding just down the glen from his father at Phawhope, married a woman almost the same name as his mother, Christina Scott, and in 1840 took sheep out to Kilmory on the Isle of Arran. Nor did this generation fail on family tradition, Peter and Christina produced nine children, and of five boys, four were shepherds. The lure of dog and stick seemed endemic, even the girls succumbed to shepherd's desires and married into the 'profession.' Sadly are records of child deaths. Charles Boa, diphtheria, aged 8. William, aged 10, Joan Boa aged 13, of 'watering of the brain.' Modern families are largely spared the grief that once held couples together through shared sadness. Divorce is a disease of selfishness.

Peter's son James, an Ettrick offspring of 1826, having learnt his shepherding craft in Arran at his father's heel, came north with the 'white tide' and by 1856 reached the remote Glen Affric hirsle of Camban in the spacious Parish of Kilmorack. Now a fatal charm follows hill men, soon a local girl was in James's arms. He and Margaret McRae, daughter of a Kintail fisherman were married at the Manse of Glenshiel that year and made a home at Camban. Fresh air and healthy living produce children. In their case, one every two years, until there were eight. James Boa and his family came to play a roll in the last hundred and forty years of life in two noted Highland glens, Cannich and Strathfarrar.

James's third child John, born at Kiltarlity in 1862, spent his childhood in Glen Affric and became an itinerant worker at sheep fank and gatherings throughout the hirsels of Kintail. Not big but tough by any standards, as a young man he was one of the last to drove sheep from the Highland straths before railways killed the trade. A fortnight south, Glenmoriston to Falkirk, three days to walk home, stepping the forty-five miles to Inverness with sheep, which he did regularly, a mere stroll.

Peter W. MacCallum, doyen of Dingwall auctioneers and known, for good reason with some reverence, as P.W., consigned Highland bullocks each summer to the broad green flats at the head of Loch Longard. Boa and P.W. were great pals and the excitement of droving these shaggy, horn clashing brutes through Beauly, up Strathglass and into the hill country of Glen Cannich would have the kids following for miles. But thoughts of home making eventually tame many wanderers and 'Old Boa' as I heard John called, was destined to find a wife to equal him in hardiness.

Glen Cannich and Glen Strathfarrar lie close at their western watersheds. Between them dips a bealach crossable only after a strenuous climb of two and half thousand feet. 'Old MacLean', as Boa came to call him, and as my mother used to warn, "when you're young boy you think you'll never grow old, but your turn will come." Well, well, 'Old MacLean' shepherded a hirsle on the Pait ground of Strathfarrar where the wide slopes of Coireach run out to the Kintail march, far above the Falls of Glomach. To the foot of this corrie and a thatched 'but and ben', no great distance from Pol a Soisal, of which I have told you, Hugh MacLean brought a bride of nineteen.

Gable stones of MacLean's home remain defiant of frost and gale. In shepherding days I stopped by them often, and taking my piece in their shelter, would look down to the wide growling burn that gnawed the remaining banks of Old MacLean's one time hay meadows. In his day there were no deer on the hill to ravage a precious hay crop, and the stone and turf dykes that took my eye as I ate would have kept out any ewes, doubtless with the help of a noisy collie. I was told children once would jump across the burn when they played amongst hand made 'coilacks' of hay. Seasons change, no child could jump it today but, as an old neighbour would say looking up from the fire as his rambling tale veered from the point, 'Wait you, I went through my story.'

A sleeping child suddenly rolled in a blanket. Hurried out, the night black, mother crying, women screaming, shouting, men swearing, sticks cracking, police or soldiers, uniforms and twisted faces in flaming torch light. Haunted, Christina Ross a terrified girl of three was to remember. Her people were driven like beasts from their Glencalvie home to clear the ground for sheep and Border shepherds. In the strange and distant connections that hold the hearts and minds of Highland folk, these Ross's, for good reason, would have known my great, great, grandmother.

Along with many another, the Ross family made what shift they could down on the coast of Easter Ross and Christina born in Glencalvie in the early 1840's stayed with her Mother until she was twelve. Needs must. At an age when today's children lounge on T.V. bean bags, she walked barefoot and alone, from Boath in Easter Ross to Durisduan in Kintail, to spend teenage years housekeeping for her brother. At nineteen, eviction by sheep proved nought before the sway of love. She left Kintail on the arm of shepherd Hugh MacLean to make a home together in Coireach, perhaps the most remote glen in the Highlands, and there, born in the tiny cottage without help beyond the man himself, was their first child, Barbara.

The shepherd's job came vacant at Corrie Mham, a tin roofed homestead under the broad shoulder of the four thousand foot Ross-shire hill An Riobhochan and handy, in a stockman's eye, to a waving spread of summer grazings at the head of what was once Loch Longard. MacLean decided to move. Though Corrie Mham lay three hours walking west of where the obscene Mullardoch Hydro dam now binds hillside to hillside across Glen Cannich, at least its connection to the outside world, be it all of twenty miles, was by cart, rather than ten miles of pony track out of Coireach to Kintail.

Term time on May 28th 1866 required MacLean to take up his new post. Barbara their daughter was six weeks old. Hardship defied by determination and devotion, the couple flitted to their new home at Corrie Mham. Shepherd and pony took bed, table, pots and pans. The nursing mother carrying her new baby slung at her breast, bound chairs and blankets to her back and trudged the last traces of greying winter snow over the high bealach to a long happy life in a new glen. The worthy descendant of a Highland clearance.

In the fullness of fate John Boa by the 1880's became shepherd at Old Benula, a small house in sight of Corrie Mham and no distance from where Glen Cannich meets Kintail in a strath of skylark meadows and childhood memory, of flower garlanded grass in the bliss of youth, in the honey scented summers of the wild bee beside the waters of Loch Longard.

Here John Boa, grandson of the sheep that wrought the Clearances, and Barbara MacLean, daughter of the misery of Glencalvie, met and loved in the fullness of manhood and womanhood, amidst a world of nature's beauty.

The status of shepherds in the era of the 'Golden hoof' of the Highlands was high. Housekeepers, even to single shepherds, thought their job a sinecure. Warm house built by the 'estate', scullery and dairy, water at the well, and for a 'privy', the decency of a wooden shed over the burn. Self respect is not squandered on rank alone and many maids being conscious of the connotations attached to living in remoteness with a healthy unattached male were at pains to emphasise their independence, and by no means least, their unimpaired virtue.

John Boa, happily married family man, was full of the tricks and pranks that made Highland humour tick in a time of innuendo and twinkling eye before the onslaught of T.V. and the universal joke. Walking being second nature to the man, he often visited Kintail and would leave Longard for the twenty mile stint well before the first fingers of sunlight, in the manner of a secret lover, one might say, could pinch the sky awake.

By the pippit's first spiral of song, Boa's jaunty step put him downhill to Kintail. The dogs of a shepherd's heather thatched abode gave warning of his approach. No smoke drifted from the stub of its lime washed chimney, a cat on the sill waited with folded paws. In the style of the times no door was passed without a word or a 'strupagh' of tea and custom would walk in with just a word of greeting. But the hour being early, John knocked.

Doorstep hens with puffed feathers waited warmth and a sound from within which meant corn. They spoke softly amongst themselves in high querulous tones. Comb blazoned, neck asheen, the cockerel attended duties. A hen scuttled, tail twitching. Pleased with his prowess, the braw bird with hearty wing flaps and proud stretching neck, saluted the glen. Boa smiled. Presently the door opened.

"Well it's yourself John. Madainn mhath, thig a' staigh, come in, come in." Jessie the amply blessed housekeeper greeted him half in English, half in her native Gaelic, as was the way. "I don't know if himself is awake yet, dean suidhe, sit down, I'll shout him," and with a formal glance at John, she knocked, "Hamish." In a voice which he knew would carry to the next room, the unexpected visitor remarked to Jessie, "A Glen Cannich shepherd is generally out on the hill by now," and taking a wooden chair from the table to the hearth he glanced through the gloom towards the box bed, "My Jove Jessie you have the sheets made up in fine time today." The inference was far from lost on the housekeeper, "I'll have you know John Boa that's my very first job in the morning and kindly keep your evil mind to yourself," she swelled with indignity. Boa sat down, left in no doubt that the door 'ben' firmly separated the shepherd from a bed of neatly tucked sheets in the corner of the kitchen which of course accommodated the housekeeper's nightly retiral.

Conversation faltered, Jessie raked the hearth, blew the peats, threw corn to keep hens from the door and took a pail to the well. A peat flame licked the lum. Boa's eye and mind fell on the poker. Three swift steps and he slipped the fire iron between the sheets.

Morning sun skipped in at one door, Hamish grunted at the other and they sat at the scrub top table to a breakfast of oatmeal porridge and the cream from last evening's milking. John soon was in Kintail.

Days grew to weeks and Boa had occasion to call again at the 'but and ben' of Hamish and the prim housekeeper. The aroma of scones fresh from the girdle and Jessie welcomed him at the door. Hamish was on the hill but come in there's a baking. They sat 'newsing' a little before Jessie stirred the fire to make the tea. "You know John, there's strange things in this house, I don't know, is it, is it the hand of another?" Jessie paused superstitiously, "the poker vanished, I've been over the whole house, not a sight." She went grumbling to the outhouse for milk. Quick as he'd placed it, Boa reached into the bed and put the poker back on the hearth.

Girdle scones, crowdie and tea, a smiling eye barely hid the laughing mind before John took the road home to Longard.

YOUR FRIEND IS
DANGEROUSLY ILL

Shepherding status reached its nadir during my sojourn in the depths of Kintyre. This gangling peninsula of spectacular seascape and single track road, in those dawdling days, had much to offer the discerning traveller not afraid to pause with a front wheel in the odd ditch. Such I suspected to be the case when on a blistering day of mirrored sea and conceited hills, five hundred ewes and lambs were telescoped before me between dry stone dykes on a stretch of road suitable for two bicycles to pass with difficulty.

Leaving my collie Shep to 'woof' at their heels, knowing that out of my sight he enjoyed a mouthful of wool, I leapt the dyke and ran to the head of the bleating queue. A large estate car straddled the road. A roof rack of leather cases, 'Cunard' stickers, conspicuous salmon rods, a dog barrier and slobbering Golden Retriever completed the blockage. From slobbering over the scenery there turned, to beam over the quaintness of shepherding duties, two 'Gentlemen' of some quality.

"Shepherd," an imperious voice cut through the bleats. Dumb insolence, a chargeable Army offense surely did not apply to struggling shepherds. Ignoring the colonial imperative, I drove a good cut of sheep and leaping lambs past the 'sahib's howdah' and ran back to where Shep, between barks, was trying to empty his mouth of wool before he thought the crime might catch my attention. The column moved on.

Shep and I brought up the tail. The last lamb skipped past a rear window streaked with retriever spittle and the voice rang out again. "I say shepherd," I looked, "tell me shepherd, which hills are we looking at, away there to the north east?" An arm extended at the angle of a Roman Emperor. Good manners prevailed. I stepped over. The voice was wearing perhaps the most expensive and well cut pea green tweed suit I had ever envied. But the view was mine everyday, I began with Ben Cruachan, Argyll-shire beauty, pencilled on the horizon.

With less aesthetic appreciation, Shep, tail up and growling, washed the car tyres. "My word shepherd, this view is truly magnificent," the voice oozed omnipotence, the eye had conquered empires. Out of the corner of mine I saw that Shep, tiring of tyres, was with a majestic salute, emptying the last of his contribution to the conversation in a thin tastefully matching squirt down an oblivious green trouser leg.

"Well Shep boy," I bent and pulled his ear as we followed the sheep, "great minds think alike." Never again did I underestimate canine perspicacity.

Some days later I was told, apocryphally no doubt, that two scenically inspired gentlemen, of some quality, entered the wayside Inn at Grogport. "What'll you have Charles?" "No old chap, it's my round." "No, no, I insist, marvellous day, do let me." "No Charles, absolutely insist, my shot." The barman polished on, the debate continued, trade was dead, at least triple whiskies, he thought, beer at one and six a pint, wasn't worth the washing up. A quick mental reckoning and he waited, poised to pour. In spite of a stammer, the brain was fast. "I say barman, may we please have two halves of lager?" Such an inconsequential resolution of the gentlemen's dilemma stunned the barman, but courtesy being the code of the bar, two 'halfs' were set down with a smile. Payment seemed slow.

A ruler of evening light caught cobweb and counter. The contents of one tumbler full of the investment were held up for a laser beam inspection. "I say barman, it's a trifle cloudy." Ignoring the glass the barman glared through the window at a louring sky. "W,w,what do y,you exp,p, pect for one and s,sixpence, th, th, thunder and f, f,—— lightning?"

Shepherds were becoming hard to find. My advert for help with the Crossaig hirsels drew response from a London policeman. A two-stroke engine propelling a globule of glass and metal in the form of a minute French bubble car arrived in the yard. With all the mystery of unravelling D.N.A., a fifteen stone flat-foot, wife, child, grandmamma and grandpapa untwisted from this molecule. John Kinghorn and family had arrived in Kintyre.

I found the demarcation line between white shirt and face hard to spot, the handshake, a putty squeeze, but the eye under a shock of fair curly hair was bright and knowing. I took to John immediately and hired him on the spot, though his knowledge of sheep rested on readings of 'Little Bo Peep' at the age of six. Three months on the hill, three stone lighter, bronzed and handsome, I enjoyed his inclination to play the accordion and take a dram, we got along famously.

'Accident prone' might be one way to describe another of Kinghorn's natural leanings as he lay groaning in bed following two inches of tetanus injection into his backside after falling at speed from a foolish tractor bonnet ride. Compassionate to a fault, certainly in the eyes of his Staff Nurse wife, I slipped a 'half bottle' under his pillow and trusted he would be fit by next week when twelve hundred stock ewes and eight hundred lambs were to leave Crossaig for the sale ring at Lanark.

Ten gear grinding floats hauled the heavily laden hearts of two thousand sheep out of Crossaig yard. Kinghorn and I with the prospect of a couple of nights in town followed by Land Rover in a more lightsome frame of mind. Shep curled in the back seemed somewhat preoccupied. The journey progressed, John and I whistling, singing and plotting our night's entertainment, Shep, silent, almost baleful, quite out of sorts.

The dastardly attacks started outside Dumbarton. Without warning we were assailed by an asphyxiating stench. A nauseating cocktail of rotten eggs, dead rats and putrid carcass enveloped our cab. Gasping for breath we flung open the windows and drove, heads craned out on either side, much to the mystery of oncoming traffic. When speech returned, over my shoulder I counter attacked with a blast of invective that would have a Sergeant-Major taking notes. Shep, head stretched flat along the floor of the Land Rover, flicked the white of eye in my direction as the flow of rhetoric reached fresh heights. Otherwise he gazed absently ahead in a fond recapture of the rapturous feed of stinking venison which was currently upsetting his stomach. Twenty minutes and three attacks later I looked across at Kinghorn. His face bore a shade normally reserved for inspection by a mortician. "Are you O.K. John?" "No," he croaked, "I'm not too good, bloody dog." Another wave of gas, I saw Kinghorn's lips were swelling and turning a deep blue. Hell's teeth I thought, shepherd killed by flatulent collie, great headline, but not handy for the morrow.

Lanark swung into view. I helped a shambling Kinghorn up to our hotel room, dodging with a smile the hostile look of a receptionist, perhaps more accustomed to seeing her clientele carried out than carried in. Poor John, shaking violently, lay on the bed. Aspirin or undertaker? Former for the moment. He sat up, grasped the glass in both quaking hands, couldn't swallow and fell back with a body racking tremble. Awaiting the attention of myself and Shep the assassin, were two thousand sheep in the sale yard. "There's the emergency button John." I guided his hand to the bed head, he smiled a weak thank you and I dashed downstairs marvelling at the potency of Shep's fetid performance.

Several hours and a thousand 'shedded' ewes later the darkness outside the hotel oscillated to a flashing blue light. An ambulance, "Oh my God," I tore up the stairs. Two uniformed men struggled to negotiate the bend with a stretcher. I stood to one side and looked down upon Kinghorn's ashen countenance. At least it wasn't covered. Yet. His eyes were closed but he must have caught the smell of sheep and raised a limp hand.

"Your friend is dangerously ill," a white coat, combining the gravity of stethoscope and half glasses, informed me. "We are at some loss, can you explain anything?" Knowing but a piece of paper separates witch doctor from medical practitioner, I mentioned Shep's rancid expulsions. "H'm," he flicked through mental pages of Black's Tropical and Obscure Diseases, "I think not, this is a serious matter." "Well he had a tetanus injection ten days ago." "That's it, serum sickness," he shot through the swing doors white tails flying.

Three cover to cover reading of old 'Scot's Magazines' and the doctor reappeared. " Look in later today, he'll still be sickly, but the crisis has passed." Good. Now I thought it safe to phone the Staff Nurse, otherwise known as his wife. I left the kiosk weakened by the experience.

About the middle of last century the shepherds on the steep snow drifted hills at the top of Glen Cannich were gathering their ewes to safety as the first aimless snowflake heralded a fresh storm. White sheets of ridge and peak hung taut from the grey of a cavernous sky. Stillness fell to a silence that carried only the raven's croak. Solitary bird of wild places, the harbinger of death.

The blizzard struck with a ferocity which drove sheep and shepherds down from smothering slopes onto the homeward path in the last of the daylight. Deepening snow forced the men to abandon a large cut of ewes in the lea of a stone fank. The animals coats were a cake of snow, driving them further would be folly, any which floundered off the path might be lost. Drawn together they would lie close and wait out the storm. The shepherds, coated as their sheep, must look to themselves lest the boulder marked path become obliterated. Well they knew in unspoken thought the penalty of its loss. Snow, swirling and blinding, they hurried, single file, hand cupped over mouths, stick prodding, tapping for stones that told the track.

Tricks are the toys of fate. The whim beyond random that holds humans in its power. For a moment the blizzard lifted, the eye of a storm that still spiralled off snow face and cornice gave them respite. In that brief space before the stinging fury again bent heads and drew eyes to slits, the shepherds caught the movement of someone coming off the hill. To seek contact, impossible, only innate senses got the men down to the nearest house. They warmed, ate and fretted over the figure seen, stumbling, crouched and desperate, in the glimmer of snow light.

Midnight and moonlight flooded the glen, the blizzard a million years ago. Stars dancing on crackling ridges, dressed the snow. Shepherds pulled on solid boots, retraced the steps of another era. Dogs bounced, breath hung, nostrils narrowed, intense frost gripped a silver world.

Behind the shelter stone, the dogs found a body. Dead? In the kitchen the wife cut off frozen clothes. In the back room her two teenage daughters huddled under blankets. The shepherds carried through a body. Breathing? "Take that man between you," demanded their father.

The daughters cuddled. The body lived. Who warmed the Raven's wing?

Six weeks of a booming cough that frightened the children, aching limbs that defied a scorching by Elman's Horse Embrocation, oh boy, it was a 'flu fit to carry 'Old Boa' across his last river. He was a worried man. Empty bottles of Friar's Balsam patent Cough Cure littered the kitchen cupboard, a half empty bottle of Fenning's Fever Curer, a tablespoon and the open Bible graced his bedside chair. One glance at his trousers hanging from the bedpost by their braces and his red flannel semmit steamed with sweat. Man, man, things were bad.

March came in, the season was moving on, and Boa must rise from his sickbed. Across the Longard river cattle required attention. The old man's customary mode of crossing the rock strewn water in drought or flood was on a pair of homemade wooden stilts. Not only would 'himself' get over dry shod but a boll of meal carried on his back also stayed dry. Anybody with a head for heights who wished to avoid wet feet climbed aboard this walking ferry. John never stumbled. A legend in its day as a feat of strength and agility, it was not an antic for a man still spluttering with 'flu.

A leaky black tarred rowing boat kept at the head of the loch some distance from the house, served as the alternative crossing. Boa tottered down the path and paddled his way across to inspect the cattle. They were spread about the river flats filling themselves with an evening feed of lank grass and longing for the first blade of green. A ruddy sun fell behind the hills of Kintail, the eastern horizon shaded into the purple sheen of a keen frost. Boa made back to the boat, a trail of steaming sweat in the snapping air. Rimy gunwales and a slippery seat, one gingerly step and an unsuspected sneeze, and 'Old Boa', with the wail of death, plunged head first into deep water. Upon which, he was wont to tell, a tissue of ice had just neatly formed.

His clothes were frozen stiff even half way to the house and John had little doubt he would not be long behind them. Stripped and shuddering before the glowing range, he assured his wife in prophetic tone, "Ah Dia, this'll finish me, I'm done for woman, doomed I tell you, doomed!." A stone hot bottle to either side, a warm brick at his feet, Boa composed himself for the long sleep with an extra large 'toddy' and a couple of his favourite Chapters.

Greatly to his surprise, the man wakened next morning. Every fatal symptom had vanished, 'Old Boa' felt young again and whilst drawing a veil over his powers as a prophet of doom, he convinced everybody that a freezing immersion was the cure for the 'flu.

Highland stories tended to be convoluted, for the nature of their telling, often of an evening with legs stretched at the fire, put no pressure on the company. People once listened, the burning peats were the measure of time, a cup of tea would come to the hand or sometimes a glass, and the teller could weave facts with perhaps a dash of fiction into a tale which might have several starting points and sometimes many, many obscure connections. This story, I'm afraid, bears some of these hallmarks, and in the spirit of a ceilidh of old, you must be patient and pay attention. If only I could offer you a dram you might follow me better, anyway.

The father of Hugh MacLean, the shepherd who took the nineteen year old bride and baby over the bealach to Corrie Mham in Glen Cannich, came from the Isle of Mull to Strathglass and married a Barbara Chisholm, daughter of the clan chief, by whom he produced a family of four boys and five girls. Many descendants of this union still live in the Strathglass area today. "But that's not what I was going to tell you," a phrase I still hear my long dead crofting neighbour say when his story wandered a little and required pulling back on track.

Barbara MacLean the baby of six weeks carried to Corrie Mham at her mother's breast grew up in the three roomed shepherd's house, the first of a family of nine girls and one boy. She knew sadness in early years when three of her younger sisters died in their teens, and as a girl of twelve, came close to losing her own life on a night of singular storm.

December blew gales as sure as January brought snow, and Hugh MacLean, a shepherd of the hills, needed no weather forecast to predict the vagaries of an element which he watched each day. A gale was building. The sky to the south, a tower of white across which flew tattered fragments of black cloud. In failing light the writhing streaks coiled and lashed across the heavens as only the Norse Gods of his forebears could drive them. The shepherd feared, his instinct keen as the crows he watched scud before the rising wind to seek shelter in bending pines down the glen.

At nine that night MacLean fought a gale of demonic power, struggling with stone and rope to secure the roof on his byre. Down in the house frightened children huddled round their mother, the wind moaning and screeching in turn, beat on the walls, found its way between stones and moss and lifted curtain and dish.

What of their father? Barbara could stand no more. She rushed into the storm. At the corner of the house the wind took her, caught her nightgown. Though a sturdy twelve year old, it lifted her bodily, and holus-bolus she was carried down to the loch. A flailing figure caught for a second in shuddering lantern light. The tempest took her scream. It lulled, gloated, another fury, she was powerless in its grip, it would drown her. MacLean ran, the water lifted from the surface of Loch Longard, a twirling sheet to a racing sky. He held her waist, his arm circled a boulder, they lay flat, a cheated wind rose shrieking to the hills. Together they struggled up to the house.

It took a week for the news to reach Corrie Mham but the shepherd knew too well the day and time of his daughter's escape from the freak blast. On the 28th of December in 1879 at 8.30pm. seventy-five souls were drowned, the Tay Bridge collapsed.

Well, as I told you already, Barbara MacLean had but to cross the loch which almost claimed her life to marry and make her home with John Boa in Old Benula. Many might consider her hardier than her man, for she bore him two daughters and ten sons, all born in Longard at the west end of Glen Cannich with no more than hot water and the help of a neighbouring shepherd's wife. A generation further back, again in the isolation of Longard, lived a shepherd's wife whose heavy pregnancy did not prevent her continuing the work expected of women folk in the glens. Each family had cattle, two or three cows, a 'perk' with the job but really a vital factor in remoteness living. The daily milking for the house, butter and cheese making and until there were children big enough, herding the cows to and from the grazings, was woman's work. A teenaged girl, either belonging to the family or from a neighbouring household, helped in most homes with the thousand chores of a sinkless kitchen and no plumbing.

Early on a fine June morning, pregnant or not the housewife went away to the hill for the cattle, leaving the 'girl' to manage her sprawling brood. Breakfast passed, middle morning came, sun warmed the stones, cows ambled into the byre. Quietly the wife appeared in the doorway, "What kept you?" queried the girl. The woman opened her shawl. The new born baby, licked and clean, made little sucking noises. Excited children gathered round to see their present. "I found it on the hill," the happy mother told them.

Not so lucky the first born baby to a young shepherd's wife at Allt Cam, who after a stressful confinement became seriously ill and was taken by cart down Glen Cannich to the hospital. An innocent husband, and perhaps a little stupid, left with a wailing, wriggling heap, made what he could of it. Days of crying went by and local shepherds, calling in the passing, noticed the baby thin and far from thriving. A discreet message went down to Dr. MacRae, who came up by pony from Kintail, and called on the sleep starved father in quite a casual manner. The baby was a skeleton. "What are you feeding her on?" "Well Doctor, I'm giving her oatmeal brose, but she doesn't seem keen on it." MacRae, a wise man, said gently, "Just give her warm milk until your wife gets back," and the baby survived to tell the tale.

Very often a friend or relation would help at a birth, sometimes travelling long distances to be present, and as the inner promptings of Kintail woman were to suggest, did intuition play a part? Did the emotional peaks of human experience, love, birth or tragic death, communicate their intensity more readily across the void between minds, in an age before 'lifting the receiver' cheapened companionship.

Propped against a stone on the high ridge of Meall Mhor, in shepherding days I would put my 'glass' on the empty gables of Maol Bhuidhe and watch deer grazing undisturbed on the green ground which once grew tatties and corn for a self contained world. Home it once was to a shepherd's family and lay far to the west of Pait Forest above the trout dimpled waters of Loch Cruishe.

The Shepherd's wife had a young cousin, of whom she was fond, living many glens to the east in an outlandish keepers house at the back of Beinn a' Bha'ach Ard on the drove road to Muir of Ord. She knew the woman's 'time' to be near. Communication, there could be none short of walking. Leaving her family early one morning, for she felt the pains to be on her friend, the shepherd's wife took lonely hill tracks the thirty miles to Glen Orrin. That night the baby came, just as she knew it would, without the help of co-incidence.

A family closeness to birth and death in remote homes gave a dignity to life, and a depth to love and caring that a hedonistic world has lost. On a knoll above Loch Monar, before Hydro times, I could have taken you to a scatter of stones where infant deaths were buried without a record, save in sorrow.

The Gaelic language, mother of feeling, father of poetry, lived in a land of simple lifestyle and humble estate. The people for whom it was the common tongue had their roots in subsistence living, knew the risks of a life dependent on the cycle of soil and season. Unashamedly romantic in the heartfelt expression of eternal emotions, its values were once the currency of the Highland people and their culture.

James Boa and scores of other families arriving in Kintail with the sheep from the south during the 1820's, found themselves in foreign parts. The natives had no English. Within twelve months however, Boa, with the help of sign language, just had sufficient of the lingo to propose to a local girl, and in three years, as a fluent Gaelic speaker, he also mastered the difficult task of reading and writing the language. His family by turn had no English. The Gaelic tongue sufficed the shepherding years spent by James's son John at Loch Longard but this man's twelve children born and reared in the glen, spanned the twilight period of the language on the mainland of Scotland. The first three arrivals in the 1880's had no English until they approached their youth, the last to be born after the turn of the century had little Gaelic.

Few of the indigenous lairds, such as were left in the eighteen hundreds, bothered with the language and relied on bi-lingual factors and ministers to relay their wishes to the common people. The 'Toff', a wealthy English sporting type who arrived in the Highlands on the heels of Victoria and Albert, of course had no Gaelic and spoke a strangled form of English in an accent synonymous with authority. This tone and demeanour, still affected to cower the natives at home and abroad, is much sought after by those who aspire to social advancement.

Upwards of a hundred families swept from Chisholm lands in Glen Cannich on the wave of southern sheep had barely settled in on the Lovat lands of Strathfarrar when in walked the 'Toff 'with his sporting rifle looking for red deer. A spate of 'sporting gentlemen' poured into northern properties a hundred and thirty years ago, waving cheque books, clearing sheep and building sandstone lodges. Displaced shepherds suddenly knew all about stalking. The 'keeper' in liveried tweeds got a job which towered above his neighbours, but only if he spoke English. Ghillies and pony men, stuck with 'the Gaelic', did the skinning.

Deer forest etiquette for the 'Toff' entwined the blue 'puff' of Mannlicher rifles with the heady curls of Havana rolled leaf into expansive evenings of brandy and cigars before a roaring log fire. An indulgence not always without penalty.

A heavy 'Gentleman' toiled his way up to Bealach Bhearnais, one of the high passes to the west of the Strathmore ground in Glen Strathfarrar. The previous evenings conviviality and now the 'close' day, complimented the man's weight in a neat triangle of conspiracy. Copious sweat, of a measurable 'proof', soon soaked the red polkadot handkerchief, swept with shaking hand round a florid, nay, a purple countenance. A worried keeper watched. The 'Gentleman' with a final flourish of his hankie sat on a stone, fell back, and promptly demonstrated the distinction between perspiring and expiring.

Keeper, ghillie, and a twelve year old boy, six wide eyes gazed down upon the two staring eyes and sagging mouth of their hurriedly departed shooting guest. Each viewed the stiffening 'Gent' from differing perspectives. The stalker thought of his job. Killing the wrong stag was one thing, walking a guest to death, quite another. The ghillie considered the man's ungralloched weight on the end of a drag rope, and the boy, who had carried the rifle for the previous five hours in the hope of a tip, saw his prospect of any remuneration deferred to the 'hereafter.'

"Well boys he'll have to be down out of here before dark," the keeper spoke in Gaelic, and thinking of hoodie crows pulled the 'Toff's fore and aft bonnet over the unpleasantly popping eyes. "We'll never drag him," replied the ghillie, wondering if he would fix the rope around the neck and through the man's jaw as they did with a stag. The boy had no Gaelic. He was son of a Border shepherd, Burnett to name, who had recently come to Maol Bhuidhe and language had its problems.

"Now boy you'll run down to Loch Carron," the keeper gave his instructions in English, "and take as many men as you can get from the Arinachaig crofts and a pony if you can get one." A tired agitated boy reached the first house, no English spoken, on to the next, no English. He was unable to find a person who spoke his tongue and far less might understand his broad Border twang. Finally miming and waving arms secured two men, and a pony.

Late that evening the 'Toff', strapped unceremoniously across a deer saddle, occupied the eminence of the stag he'd hoped to kill.

Just a handful of old people in Strathglass by the early nineteen hundreds spoke only Gaelic, and one woodcutter without English who worked all his days on the Lovat estates decided to retire on his seventieth birthday. "What would you care to have to mark your retirement," asked Lovat, about the only laird left in the Highlands who did 'have the Gaelic', "Oh well, I've never been past the town," the man said, meaning Inverness, and bitten by wanderlust on the spur of the moment continued, "I'd like to travel to London." A puzzled Lovat gave him the train fare and something to spend.

At Edinburgh the old boy turned, beaten, not by a platform barrier but a language barrier. Come the Great War, English would take you anywhere in the Highlands, the Gaelic wouldn't take you past Beauly. In keeping with the trend, my grandmother, when I was a boy, could still gabble away to her old neighbours, my father could shout at me in suitable phrases when the occasion demanded, whilst I have little beyond token greetings and goodbyes.

Warmth and cooking in these old rough stone houses was far from today's thoughtless flick of a switch. The peat fire on a open hearth played a central role in domestic comfort, drawing a reverential attention not unmixed with a dash of superstition. Christine Boa born in 1891 and rightly called for her maternal granny, was the fourth child and first girl of 'Old Boa's' dozen offspring. I knew her well, she seemed like a mother to me, kindly and wise, especially in the ways of children, and for good reason. From the age of four she nursed each child as it appeared, washed, fed and dressed them. Put them to bed, recited reams of poetry, and if there had been no drouth outside that day, set about drying nappies and clothes at the open fire.

Laughter and fun followed 'Teenie' to the end of her days, and that's the way it was in Longard. One Hogmanay the whole troop of Boa's put in the celebrations across the river at Corrie Mham, the childhood home of Old Boa's wife. The night waxed well, not with drink, but songs, dance, story and friendship. On the stroke of twelve the solemn toast to absent friends had meaning. Contact with loved ones crossed oceans in the mind. Moments later, grabbing guns, the men hurried outside and fired a shot into the night. If the air were still, the crack, crack, would ring from house to house down the glen. Whoopee, a Guid New Year, and straight into an Eightsome Reel.

Nobody wanted to break up the party, the children drifted 'ben' the room as sleep beat them, the grown ups sat at the fire and began to talk of happenings and characters of 'lang syne.' Memory and nostalgia went hand in hand. Eventually Old Boa stood up, "Well, well, a grand night, whatever the year will bring, we'd better make over." He made a move to gather his family. "Wait, wait, what's your hurry, you'll take breakfast," "Ach no, we'd better not." The Scotts prevailed, the fire was stirred to life, porridge soon bubbled, ham and eggs tickled the nostrils and the Boa family lingered over a hefty meal.

The sky was bright, Old John pushed open the door at home. It felt cold. "Ah Dhia," he strode to the hearth, only a tiny heap a white ash, "Ah Dhia," down on his knees, blowing ever so softly, not a ember came alive. The fire was dead. The family stood silently. He cleared the stone flag with much lamentation, a bad start to the year. The fire, caringly 'smoored' each night had not been out since they came to the house. He uneasily struck the first match in over twenty years.

Dr. Johnson remarked to Boswell during their excursion through Skye "There are more gentlemen than shoes in the Highlands," and sure enough, to save leather, shepherds in the summer often went barefoot to the hill. All the kids, even to my father's day, put off their shoes in May, and apart from squeezing them on for church their hardened feet didn't feel leather again until the first frosts. For Highland folk at the turn of the century, shoes were something of a luxury and as travelling by 'Shanks's pony' was the norm, savings could be made and shoes hung round necks on a long walk. Feet would outlast footwear.

The pace of people's lives is governed by the speed at which they travel and communicate. Until well into this century, in country districts, walking was 'King of the Road.' For most folk, daily life raced at three miles an hour, but the prowess of Old Boa as a walker gave topic to many's the ceilidh. The speed of his step was phenomenal and moreover he passed the trait down to his grandson Iain MacKay. At hundred yards or hill race in any Highland games, Iain often claimed the trophies. We shepherded together in the 1950's and 'keeping to him' on the hill, I had to 'go some.'

Heavy snow choked the Highlands early one February, and Boa who managed the Benula sheep hirsels in Glen Cannich, became concerned over the stock ewe hoggs which he'd put away to wintering at Bunchrew a few miles outside Inverness. An oval moon made silver daylight of the snow. An inside pocket held three rounds of roast venison piece. Old Boa set out, "Don't worry I'll hardly make back tonight." Strathglass hushed and dormant trickled blue morning plumes into a glossy sky. He took the river bank, blown clear and crisp. By middle day cross country tracks brought him down to the hoggs, thirty odd miles from home. They were safe and being fed.

Late that night the children wakened, someone was kicking snow from boots at the back porch. A tired seventy miles, it was Dad. Bright faces peeped round a door and ran to hug his wet legs.

Only the evening sun of early summer could linger so lovingly on the waters of Longard and blend shadows of hillside and crag in the rosy blush of a beauty fulfiled.

John Boa sat on the edge of his boat. A tin of home made fishing flies open on the thwart. He looked at the water, back to the tin, took out a fly and began to tie the cast. A sandpiper flicked amongst the loch side stones, white belly, bouncing tail, it gathered insect for a demanding brood. At its staccato call and flitting wing beat, Boa glanced up.

Along the track a boy approached. It would be a telegram. Seldom welcome news, terse, typed and sudden, a form of communication ill suited to a word of mouth community.

The young boy handed Boa the yellow Post Office envelope. At a time when children stravaiged the countryside for pleasure, and worked cheerfully without expecting reward, this boy, still in school, would walk barefoot the twenty-eight mile round from Cannich to Longard and back for a few 'coppers.'

John hesitated, then slowly tore open the envelope. 'Father died today, Tuesday. Funeral, Ardgour church Thursday.' James Boa, a Border shepherd who helped the tide of Cheviot sheep sweep the Highlands, was dead.

Brief though the sun rests behind the wide shoulders of An Riabhachan in a Longard summer, Boa was afoot before its awakening glimmer crimsoned for a moment the north corrie snows of Mam Souhal and Carnaig. Taking the high road by the head of Glen Affric to the Cluanie watershed in Glen Moriston, he crossed into the Cameron country of Lochiel and down the bonnie wooded Glengarry to Loch Arkaig. In the peace and solitude of the hill country the spirit of his shepherd father walked in his step, and they journeyed together.

The tailor's shop in Fort William closed at half past five. Boa tapped on the window, the tailor shook his head but catching the shepherd's face, relented. "What's the problem?"

"Well I've walked from Glen Cannich today, my father's funeral is tomorrow across in Ardgour and I haven't a black suit."

Measuring tape, material and cutting table, the tailor and his young assistant stitched most of the night. John walked on.

The tide had turned at the Corran ferry, John's last step to Ardgour. It was late evening, the ferrymen rowed him across the fast rippling narrows. Down the darkening waters of Loch Linnie, beyond the hills of Mull, the crimson robes of a long day's sun knelt in requiem light.

As good as his word, next morning the tailor's boy arrived with the freshly made suit. To the grave side John Boa led his grieving mother. A Kintail MacRae, a Highland lady who hadn't deigned to learn the English, sadly buried her Border shepherd husband under the shadow of the Ardgour hills. The year was 1901.

Today only fallen stones above the scars of Hydro flooding recall the lost beauty of Longard, sad in memory for the happiness of its people.

AS FAR AS THE EYE CAN SEE!

The man isn't cold yet," Iain MacKay, shepherding comrade and quick thinker on the line from his Kilmorack croft to Kintyre. "Hot news though Iain," I laughed unkindly, "who are you speaking about?" MacKay was not of the fashion to waste money on idle phone calls. "Willie Chisholm, they got him dead this afternoon in his turnip shed up at Cluanie." "Who?" "Chisholm Teanassie, you know, the 'Teachdaire.'" Ah, a vital clue, the deceased man's 'by name'. I had him at once. The literal translation means 'gatherer', innocuous enough, but the Highland style of inference, rather than statement, implied a capacious interest in gossip. Such unflattering descriptions rarely reached the ear of the owner, but in a land where every second person was Iain, every third person Fraser and no lack of Chisholms either, it provided necessary, often colourful and generally perceptive identification. Sample 'by names' from the Kilmorack of the day included, the 'Rathad', Gaelic for road but unfortunately pronounced 'rat', the 'Monkeys', the 'Hurlys', the 'Fox', and several better left unprinted.

MacKay spoke at speed, "You'd be in with a good chance boy, the 'Teachdaire' was a tenant of your pal Baron Stackelberg. He'd one of the Baron's crofts at Breakachy and farmed Cluanie as well. Cluanie's not a big place but it's good ground, a bit steep though, I look up to the house from the fields here. He'd no family, stayed down at the croft with his sister, the Cluanie house's been empty for fifty years but the roof looks O.K., from here anyway, great flock of ewes," details rattled on. "Sounds the very place Iain, thanks just now." Click.

A man in a hurry, at twenty-one I'd saluted farewell to the Queen's Colours, caught the north train, wife, child, and fifty pounds. A claustrophobic spell as the Baron's dairy cattleman and we headed for open space. For a number of years I shepherded the high western marches of Glen Strathfarrar. Frugal living, venison, tatties, an eight pound a week wage, a pack of sheep and the keep of cows. It put a thousand in the bank. The Hydro Board flooded Loch Monar, we took an ark to Kintyre. Fine friendly place, grand folk, too far south, MacKay's phone pointed the exit north. I was twenty-eight years and a month the night of the message. If not farming for myself at thirty, I'd vowed to give it up. Here's your chance Thomson boy. Down phone, up pen, lick a stamp. 'Dear Baron Stackelberg, Would you consider me as a tenant?'

The business of living in a rambling crofter style took time to observe the portents of weather, crop and wildlife. Time also to scrutinise the activities, and sometimes the antics of fellow crofters. An hour here, a 'strupagh' of tea there, 'news and views' filtered through fireside and sheep fank, hay field and harvest, neighbourly gatherings of help, and perhaps hindrance, which bound together the Braes of Kilmorack in a way of life as wholesome and satisfying as a well set stook of corn.

Boxing day in 1961 turned to a bright morning with a north-east wind that would hang a 'dreep' on the best mannered nostril. 'Sleepy Sandy', glad of the shelter of his byre door, paused after flinging the last shovel flop of dung onto a squelchy midden. He crofted his days on the Kilmorack 'Braes' by methods, which far from lacking in hard labour, did not include undue haste.

Each morning the spread of Breakachy appeared through the smoke of Sandy's first pipe. The 'speckled fields' would be closest in English, a fitting description, for the cropping ways of those days coloured each field according to the season, and the tenants of Breakachy down the generations worked their land with hands that cared for its fertility and its place in the cycle of nature's ordination. Under the crofter's gaze, chequered fields, edged with pine and birch, drifted into heather hills and, out by a climbing burn, to the deer grazings and grouse knolls that sheltered below the shapely peak of Beinn a'Bha'ach Ard, the hill of the high pastures.

There was always something 'doing' over the way which merited five minutes and a pipe. Sandy settled against the door post. October's tooth combed stubbles sloped to a deep sunless burn which bounded his fields from the crofts of Breakachy. Slippery ground for the binder in the glaur of last autumn Sandy reflected, struggling again amongst its tangle of sheaves. A thrumming on the wind drew his mind from harvest tussle and he watched spindles of sunshine blush the rosy underwings of an alighting flock of far travelled birds. The Artic thrush, down from the north. Sandy knew of their coming each year and looked beyond the byre gable to a flat grey sky above the maroon tipped birch, "Aye birdies, I doubt there'll soon be snow in your tail."

Sure as the bird's foretold, a few days before Hogmanay the Braes of Kilmorack laboured under two feet of snow. Crofters with bales on their backs plodded 'yeti' footsteps to immobilized sheep, 'Wifies' shuffled to hen sheds with steaming pails of water for complaining hens, and about drifted byre doors hung the whiff of turnip breath and hayfield glory. Warm and content from a night's cudding the cows grunted, filled the 'grip', and provided the crofter with his morning chore.

'Sleepy Sandy' flung a dollop of dung onto the midden and watched for a moment its oozy brown trickles cut canyons through humps of white desert. He stood the shovel against the wall and felt for his pipe. The first curve of an orange sun haloed the fence posts and trunks which led down an overgrown track to to the Breakachy burn and Calan's ford. It once was the highway to Strathglass and the cluster of ruins at the foot of Calan's field were known as Spittal Street, a hostelry, as the name would tell. That morning, amongst its snow dusty thickets, the birds of the north wind fed on blood red berries, burnished gems set in purest white, pride of the wild Dog Rose. The boisterous squabbling of hungry birds sent little showers of snow from laden branches, the cackle of their voices was the only sound which stirred.

A smoking match hissed in the snow. Sandy pulled his pipe and smiled the smile inner of pleasure at having a private window on the busy world of fellow creatures, "Well birdies, enjoy your feed, you're fair judges o' weather." As he was himself.

Away to the west, out of the blue of rising dawn, the chiselled ridges and snow filled corries of Beinn a' Bha'ach Ard crackled with cold light. Sandy smoked. His eye turned to the gleaming white slopes. Slowly, so slowly, from softest pink, grew a shade, deeper, fuller and richer, until the whole hill glowed with a saffron sheen, passionate beyond the dreams of human palette. The colour of a plaintive melody, of painful longing unfulfilled. Distant, untouchable, but still calling, calling, an evocation to eternal beauty. Then, as slowly, the colour drained, the endless spinning majesty of the universe became a fading emotion, another sunrise sank into the daily cares and squalor of a busy world. A cow chain clinked in the byre, the kye needed out for water. Sandy stirred.

Across the muted burn, he caught sight of the 'Teachdaire' knee deep in fleecy snow toiling up the steep fields to Cluanie. The heavy man paused and put a hand on every second post. Sandy knew Chisholm's routine. At first light each morning a tuft of smoke from the east chimney of their Cruinassie croft told him that Kate the sister had stoked the old black range. In her younger days she kept house at the Lovat family's London home and early rising remained her habit. The 'Teachdaire' would be at the porridge before setting out, as he did that morning to feed his cattle.

With leaden steps, Chisholm struggled, it was steep and breath catching. The fence that climbed the side of the Stackyard field gave him support. Nearing the house he floundered into a drift. Through the straggle of purple branches on the far edge of his field, the peak of Beinn a' Bha'ach Ard reflected the glory of a risen sun, as in all his life he had never before seen it. He lay a moment in the snow. The call of expectant cattle drifted down on thin air, the beasts waited, impatient in their dank steading. Chisholm pulled himself up the last of the slope, post by post.

In the late afternoon down at the home croft, the Teachdaire's sister worried. She phoned down to the Teanassie schoolhouse at the foot of the road. George Campbell, schoolboy son of the headmaster, tramped up the twisting track to Cluanie. The cattle were bawling. A hesitant boy pushed open the fold door. Hot breath met him, intent unblinking eyes watched him, ears cocked, the beasts stood motionless, silent at the sudden intrusion. Winter's gloom hung about the shed, filled cobwebbed corners. George's torch hovered over hay hakes and troughs. Empty. He moved a step. Hand on the latch. The yellow beam flicked along the cobbled pass. Childhood eyes widened. The 'Teachdaire', lying at the turnip shed door, circled in light, was dead..

The chug of a 'Fergie' tractor. Rod 'the trapper' hurried in, his eye followed the stabbing light. "Poor William," they looked down, "Ah well George boy," the 'Trapper' spoke slowly, "that's it, that's the way he would want. The man's not curable now but we can feed his cattle." Turnip, bruise and hay to the beasts before they loaded the body of Chisholm 'The Teachdaire' onto his old cope cart and made down the darkening road from Cluanie as the first evening stars sprinkled frosty light on the crystal snow.

Baron Stackelberg,
Erchless Castle,
Struy, by Beauly,
Inverness-shire.

12th. Jan. 1962.

Dear Thomson,

I would be delighted to have you as the tenant at Cluanie and you are free to make arrangements with my keeper Duncan Chisholm to check the house and boundaries. There are roughly 300 acres of which some 60 is arable with the balance of hill and woodland. The rent has been £51 a year, payable to my Solicitors, Innes and MacKay of Inverness, and I propose the same figure. Good luck,

Yours sincerely,
Nicholas Stackelberg.

Dressed sandstone, pink and weathered, framed the doorway and windows of the tiny pine lined house of Cluanie. Unlived in for fifty years, 'L' shaped below, attic bedrooms above, quaint but dry, it featured skirting boards neatly holed by the workmanship of Mr. Rat. No water, no electricity, no sanitation, cast iron grates for heating, the house was deemed only suitable as a summer retreat by the tenant at the turn of the century, a Mr. Morison, Beauly iron monger and 'boozing buddy' of the fabled fiddler Scott Skinner. Back to orraloon days, this time with a wife and two small children.

On June 2nd 1962 we arrived from Kintyre. The removers stuck on the twisting climb and were pulled the last hundred yards by a neighbour's tractor. The piano, lead weight but ivory keys had survived another flitting, I cut the banister, manoeuvred beds up the turn on narrow treaded stairs and made tea from the burn. The removal van crept down the road towards the sanity of tarmacadam, the men shaking their heads.

But this healthy home breathed fresh breeze or gale and took the sun round its arc from daylight to dark. Set on a curving ridge above sloping fields, with watchtower alert, it spied from haughty isolation upon the crofting Braes of Kilmorack, and beyond to the shadow of the Black Isle, dark against the sun bright waters of the Beauly Firth. No neighbour moved but a sharp eye and a handy telescope had them covered. Chisholm's father, the original 'Teachaire', read the Inverness Courier line by line, and disseminated the information throughout Breakachy. I saw how his successor to the title gathered the 'news.' On a nail at the door had always hung the dead man's spyglass.

Our first Sunday in Cluanie was bright with the freshness of early June. Murd Fraser, 'the Batten' and his son Alistair walked up the road to bid us welcome. We had a dram, Betty made them tea and we looked out across the Lovat lands. Emerald fields, tufted trees, a wink of water through their leaves. Old Murd spoke, "I knew your father when he was a boy about his Auntie's croft down there across the river."

My 'little grey Fergie', the result of a Kintyre deal, arrived the day after flitting. We had a roof, a view, a tractor but no cash on the horizon. Food came first, live off the land.

For seventy pounds I bought the implements needed to plough, cultivate and ridge the sickle shaped field that bounded the road up to the house. Five and six year old Hector and Alison climbed up from school, dropped their satchels at the door and made games of gathering the stones. The tractor roared round the clock, dust flew and harrows rattled, on every croft along the Braes the Duke of York's early potatoes were already 'through' and at the first hint of a shower turnip would be sown.

'When the birch is out it's time the tatties are down.' I knew the old folk's annual chant when the first warm mists hung over the woodland's slender stems, and the birth of yellow leaves brought a fragrance to the pale tinge of spring. But Nature's signal had long since passed and the skirt of birch around Cnoc Cluanie donned a deeper shade of green. Good luck, seed appeared in sacks from kindly neighbours, and I had the ground in trim. Late by the calender of the trees, but harrowed to a tilth, rich, thick and black, with a scent of treacle in the curls of steam that rose to a climbing sun.

In with the ridgers, run up the drills, full pail in hand, a stoop of the back, step, tattie, step, tattie, step, tattie, step, our winter's diet down in a crack. Ridgers again, close up the rows, straight as a die, leave tatties in tents, warm, dark and dry, to think about growing, watched by the crows.

Caw, caw, wakened me at four. I peeped from the skylight, the sun peeped over Eilean Dubh. Up and down my drills the black coated devils waddled, bills covered in soil to the white of their cheeks, heads to the side they probed for tatties, grave as judges passing sentence for murder. Out to the door. I gripped the .22. Little did they know I always shot from the shoulder and killed through the head. In moments, the boldest robber flopped amongst the drills. One flap and squawk took his accomplices to sit brazenly on the pylon wires wiping breakfast from their bills. A long shot brought him company. I hung the birds from sticks and poked tatties back into the holes. The morning sun gathered strength, but already the birds feathers had lost their gloss. We were in the survival business.

Taps and flushing toilet did not feature in our water system that summer. By the end of June the burn down from the house ran under rather than over its stones. Betty carried the vital liquid with care, cooked on a two burner Calor gas stove and coped with washing children and clothes in plastic pails. The concrete floored kitchen's only refinement was a cast iron boiler sometime used by the 'Teachdaire' to heat gruel for feeding his calves, and though our finances were at 'soup kitchen' level we baulked at gruel. Time for action on the domestic front. Andrew Anderson, banker, but more importantly a sympathetic Shetlander, lent a thousand pounds of Clydesdale's precious money with no more security than my enthusiasm to borrow it.

Cuckoo calls and concrete blocks thus enjoined on a June morning long before a thirsty sun could lick cool droplets from the spines of summer grass. I walked up beside the drying burn towards the 'construction site.' Echoing across the woods and moorlands of Breakachy, rival layabouts 'cuckooed' in earnest competition, but voices were tiring and one hoarse champion could only manage a 'cuck, cuck.' I laughed. Exhilaration lurks in the first breaths of clean fresh air. My footsteps scattered pendants of rainbowed light that shone in moments of life through prisms of dew. The first warmth of a waking sun fell on my back, lifting the chill of night. The world of nature seemed home and welcomed me as a friend.

By middle day my back was burnt but the dam was built. I lay on the grass. Betty walked up with tea and a piece. The children were down the road at school and we sat awhile.

The sun crept below a cloud, the birch beside us shivered, it's leaves were young. But by and by, the sun came back with a carpet of yellow warmth, the birch leaves gleamed in fresh delight, and from a hidden home, deep in the shallach boughs, the willow warbler sang its distant flute. Betty smiled, I took her hand, and only nature knew.

Drooping 'lugs, 'sunken eyes, the sick calf coughed. Squirts of pale yellow calf scour splattered the kitchen wall beside the Rayburn cooker. Under the winter glow of the Tilley's homely hiss a tracery of watery trickles matched the peeling emulsions ancient pallor with a sensitive tonal harmony. The only possible detraction could be the eye smarting smell. I rigged a sack screen to minimise further artistic effect. Redecoration was not the motive in creating a sickbay beside the stove.

Twelve living calves bounced about the byre. Every thirteenth innocent was born to die and succumbed to the plague at ten days tender age. They would stretch limp and shivering alongside the only source of heat we possessed, a roaring Rayburn. Into the mournful mouth, down a reluctant throat, were thrust pink antibiotic tablets, vitamin A powders, diluted milk laced with salt, raw eggs in their shell sand to round off this life quenching treatment, a tablespoonful of whisky as a benediction before they expired. What prayers for their deliverance, oh the vain hope of binding straining bowels. In desperation Plaster of Paris crossed my mind, even corks. All to no avail. I was to bury five calves before my spade broke on that first winter's frost. The bottom rung of farming's ladder seemed about to break under the weight of bad luck and bank borrowing.

Kilmorack abounded in characters, who stood out, fables or foibles, warts or wigs, as individually as the crofts they farmed. 'Big Jim Teanlonaig', he was known to the Braes by his farm, or Jimmy Fraser, his baptismal title, was a genial bald headed man of great good humour, a fortunate turn of character, for he was also a man of mouth gaping strength. To him, hundred weight sacks off the back of a combine were but bags of sugar to a Supermarket check out. Fifty-six pound weights, the kindergarten toys of Hercules, he would lift high above his head, without apparent fear of his toes, in the crook of each 'pinkie'. And, if prompted by suitable gasps of astonishment, Jim, as an encore, would lift a hundred weight and a half sack of grain in his teeth. His own of course.

Arch rival in these fairground feats, 'Dunc Oldtown', a worthy representative of the wild MacRae's, lived at Aigas further up Strathglass. He and Big Jim vied in such facially expressive performances as lifting the rear end of a Ferguson tractor clear off the ground. During this spectacle, Jim's contorted visage would assume a complexion fit to blanch the face of a rising sun, but Dunc, a man of raptorial profile, could extend a curving tongue to the tip of his nose and lick away any bead of sweat which 'au rigueur' might course to its point. I judged 'Oldtown' the winner.

Contracting work with my grey Fergie tractor, rather than risking a rupture, seemed the one way to find cash to buy the weekly groceries. 'Big Jim' booked my first assignment. His neighbour up the brae, unwilling to move into the machinery age, had found that horse power alone was letting the farm work fall behind. Hurriedly, for ten pounds, I bought a plough and announced my status as contractor to unsuspecting crofters.

At six on a Monday morning I roared up Teanlonaig brae. The farmer stood waiting in the yard. A small wiry man stained with hard work. He spoke. The voice startled me, and a wide radius of sleeping Kilmorack. How could such a volume of sound emerge from such a modest container? A warning to fog bound shipping? Without a sight of mist, far less fog, the voice addressed me at unreduced decibels. Twenty acres to plough for turnip. A pound an acre? I agreed, set up the 'feerings' and soon burnished mould boards turned the crackling soil into a tug of worm breakfast for a line of squawking gulls. By dinnertime, I had pulled a week's 'rations' for the family. The old 'cuddy' at the fence over the road slouched a hip, hung a lip, and balefully eyed my progress.

The socially disruptive racket of clipping machines had still to ruin the pleasure of a day's steady hand shearing. Tongues and shears clacking away, the banter of shepherds at communal clippings took minds off the work and occasionally, in fits of laughter, the point off a sheep's ear. Finding work for my shears proved easy, keeping up much harder. Tootling back to Kintyre in the Austin van on my first clipping contract, I realised the truth of the Campbell saying, 'It's a far cry to Loch Awe.'

Down Loch Ness side we sped, dog at the window spying for sheep, me at the wheel swinging the bends. Through Fort William, sprawled amidst grandeur, swirled across Loch Leven on the Balachullish ferry, a sniff of the sea before the long thoughtful climb past the Sisters of Glen Coe in a sunless Glen o' Weeping. Rannoch Moor, bog, grouse and baggy breeks. Ruined Kilchoan castle at the head of Loch Awe, guardian of Clan Diarmid country, subject of McCulloch's romantic painting in Scotland's National Gallery. Whoops, mind wandering, it's right over a single track hump above the turrets of tarty Inverarry castle, sharp as swords against the stretching waters of lazy old Loch Fyne, seaway of 'Para Handy's puffer' days. Sixty twisting miles to buzz down the Duke of Argyll's rhododendron ridden peninsula, all lush green, purple bloom and long perspective. Seascapes, islands, and a sleeping dog on the seat.

Four in the afternoon, seven and a half hours of revolving scenery and the dog and myself land back in the familiar surroundings of Crossaig, the farm we'd left a month before. Nancy, tail up, ran round her favourite sniffing posts making little unladylike squirts of glee. More sombrely I greeted the nose pinching stench of packed sheep with a drink of tea and a look over makeshift pens at the darker end of a clipping shed. The yellow orbs of a hundred and thirty apprehensive Black faced hoggs stared brightly over knitted backs.

Nothing for it, oil on the sharpening stone, shears honed to a edge to thrill any demon barber, wool sack doubled on the concrete, one concession to comfort, the last straight back for awhile, O.K. The first prancing hogg is dragged from its friends by the 'catcher', turned with a flick, plonked with a dunt, down on its 'bahooky', and it's ready at your feet. Grab horn and "lug" together in your vice grip, it saves the "handle" breaking off and leaving a pulsating hole in the sheep's head, dig a knee into its spine, force an elbow into it's neck, growl into a frozen black face, "settle now you dancing bitch," and you're away.

Bend your back, and stay bent, or your back'll give way by night. In you go. The shears part a pure white cleavage down a sweep of the hind leg, a great 'rise' you say with relief, plenty wool to clip in, but 'strong.' Your wrist'll know that as well by night. Fill the blades to the neck, slowly first till you get the pace, then. Shirt off, into the swing, into the sweat, into the smell, sheep shit, sweet sweat, grease. Smell, shit, sweat, grease. Turn the sheep, twist the sheep, balance and knack, clak, clak, open, close, open, close, open, close, aching wrist, sweat trickles down your chest, salt bites your eyes, muscle, rhythm, man and sheep, strength and power. Or as the Aussies would say, 'head down, arse up, and go for your life.'

Eight o' clock, a generation of Kintyre midges had bred in my sweat, thirty Black face hoggs, a red splodge of 'buist' on their backs had sprung to freedom and it's supper time, dram time, story time, dram time, bedtime.

The frying of bacon drifted down to the clipping shed from Crossaig kitchen on skylark sharp air with a waft of aroma that drew working men in Ganderenne rush to the breakfast table. The pleasures of the trencher are justifiably known to those who moil, and man, I could eat. Twenty hoggs had already come between me and a plateful of cholesterol. Medical fads were no substitute for physical work. With eighty 'kickers' to go, I needed twisting power.

The day turned humid and Kintyre dozed. Languid sunshine leaned on the tin roof and slept. Nancy trotted from under the wool rolling table and lay in the burn lapping water. Sweat lapped off my back, and occasionally I looked up to watch a sighing tide pencil patterns on the blue water of Kilbrannan Sound. Fifty hoggs later the midday paddle steamer swung past the Cock of Arran, making long ripples for Campbeltown. A boatload of lobster faced tourists were also heading for a clipping. Ah my, the chill wind of a shorn wallet.

At seven that evening I was three pounds lighter, seventeen pounds better off, but no thank you, I wouldn't wait my supper. Dog and I headed north, smelly, happy, and by midnight had summer stars dancing on dour Loch Ness. Their silver shepherdess popped from behind the Black Isle as a weary grey van picked its way amongst the stones up the steep Cluaine track. The 'swagman' sang Waltzing Matilda and Nancy opened a reproving eye. I slept late.

A slightly duller eye later that afternoon, looked over a pen of monstrous Aberdeenshire Half-bred ewes who glared back with 'clip me if you dare' written on their faces. Obdure animals belonging to Mary and Tony McCraith, my erstwhile Kintyre employers, for whom I'd crossed the Laigh of Moray, climbed the Pass of Kildrummie, saluted the land of 'orraloon days', and dipped across the Don, all to reach the couples new Deeside estate, intent upon divesting a hundred of these Amazons of their winter woollens. A daunting prospect, it took two of us to turn the first sheep.

Before dinner that night I lay in the bath examining the damage inflicted by twenty such strenuous encounters. A bright red weal coursed the length of my chest, a lacerating forefoot had narrowly missed my throat. An ugly mauve bruise inside my right thigh, a carefully aimed free kick, rather too close to a penalty for peace of mind. I snoozed under the taps.

Dinner was sumptuous. All candles, witty conversation and good company. I winked at Mary over the antique silver, as any enterprising shepherd might do. Brandy and port winked back. I retired to the guest wing a trifle crumpled. The pillow was soft, my mind was soft, the door opened softly, the maid tiptoed to say 'goodnight.' Softly.

Tomorrow, eighty Amazons to go, what the hell, but clipping was hard.

September's ripening glory rustled with the first breath of dawn. The night had been clear and cold with a hint of the bold stars of winter. Shy mists weaved their last mysterious trails amongst climbing birch, and a wealth of burnished light spread across the Braes of Kilmorack. A sea of golden bounty grew to a patchwork of tiny fields. Some steep on the edge of dank sunless hollows, others ragtaggle down the lea of sheltering woodland. Irregular handmade shapes strewn over the landscape by centuries of cultivation, they followed the lie of the good land and left the hillocks of gathered stone to bushy green islands of whin and broom. There, swung from thorny spike to spike, hung a crocheted trapeze of silver doilies which trembled under the first jerky inspection of Mr. Spider. Below, with barely a crackle, a russet form parted the stalks of a chill night's lair and the bright eyes of danger fell intent upon a crouching breakfast. The world was waking, and each pixied ear of corn on the bending heads of harvest glistened with a yellow jewel of morning sun.

Across the burn 'Sandy Leinassie' lent his scythe against the gable of the barn and went in search of the 'safe place' he'd put the sharpening stone. Today he would 'road' his oat field ready for cutting. High above, out from the loft door, the blue wings of summer love sat side by side and talked on wires in low twitterings. The alluring scent of apple and acorn lingered over fields of shining corn. The expectancy of harvest filled the air, and the womanhood of Autumn rested in all the fullness of her golden haired beauty.

The munificence of Mother nature blessed the Braes in bucolic bliss. Balm to the hearts of crofters as they waded waist deep in crackling harvest fields, catching a handful of corn here and there to rub between their palms, and thoughtfully bite a grain to feel its ripeness. From the Cluanie kitchen window we looked down upon five sloping acres of winnowing oats, hard, ripe and ready for cutting. Only the intrusion of a mechanical mind was to mar this swell of cornucopia. For a princely thirty pounds I bought a binder.

Let no man believe the indifference of inorganic matter to the temporal world when human ingenuity blends steel and wood, wheel, cog and canvas into the complexities of a mobile contraption for cutting corn. A row of sharp pointed fingers, six feet of reciprocating blade, cranking drive shaft, couplings, rollers, revolving wood stayed canvases, resembling large ladies corsets, and an assemblage of levers, gears and wheels that conveyed the slain stalks of oats towards the indignity of a waist band of twine and an unceremonious kick onto prickly stubbles in the form of a sheaf. Set on spindly wheels the whole menacing invention would advance on the harvest, striking terror into innocently waving corn and no small apprehension into the minds of simple rustics.

On the tail of this conveyance, perched high on a steel sprung seat of shapely cast iron proportion, which, after hours of bouncing would print the name of the machines maker on his bottom, sat the operator. Ostensibly in charge, he pulled levers with either hand, hung on by his feet, and surveyed the whole clanking process from the stately turning sails to its agitated 'kickers'. A notch more now, a shift back or forward on the 'board' and the crackling corn would flow like the contents of a tube station escalator towards the intricacies of the 'knotter' and the omnipotent judgement of the 'trip'. Here, central to this jerking animations function, lay it's brain.

A tinge of frost sharpened the autumn air and put a tingle in the blood. A freshness at each breath brought a zest to muscle and mind after the sweating hay days of summer. The white dew had dampened the crop a little, but patience prevailed. The binder, ready at the gateway below the house, sat waiting and pensive. I fussed round its nipples and chains with grease gun and oil. Two balls of twine were popped into the string box and the end of twine carefully threaded on a route of tension screws and eye holes through the secret 'bills' and 'knife' into the 'knotter's teeth'. Not a word passed between the Machiavelian machine and myself.

Oat heads shivered themselves dry in a breeze cool from the north, the sun beamed without a cloud to worry it, or me. By mid morning I jacked the binder's towing pole onto the draw bar of the 'grey Fergie' and tightened the contraption's canvas conveyors. Forward men. A touch of the tractor throttle, I let in the clutch. The sullen binder sprang to life and hurried along on our heels, an awesome clank of joints and connecting rods, each part performing its angular antics with the gusto of a fiddler's elbow in an impromptu 'eightsome.' By surprising contrast its windmill sails turned slowly, dragging the helpless crop onto an indifferent cutter bar with the inhuman gloating of an Income Tax Inspector.

Round and round we rattled. Betty rode the binder, I drove the tractor, head over my shoulder watching the whiz of moving parts, keeping the cutter bar full and waving instructions. Down the hollows, change gear for the pull, reverse at the corners, keep them square, follow the shape of the field. The operator, wild eyed and squeaking when the whole outfit tilted steeply on a side brae, bravely pulled at levers and hung on.

Proud standing corn, an army mown in its prime. Off at the knee, the slain stalks landed flat on the binder's rolling canvas to vanish up the escalator 'corsets' and lie, pummelled by 'packers', until the machine thought fit to flick it's 'trip.' A flash of insight, the 'knotter' spun, a knot was tied. Bound as a sheaf, each bundle of straw was flung by the 'strippers', with all the flourish of a nightclub 'bouncer,' onto the very ground from whence, only a round of the field before, they had stood grandly waving to our passing cavalcade.

Hearing the clack, clack of machinery, Alison and Hector ran up the brae from school, dumped their school bags at the gate, and oblivious to leg scratching stubbles, pranced after the wonder machine with the glee of tumbling puppies. At the binder's last round, almost between their legs, out bolted a handsome brown hare. Ears flat, naught to forty, a couple of swerves and straight up the hill. Two children, naught to ten, straight for the fence, ears abandoned.

Supper time, we sat on the back edge of the binder and ate cold venison sandwiches. A sloping battlefield surrounded us, row upon row, rank upon rank of fallen sheaves circled the field, ears down, butts splayed amongst the shorn stems. I looked askance at a few trailing stalks, "That damned binder's throwing loose sheaves," I grumbled to Betty. "Yes, one or two a round, but I could see you weren't of the mind to stop cutting." "Uhm," I thought of the hand made harvest knots required to rectify the binder's insolence. Did my grunt of disapproval reach the cunning machine?

We set up the sheaves, eight to a stook, lined towards a ageing sun which lent for a moment on the shoulder of Beinn a' Bha'ach Ard and promised them a drying wind from the west on the morrow. Soon the inside of our forearms stung with scratches, we worked into the chill of evening. Mist filled hollows on the Kilmorack Braes, another frost. The children, tired of sheaf tunnels and straw houses made for bed.

Homage to a dying harvest day, on the eastern horizon, close almost to the touch, rose an orange orb, held by the Goddess of Fulfilment. An exultant moon strode in majesty to bestow her glow along aisles of standing sheaves. And a simple corn sheaf, symbol of our dependence, bowed before her everlasting cycle, promise of the Ancient of Days, which as certain as the universe turns, draws life out of death.

But down at the edge of the birch, tall in silhouette, owls talked of mouse pie, and worried mice scurried to nibble new homes under sheltering stooks. Bet and I walked up the field in the last light. Stubbles crackled to our stride. A night of thin air shivered in ecstacy to the scent of chick weed, dyenettle and corn poppy, dank yet fragrant, incense to the harvest thanksgiving of the spheres.

The binder, sullen and mechanical, stank of oil. Alien from another planet.

Requests for the contracting services of my 'Sunshine' binder arrived by bicycle, word of mouth, notes with the postie and a combination of telescope and telepathy. Perspicacity and peace of mind had still to be undercut by the intrusion of the telephone. Without so much as the 'first class' post I was soon cutting corn from one end of Kilmorack to the other. Sam the Mill, Alec the

Fox, Bella Craigdhu and other worthies gauged their crop, the weather and our progress. Few of the croft fields were more than five acres and could be flattened in a day. For a pound an acre I would sell my soul and the binder's as well.

The secret was 'power drive'. Instead of this Heath Robinson's delight being driven by a huge spindled land wheel which in soggy going left a vulgar smear on a tangle of uncut crop, this wonder of the country hick, bemuser of field fence loiterer, drove through a 'power shaft' connected, no less, to the tractor transmission. Yes boy, boasting power drive 'Sunny Jim' and I could cut our way through thin, and sometimes thick, with the bravado of a machete waving Brave at a war dance. Such prowess perhaps accounted for 'Sunny's' air of conceit, if not his increasingly willful behaviour, as he swanked about the corn fields of Kilmorack. Late one evening towards the end of harvest the binder and I were cutting a 'wee fieldy' of oats down on the riverside belonging to Rita, daughter of 'The Hurly'. A dew crept over the banks, the crackle went out of the crop and pressure was on to finish. I revved 'Sunshine' to the limit of his rattle. That was it, enough's enough, without a word of explanation, 'strippers' and 'kickers' flailing like legs in a rugger scrum, he spewed untied stalks onto the ground. I slowed, another round, hopeless, straw everywhere. Drawing my language from parade ground memories I left the infernal contraption with it's character in tatters. Must be the knotter, could be the trip spring. I stopped at the gate, unwisely leaving the tractor ticking over and 'Sunshine' in power, if not in command.

Who knows, as much for a blether and the chance of a dram, but helpful as always in crofting style, the 'locals', jalousing Rita's harvest was being cut, strolled along to the field to set up stooks. Willie Grant the road man, Gordon, his old father-in-law, and Dunc Oldtown were only three of the experts who gathered round 'Sunshine' to diagnose his ailment and ruefully note the havoc of strewn straw.

"Ah well Thomson boy, it's the twine tension," Willie fiddled with the string. Oldtown had his say, "Look the bills aren't loosing the knot, you're knife's blunt." They peered at it, looked under it, tightened this, pulled that. The binder sat sourly, watchful, resentful?

I lent over the knotter to clear a bundle of strings. Did someone touch the trip? Did the machine seize it's chance? The strippers flashed faster than a Shogun scimitar, ripped my trousers, took me by the belt, flung me on top of the packers and held me tight, waiting. The arms would slash again in seconds. Gralloched, guts tied with a knot, bleeding to death, a mind picture about to fill the screen of reality.

Faster than the machine could lunge again, Dunc Oldtown leapt to the tractor and pulled the stop. The binder was foiled. Oldtown's swiftness saved my life. I undid my belt and slid down. The crowd surveyed the torn trousers, "Nearly had your balls off that time Thomson."

The salesman swore the binder would fix so I waved it goodbye on a lorry to Skye. Never trust a machine with a glint in its eye, even if it's called 'Sunshine.'

A crop of Glasgow orphans and the regular cheque through the post for rearing them, supplemented the meagre farming income provided by Highland crofting in the aftermath of the 'clearances', and for many Highland families during the dire days of the '30's' depression it proved a mainstay to keeping them on the land. From the turn of the century up to the 50's and 60's hundreds of children were sent to Highland crofts as an alternative to an orphanage amidst Scotlands industrial squalor

The orphan's treatment could vary from being 'one of the family' to a fashion, if they were boys, of keeping this fee paying labour in a 'leanto' on the gable end of the croft house. In some homes these invariably well disciplined children would seldom enter the main house and never got 'ben the room.' Meals were eaten standing at the scrub top scullery table, and whilst the diet, based on the produce of the croft might pall, turnip soup day after day, or 'braxy' mutton when a hogg died, it would undoubtedly be wholesome by comparison to the teeth rotting drinks and obesity inducing mush enjoyed by today's juveniles. Coarse wool blankets soon hardened sensitive skin and one group of children brought up in Kilmorack slept in the loft under deer skins. Clean blankets would appear only for an inspector's visit during which he checked the silent children against malnutrition and body vermin. Happiness is expectancy divided by realisation, hardy unspoilt children were often the happiest.

The majority of orphans worked on their foster parent's croft, attended the local school and became one of the community, though sometimes an untypical name marked them out. Discipline could be harsh and was generally administered along with a strict religious training. Saturday's tablespoon of sulphur and treacle, augmented on the Sabbath by three hours of sermon, ensured a weekly cleansing of body and mind. Nor did week days provide much scope for wayward behaviour. A 'worthless sinners' grace, often in the gaelic, began and finished every meal, and each evening the patriarch of the house would intone a lengthy Bible passage stressing the evils of sin. Conjecture doubtless intrigued the minds of the listening circle, but kneeling twenty minutes bare kneed on concrete provided a measure of atonement for any wicked thoughts. Cash with which to even glimpse the prospect of a little harmless sinning seldom found its way to the orphan's pocket. Life in Highland homes of that era was spartan for all. Yet out of this rigorous system grew many fine, unselfish men and women who brought credit to the land of their adoption.

Not all orphans had the benefit of this style of upbringing and my grandfather did much 'good work' for those he thought less fortunately loitering the streets of Inverness. He had sound reason to care for orphans. My great grandfather, a man of artistic and freedom loving temperament, untrammelled by a sense of responsibility, took his wife and son down to Leith in the second half of last century. There great granny was to awaken one morning in their dock land lodgings to a husband vanished and a sail on the horizon. The trek back north to live the poor relations on a croft at Summerton near Tain in Easter Ross must have been a sharp experience for a small boy.

As a business man in Inverness with a drapers shop on Church Street, grandfather devoted much time to his Boys Brigade Company and the welfare of underprivileged kids. My father told how he and his brothers, with the Inverness 'B.B.' Companies, would march out of town through Clachnaharry, kilts swinging, pipes playing, pulling handcarts of kit to camp on the Muir of Ord near the old market stance of cattle droving days. Grandfather paid too little attention to his business and went bankrupt, great grandfather, the absconder, eventually surfaced in America after producing a large family in a bigamous marriage, and the Boy's Brigade camp site is today an unsightly industrial estate.

Without knowledge of parenthood or pedigree Alec Murray came, an orphan from Glasgow, to a Kilmorack croft just before the last war. There he was reared with the family of Neil Campbell by a Gracie MacDiarmid, herself an orphan of an earlier addition to a bannock and cheese, tea caddy on the mantlepiece Highland household. Gracie, her hair drawn tightly to a grey bun, was a small walnut, hard working woman, known unkindly as the 'whiprak'. The last authentic Gaelic speaker on Kilmorack Braes, she imparted a smattering of the language to young Murray and more importantly perhaps, encouraged him by foot on the neck thrashings, towards a surprising turn of enterprise, and a bent for unremitting work, which when coupled to a predacious attitude towards Lord Lovat's spacious patrimony, singled him out amongst the Kilmorack 'loons'. Moreover he was a born shepherd, and as his life has since proved, 'a lad o' pairts'

For the past hundred years the largest one day auction of lambs in Europe takes place every August on an airy Sutherland-shire hillside above the honoured village of Lairg. Over thirty thousand lambs bereft of mothers, mist and moorland, bleat in swarms through the sale ring, and at the rap of a hammer, head south to kinder climes.

A nose nipping stench of dung and dip swirls through curls of fag smoke and 'confab' to hang in a blue haze of hub-bub over a ringside pack of swivelling eyes. Portly mole skinned farmers up from the lowlands, lean tweedy hill men down from the glens, and pink fleshy gentry drawn from the gun room, they jostle elbows around the rail and crane necks over heads. Baggy plus-four trousers or plus two knickerbockers, the social divide dissolves for a day, and out at the pens or in from the bar, shepherd and master assess the bright eyed progeny of a year's labour.

Conducting the cacophony from his 'box' in a manner not too far removed from the rantings of a hellfire and damnation preacher, an auctioneer sweeps the ring with eye and hammer, sways to the bids, crouches, bounces, sings staccato, raises pitch and tempo. A crescendo call, a last sweep, and crack, sold to that gentleman in the flat cap. "Yes Sir, you Sir, thank you. Now we have lot eighty-five, straight off Cape Wrath." A fresh jumping, bundling bunch of woolly bodies fill the ring, racing hearts, popping eyes, all wishing they could be the middle of the pack. Anticipation on edge, man and beast, attention rapt. At a well timed nod money changes hands in thousands. From moorland to Monte Carlo, it's a cert for electric excitement. Waving or winking at sheep sales should carry a health warning for wallets. Enter young Murray, sixteen, keen as a new charged battery. Wires cross, up jerks hand, down smacks hammer, two hundred lambs, fresh as paint, smartly switch owners in a flash of bidding fever.

Up looms James Fraser, Mart Manager, man of principle and foreboding manner. "No lambs leave this mart without payment." The budding shepherd studies his boots. A saviour arrives, Johnagh MacKenzie, wealthy sheep farmer from Glen Cannich, likes Murray's style, admires his ability to run on the hill at small cost. A word from MacKenzie, Murray looks up, tick money falls, manna from the mart. Alex puts his foot on the first rung of the farming ladder.

Late that night a lorry load of lambs trundles out of Lairg with Murray in the cab, thinking hard.

Lying across the Beauly river from the Braes of Kilmorack is an extensive ridge of woodland known as the Ruttle. The Lovat Estate had newly felled its mature pine and a spindle-shanked wooden bridge crossing the river gave access to a sawmill used during the work. No sheep thrive better than those which enjoy the clean grazing of a freshly cut wood.

Sometime after midnight a lorry load of lambs stops on the banks of the Beauly river. White backs bob in the moonlight, little boarding hooves rattle on wooden cladding. Within minutes two hundred hungry pirates swarm over his Lordship's woodland policies.

Several months passed. The squatters were shepherded out of sight of the road as far as possible until one bright day Lord Lovat driving up Strathglass accompanied by Jim MacLean his head shepherd looked across, "My Jove MacLean your hoggs are doing well in the Ruttle, what a splendid idea." MacLean mumbled a comment but silently ground his teeth. A week later and the sheep were through the Inverness mart. Murray had caught his first crumb.

Such familiar usage of Lovat's broad acres continued over a number of years, with particular attention paid to his Lordship's boundless stock of red deer. The day came when fledgling Murray, now married to a daughter of the Estate's river baillie, decided upon a safety zone between himself and the land of his depredations. A farm tenancy with Sir Ivor Colquhoun far away at Luss on the 'bonnie banks of Loch Lomond' seemed the appropriate distance.

Hardly was the flitting unpacked when a fresh enterprise presented itself to the pioneering Murray. Tents and midge scratching tourists abounded and he was soon collecting camping rents from his own ground and Sir Ivor's as well.

By and by the two aristocrats happened to meet and Colquhoun remarked huffily to Lovat, "You know Shimi that's a hell of a man you sent me after the glowing reference you gave him."

"You're right Ivor," smiled Lovat, "and you'll need to give a better one to get rid of him."

Dr. Johnson, noted London 'one liner' and Scotsaphobe, remarked when visiting the Highlands thirty years after Culloden, "My dear Boswell, here there are more gentlemen than shoes." Any such lack of stout brogues did not prevent the widespread Fraser aristocracy tramping through the law courts in pursuit of the coveted Lovat title. Today's Lovat line trace their recent ancestry to an astute but obscure sixteenth century gentleman, Thomas Alexander Fraser the Laird of Knockie, a bleak but picturesque estate lying high above Foyers on the south side of Loch Ness. In an age when fortunes were won as often by penis as pistol, Thomas put ear to bedpost and caught the distant knocking of a connubial opportunity, for it would seem across in the fertile spread of Aberdeenshire all was not well within another branch of the Fraser fraternity.

Some little time previously Chalmers the Laird of Strichen died and his widow Isabel Forbes, without letting her feet get cold, married Thomas Fraser, a son of Fraser of Philorth. Naturally the new bridegroom sought to swing the Strichen inheritance in favour of his own loins, but the bereaved daughters of Chalmers, peeved at the prospect of their 'tocher' being lost between the sheets, shrewdly called on Gordon of Gight to fight their case. Meeting young Philorth at Old Deer in 1576, Gordon achieved the desired result without resort to any tedious legal compromise by drawing his sword and neatly dropping stepfather Fraser on the spot.

Twice widowed, distraught, vengeful or both, Isabel dried her tears and in the interests of continuity promptly married Thomas Fraser of Knockie, a smoothy with a sympathetic shoulder and a plump wallet. Taking care not to arrange a meeting with Mr. Gordon, Thomas hastily paid 12,000 marks to the grieving old Laird of Philorth for the transfer of the Strichen rights to his own heirs, and with equal promptitude bought out the inheritancies of the two Chalmers girls, Catherine for 5000 marks and Violet for 3500 marks. The disparity in the girls valuation must be left to conjecture but at one gentle stroke Knockie secured the succession, albeit on a gamble with the Goddess fertility.

Back home at Beauly the Lovat succession seemed equally subject to the 'schemes o' mice and men.' For his sterling service to the nation, General Fraser, son of the wily Simon of the '45' retrieved the Lovat lands and title from the Government in 1774 but died without issue in 1782. The plum dropped on the Hon. Archibald Campbell Fraser, half brother of the General and youngest son of the beheaded Lord Lovat. This man and his wife Jane Fraser, a sister of Sir William Fraser of Ledclune were sadly preceded to the grave by their five children. Whereupon the death of the Hon. Archibald in 1815, under the terms of a mysterious deed of entail drawn up by the General on the restoration of property and title, all things bright and beautiful, all creatures great and small fell, as though by Almighty whim, to a thirteen year old boy, Thomas Alexander Fraser, son of the 9th Fraser of Strichen and direct descendant of our compassionate suitor. Two hundred years watching from the wings, old Thomas of Knockie smiled.

Coming of age in 1823 and thus into legal possession of the Lovat lands, the 'Strichen loon' put his Aberdeen-shire origins emphatically behind him by selling the Strichen Estate and devoting the £140,000 it raised to the improvement and expansion of his new found territory. Adjoining farms were purchased, farm houses and steadings built and vast upland areas of the estate given over to afforestation. At twenty-one he further distanced himself from the 'Doric' of his native Northeast by marrying the daughter of the eighth Lord Stafford, a mighty Norfolk nobleman whose ancestors sacrificed their lives during the factious Wars of the Roses. More modestly the bride contented herself by bringing north a pair of squirrels whose descendants, in due course, ravaged the woodlands so diligently planted by her husband.

In spite of this up market English marriage, Culloden and Catholicism still soured southern tastes, and Thomas, though legal owner of the Estates, failed to establish his descent and right to the Lovat peerage. Prudently he supported the Whig party and by 1837, on the accession of the Whig's to

Westminster office, their faithful adherent Thomas was soon looking in at the House of Lords as Lord Fraser of Lovat with the distinction of being the first Catholic to be created a Peer of the Realm since Henry the Eighth's Reformation Act of 1533 ditched Papal power. It took a further twenty years however before the stain of Attainder for Treason was removed from the Beaufort escutcheon plate and an erstwhile Aberdeen-shire laird could emerge Baron Lovat.

Thus when Thomas of Strichen died in 1876 he left his son, Simon, Master of Lovat, the Beaufort inheritancy, the title, and the proceeds from a Life Policy specifically for the purpose of building a residence to match their acquired family status. For £300 the burnt out ruins of old Castle Dounie had been replaced by the Commissioners of the Forfeited Estates with a small square building from which they administered lands confiscated after the 'Rebellions.' Hardly a comfortable residence mentally or physically for the new incumbents, a hundred years had passed, at last prosperity beckoned. Agricultural and sporting rents had never been higher. Pride did the rest. Castles in the Scottish Baronial style were all the rage, no great estate should be without one. A Mr. Wardrup was called in. Fresh from building a family seat for the Earl of Stair, he knew about these things.

In 1880 the Beaufort foundations were laid, much to the delight of local masons and labourers who marvelled at it's size and thought of their pay packets, much to the hand rubbing of Beauly shopkeepers who thought of its boost to the economy of the district. Only a few petty aristocracy hid their envy by describing it an idiosyncratic pile of monumental folly, and to be sure, that year as prairie busting ploughs were turning Canada into a world bread basket the first shipments of frozen beef from Australia were sold in Smithfield. From mock battlements the horizon for agrarian based wealth was clouding.

However with that unswerving family flair for matters d'amour, Simon had already married into an influential Catholic family, the Weld Blundells of Lulworth Castle in Dorset and happily after six hundred years found himself able to overlook the indiscretions of the Weld's campaigning progenitor, Edward 1st, 'Hammer of the Scots.' Less content were those who thought the Strichen Fraser's connection to the Lovat lands and lineage somewhat slender and indeed, given heraldic timescales, the ink was barely dusted on their pedigree scroll when expensive lawsuits of a disquieting nature were to unroll.

For many years a horsefly of a New York clergyman hovered over the Inverness legal scene raising suits in support of his claim to be, by nearer descent, the rightful Lord Lovat. A minor irritation, more easily swatted than the man from Angelsey who sweated up from Wales in 1881 buzzed by Messrs Giffard and Russell, a learned counsel of the day. To finance this claim a syndicate had been formed to which many of the estate tenantry surprisingly subscribed, inspite of the new line of Lairds proving themselves caring and considerate.

Perhaps the Welshman's tale jogged the folklore and local loyalties that lay at the back of old memories.

——————

Hard by the bank of the Beauly river, west of the village, lay the long thatched farmhouse of Teawig. On a dark winter's night its windows flickered with reed lamps, leaping reels and laughter. The fiddler weaved a web rich in Highland tune, dashing river, tumbling torrent and swirling tide. The door burst open, in strode young Fraser, wild and fresh faced. The dance paused. The bow took a different note, a slurring sneer played a tune, slow and insulting. The 'Battle of the Shirts,' still full in memory, stalked the earthen floor. A Fraser felt the slap. The fiddler, a MacDonald, leered across his glinting wood. Eye to eye, Fraser, MacDonald. The fiddler struck his bow, Fraser struck his dirk. A pool of blood seeped dull red through the silent crowd. In a swirl of kilt, Fraser softly closed the door. In a cough of pride the fiddler slowly died.

Without a turn of his head Fraser made easy strides down to the river and hailed the ferry. The creak of pulley blocks told he was instantly obeyed, for this was the younger son of a Lovat of the sixteenth century. Black and bent the ferryman pulled his dipping line. A crystal frost clung to the boat and white as a wisp river fog it slid to the bank at Fraser's feet. He stepped down. No words passed, the ferryman knew his place and returned to the rhythm of his ropes.

Presently the young man knelt at the gunwale to wash the blood from his hands. Soft eddies murmured. Tiny whirls of space in the river's life. Alive a moment, then swallowed, each a choking vortex in it's endless flow. From the water rose a face, a gargoyle in the moonlight mirror of his mind. Coils of crimson death spewed from its mouth staining the silver river into streaks of a sleepless dawn. By middle day the Grampian hills were underfoot and flight the lesser price of pride.

Angelsey of that era must have been as remote from the Highlands as the Gobi desert might seem today, and there in the Land of the Leek Fraser paused for breath. Return home? retribution would swiftly slit his throat, he worked his days as a miner, found energy enough to marry at the age of eighty and produce a line of sons. By now it's 1881, safe to surface, sing Cwmn Rhondda. A plausible 'Taffy' from Wales, that warren of windbags, inflated his ego sufficiently to retrace the fleeing footsteps of his priapic ancestor.

Such was the tale told by this supposed descendant of the sprightly octogenarian standing hands outstretched, eyes beseeching, before a Judge of the Edinburgh High Court. In a lyrical Celtic peroration, by the closer consanguinity, he claimed Lovat's land and title. Not a happy 'yakki daa' situation. Strichen's hand clutched smelling salts. Title just signed, new castle, scaffold straddled walls, mortar still setting, strewn sandstone blocks, grand turret half built. To say there was panic at the portcullis would describe dysentery as dyspepsia. Dust rose in feverish clouds from ancient Kilmorack and Kiltarlity Parish papers. The death record of this reputed murderer must arise, slay this spectre from the vaults of vengeance. Loss loomed from the Land of my Fathers.

The case reached the House of Lords. The Judge looked up, beakish and bewigged. He cleared his throat, "I find." In dashed Mr. Biscoe of Kinghillie waving a document he'd discovered deep amongst Kirkhill Parish papers. The judge perused the vital entry. "Ahem, ahem," he coughed. A wise and pensive cough below gold half spectacles. Judgement was delivered in favour of the defendant. Lovat sat down with the sigh of a surfacing whale. Unfortunately the expenses which surfaced proved equally vast.

Baron Nicolas Stackleberg stood on an eminence overlooking his Estate. Suitably eminent himself, powerful arms folded on a barrel chest, shirt sleeves flapping to a June breeze which had yet to lose its taste for snow. Plus foured, head high, just a tilt, every inch a gentleman and a fine figure of manhood to boot. The Baron surveyed a domain over which artists and estate agents might drool. His castle smiled up. Also eminently perched with equally commanding mien, from lead lighted windows its haughty gaze swept above the bowing woodlands of Strathglass to dwell on the heights of Scotland's Byronic grandeur. From the opposite angle an admiring sun smiled down, drenching the river with diamonds, turning trees into shadows and lighting the emerald green swards, appropriately dotted with Erchless dairy cattle. All in all, a most eminent day. A ruddy tinge on the Baron's full neck hinted he was fuelled for the occasion.

Huddled in the lea of the Baron were Jason and Henrietta, fourth generation Chisholm's from 'back home,' and 'ah gee' just yearning to buy us a homestead in 'yur lil ol' country.' The civilising effects of eighty years in the world's most facile democracy ensured the arctic gale had yet to blow which could penetrate the exiles summer. apparel. Nostalgia for them seemed best viewed from the privation of padded storm coats, and a camera peeping between buttons would ensure, in due course, that the Highlands could relax to the snores of a Virginian drawing room.

Just a measured pace behind the trio stooped Rory MacKay, solicitor to the Baron and dutiful son of Captain 'Whistling Willie' MacKay, noted lawyer, peddler of tuneless piobroch about the streets of Inverness and the acknowledged historian of Clan Chisholm. Rory, a man of wit rather than letters and styling himself Corporal Mackay, stood dejected and shivering. The thermal limitations of his grandfather's threadbare Inverness cape and moth trimmed kilt made apparent by the crop of goosepimples which likened his legs to those of a poorly plucked chicken. Gaelophile and Mod rouser, Rory mused sadly over the demise of yet another slice of Gaeldom and, a Highlander to the till, 'prepared to go down with his people' as he braced himself to ring up another fee.

"Gee Baron," Jason turned slowly, drawing in the scale and sublimity of the scene through the view finder of his Pentax Mk.10. "Gee Baron," he repeated between clicks, "this sure is a swell lil' bit of land space." The Baron swelled with pride, the panorama swelled with pride, Rory, with silent Highland perspicacity, shrank with apprehension. "Say Baron," Jason lingered over the title to emphasis the egalitarian principles of Uncle Sam, "where's about the frontiers of your territory?" Nicholas Stackleberg a crack cavalryman of noble blood who had soldiered from the Steppes of Russia to the Plains of Poland raised an arm. With a sweep that would have signalled the charge of a line of Hussars he encompassed the horizon. Hill upon hill fell to his command, the Beauly Firth, the Lovat Estates, the Corrieyarrick Pass, he paused and looked down on the speechless Yanks, "As far as the eye can see," he boomed and strode down to his castle.

Rory gulped and thought of the missives. Another deal was blown, until sadly one day, for a reputed £60,000, the boundless Erchless Estate fell from the hands of a puissant character into the pin striped mundanity of a mere Edinburgh solicitor.

I COULD STILL BE DYING

A hedge of the yellow dog rose greeted a visitor to the croft of Ardochy. A welcome, not brash as the floribunda, nor gushing as the daffodil, but shy, in a shade of sunshine yellow that told of natural days and a style of living which held time in its hands at the end of a hedge lined road. Happy flowers, they lived with the hum of the bee in their petals and the song thrush nest in their secret tangle. Once the road at their feet had carried cart and pony, sheep drove and cattle on rutted tracks between the fields of Breakachy to the wide spaces of Strathglass. But no more, ash and birch leaned heads together, Herb Robert and Star of Bethlehem stretched pink and white on grassy banks where the grasshopper churred in blinks of hot sun and the mossing path led only into the green years of yesterday.

Seldom a day passed but I called at the croft of the yellow roses. Summer mornings bright I caught their breath, sweet under the rowans that twined about the gate, soft and calling as the nape of a lover's neck as they opened to the first tender light. Sometimes I would stop by when the midday shimmer sent Archie's hens to drowse one legged in the cool of the cart shed, and down in the dust at the garden edge dowdy sparrows would fluff hollows amongst Alec's drills of carrot. Scruffy, squabbling delinquents they dashed for cover as I turned at the hedge.

Or perhaps I came of a June evening when the breeze stole away to the pines on the cnoc and sounds of the hills drew close. Clear from the lonely

The Lovat Fraser family at Beaufort.
Left to right: Tessa, Kim, Lady Lovat, The Master of Lovat, Andrew, Sir Hugh Fraser, Lord Lovat, Hugh.

Beaufort Castle under construction, 1880.

The Beaufort battlements above the Beauly.

Lovat of the '45 from the original by Hogarth.

Eilean Mhuilie, in the cradle of the Strathfarrar hills.

The Red Fox's retreat on Eilean Mhuilie.

Four Good Reasons

Why you should call at

T. MACKENZIE'S

DISPENSING ESTABLISHMENT,

4 and 6 Church Street, Inverness.

I.—It is one of the oldest Chemist's Shops in the North of Scotland, and is now owned by one of the foremost Chemists of the times.

II.—The dispensing only of Drugs and Chemicals of known and full Medicinal and Chemical power. No second or third-rate Drugs or Goods stocked.

III.—The chemical and accurate skill in compounding Prescriptions, to give equivalents in doses, &c.

IV.—The effectiveness with which we have met modern competition, in charging moderate prices compatible with the above conditions.

We hold a Large Stock of Sponges, Rubber Bottles, Sponge Bags, Waterproof Sheeting, Perfumes, Nail, Tooth, and Hair Brushes, Soaps, &c.

Visit our Photographic Department. Send for Lists.

Eyesight. **Spectacles.**

THE EYE is the most important organ of the Human Body, and is frequently the most neglected. Very few have perfect Eyes, and in most cases the two eyes have different errors. Please note that 90 per cent. of DEFECTIVE EYES are due to REFRACTIVE ERRORS only, and these can be remedied by SCIENTIFIC EXAMINATION and construction of Suitable Lenses to correct the different Refractive Meridians of each eye.

Mr MACKENZIE is an EXPERT REFRACTIONIST and has devoted many years' study to Light and Sight, is certified and recommended by the London Worshipful Company of Spectaclemakers.

Sight-Testing Room with all the latest appliances Free to Customers

T. MACKENZIE,

F.C.S., Ph.C., F.S.M.C., B.O.A., &c.,

4 Church Street, INVERNESS

Uncle Tom, a very important man.

My son, Hector Fraser Thomson

My father, Hector Fraser
Thomson, Malta 1944

The Falls of Kilmorack, which provided a site for the dam.

Lonbuie, Auntie Jeanie's croft.

The Kilmorack dam.

The Aigas dam.

Harvest at Whitlums, Gartly, Aberdeenshire, in 1948, with the Beattie family. *Left to right:* Margaret, Sandy, the 'Orraloon' and Hugh.

Erchless Castle, home to Baron and Baroness Stackelberg, once seat of 'the Chisholm'.

The Jersey heifers, ready for off.

John Boa, his wife, Barbara, and their family in 1907, all born at Longard, Glen Cannich.

The Longard shepherds' home, cleared for the hydro, 1947.

John Boa on his eightieth birthday, on top of Ben Wyvis

Flood in the Highlands, by Sir Edwin Landseer (Aberdeen City Art Gallery and Museums Collection).

The Aigas dam, the morning after the flood, 1966.

The waterspout on the forecourt of Aigas dam during the 1966 flood.

The Mullardoch dam straddling Glen Cannich.

Strathglass under water.

Cluanie croft, on the skyline under the tip of Beinn a' Bha'ach Ard, 'spies' on the Braes of Kilmorack and the Beauly river.

Alec 'the Councillor', Archie and 'Bossy Flossy' at Ardochy.

Looking to Breakachy from Erchless Hill, and a fine stag grassed by Duncan Chisholm.

Duncan Chisholm, keeper to Baron Stackelberg on Erchless Forest and Betsy, the 'white pony'.

A show-winning blackface ewe lamb bred by Alex Murray in Strathtay.

Alex Murray, ex-provost of Perth, at the shearing.

The Californian Frasers at Beaufort, welcomed by Lord Lovat and a good sprinkling of locals.

Lord Lovat and Duncan Fraser, stalker in Strathfarrar.

Cattle ranching in Glenstrathfarrar, 1949.

Eskdale Church, built by the Lovat family.

The Lovat graves and the hills of Strathglass.

Struy Church and the pub below Beinn a' Bha' ch Ard, in the heart of Strathglass.

The great hills of Glenstrathfarrar.

Simon Fraser, Lord Lovat, at his coming of age, 1998.

moors of Breackachy came a curlew's lament, the loss of the Highlands sad in its fading note. Safe under a heather tuft the plover fondly turned her fated clutch and high against the lingering northern sky a snipe fell sobbing over the world of dying hills that ere long were to know their cries no more.

In the shadows of the crofthouse, swifts, dark on sickle wing, screamed about the gables and swallows that built each year in the crook of the byre, skimmed for midges above a midden of winter's dung that lay in the elbow of the yard. Each evening Archie would 'shut the hens' but the swallows nest in his hen shed packed a pink mouthed straining brood, and to help the ceaseless caring of the harried parents he left the door ajar.

Days drew by and Archie one morning lamented to me the killing of some hens. Feathers marked a trail over the burn and into the Coille Dhu, a steep woodland across from the house. A trap was set tight to the corner, lightly covered with litter and left. I took the rifle on the following morning. The door was shut. "The trap has him." I peered into the gloom, green eyes spat with fury. From the shoulder I put a bullet between them. It was a beauty of a wild cat, dark marks down the back, perfect black rings to the tip of his tail. Perhaps he was carrying to kittens over in the black wood and I was sad.

Pennycross House,
County of Argyll.

2nd April, 1862,

Mr. Finlay MacRae,

This is to certify that you have been a tenant on this estate seven years at the term of Whit Sunday next, during which time I have found you an honest, industrious, sober, judicious farmer and payed your rent in full; and I will be glad to learn that you got a farm to your mind in the County of your nativity, as you seem so anxious and will prefer over there.

Truly
Alan MacLean, L.D.

Copper plate reference, copper plate writing, style of the times, it helped Finlay MacRae obtain the tenancy of Ardochy, a desirable forty acre croft with an outrun of pine clad heathery hill which rose to the western edge of the populous and long settled community of Breakachy. The Highlander has always been prone to wander, and MacRae, a Kintail man, in his early years proved no exception. His mother's people, MacLennan to name, one time Tacks men at Lienassie, had farmed in the shadow of Kintail's shapely Five Sister's, but horizons beyond Wester Ross beckoned and a member of the family reached Demerara in the days of sugar and slavery. On his death this adventurer left provision in his will for the child of a slave woman who worked on the plantation. Finlay, though lacking the plumes of a conquistador, crossed the Minch to Lewis during the tattie failure years of the mid 1830's and took a croft at Arnish on the shores of Stornaway bay. By the 1850's he farmed at Carsaig on the green Isle of Mull and ten years later, MacRae taking a chance to better himself as they say, made for Kilmorack. A resolute step, the Doctor of Letters passport in his pouch and no removal van.

Hidden away to the west of Ardochy amidst a swell of purple hill crowned with ageing pine, huddled the tiny croft called Yellowbrook. A speck of green ground, sloping and sunny, had been toiled from the moor. A burn, brown from the peat lands, carried the symphony of winter's spate or the distant tinkle of summer drought to the foot of this Highland home. Perhaps a couple of acres, hand dug, pick and spade, soil for crop, stone for dyke, I would pause where the trenching ended. Above me, on the crest of the full breasted slope, ruins tumbled, bramble and bracken strove to cover their sorrow, I would think of the seasons in a life that once had been. The spring air yet breathed heavy with the almond scent of yellow flowered whins, guardians of empty gables, and on the mellow banks of Yellowbrook a late summer heat would pop the pods of broom on a lazy afternoon. Deep in the care of a red berried rowan the thin song of an autumn Robin waited the returning joy of children at a winter window.

For over a century ago this forgotten croft had lived, vibrant with voice and people, the birthplace to a numerous family of hardy children. Slim, shy, barefoot bairns in hand-me-down home spuns, they grew, nature their companion and mentor, in a playground of fields, dandelion clocks and daisy chains. Helping at hay time, hut stooks at harvest, in sunshine breeze and dapple cloud they'd ramble the hills, hunt the wild bees' nest and stretch the summer evenings until laughter floated away beyond bedtime. Or with the children of Breakachy, friendship and squabble, they'd follow burns through pool and shallow, guddle trout that winnowed the shade and swim the Mill pool where it took their breath away under the falls. Or reaching toes to the winter's scudding fire they'd catch a hand at the old folk's tales. Ghosts and goblins weaved by wizened faces grew in the smoke of the peat, till at last the Gaelic songs would lull tired eyes to a box bed and happy with little, they'd sleep in the comfort of family warmth.

Longevity is a gift of the genes. Add a spartan upbringing, an active healthy lifestyle and, accidents apart, you shorten the odds of beating the bookie's favourite in the compulsory life span stakes. When 'Sandy' Chisholm moved from Glassburn in the heart of Strathglass to the croft of Yellowbrook well over a century and a half ago, he left behind his weaving trade, brought an eighteen year old bride and set about proving the point. Sandy's wife died at eighty-eight, himself at ninety-two, and in their thatched crofthouse of two front windows and one doorway, people in, peat smoke out, they bred twenty-one children. In the way of crofting life the wife would have milked the cow, fed the family, washed clothes in the burn and worked to the day of each birth. No epidurals, kettle on the hook, into the 'big bed' and press. Two of the children died in infancy, three as teenagers but the remaining sixteen offspring all lived to be over eighty. William the last to die in 1927, reached ninety-seven and the average of that group was an astounding eighty-five. All enjoyed perfect health until their deaths, which in at least twelve of the cases, came by sudden heart attack. But the weaving trade lives on. A descendant of this tenacious strain of Clan Chisholm is today a prominent Inverness kilt maker with world wide connections.

The Yellowbrooks were the breed of people amongst whom Finlay MacRae found himself after trundling goods and chattels from Mull to Ardochy. In due course 'Old Macrae' died and returned at last to Kintail. His son Ewen took on the tenancy and chose to go no further than the Yellowbrook croft to find a comely and kindly wife. 'Fair Jane' Chisholm inherited something approaching her mother's fecundity and bore him ten boys and one girl in a brood that included two sets of twins. A triumph of love and compromise over religious barriers, for the Macraes were staunch Free Presbyterian, the Chisholms devout Roman Catholic and the resulting family, between the two Faiths, was duly divided. Fate played a different role. At four months of age their only baby girl, lying in her crib beside the fire, choked to death on a feed bottle.

One of the great pleasures of farming at Cluanie was the mutual interests and affability of the neighbourhood. Ewen and Jane were long dead but grandsons of 'Old Finlay Macrae' still crofted Ardochy and I had only to climb my top fields, pass the ruins of Ali Cluanie's, the name a remembrance, the man long forgotten, and drop down through pines at the Paddy's wood to a seallach bordered track which took me to the barking welcome from 'Flossy.' According to season the wooden porch smelt of pet lamb pee, sheep dip or onions. One knock, "Hello, it's only me," and two steps brought back a Victorian era.

I first met Alec MacRae, 'The Councillor' on a day in January. Lost snowflakes flecked the ground as Duncan Chisholm, the Erchless keeper showed me the boundaries of Cluanie and we called at Ardochy. MacRae bent in the doorway of his tin roofed cart shed filling a barrow with turnip which he deftly halved in his hand with a 'clipper.' The shafts of an iron shod farm cart hung on their 'back chain' from a rafter above his head, sacks spread drying on ropes, and further into straw strand and cobweb, amongst wire tattie baskets and old stack ropes, from the era of polished gaiter and oil wick side lamps, hid a lightly sprung varnished gig.

'The Councillor' straightened at our approach, "Well Dunc, will it make a fall?" he looked round at the weather and then at me. Hooded eyes, questioning but discreet, a strong jutting jaw dominated the fresh skinned face of sound health and unimpaired constitution. A white haired man touching seventy, powerful of frame, knowing of mind and both attributes amply justified. As a young man he caught a neighbour's yearling colt feeding in his cornfield and lifted it bodily back over the fence. An older man, as a Governor of the North of Scotland College of Agriculture and longest serving member of the old Inverness County Council, hence the widely used byname, his brand of archaic wisdom won weight and respect. Only once did 'The Councillor' fight an election for a place on the Council. When questioned as to the suitability of his candidacy a school days companion, 'Old Murd Batten' known for his tongue, remarked gravely, "Well boy, Ardochy has the time and the clothes."

Tight coated cheviot ewes, flicking snow off their ears, watched and bleated. A bold one, perhaps an ex pet, pawed the gate. Flossy paused from wagging at us and turned a threatening eye. MacRae in neck banded linen shirt, brass collar stud, waistcoat and spacious plus fours politely untied the hessian sack from about his waist and we shook hands. In that simple grip and glance his whole manner embodied the concern for land and livestock that made existence possible down the generations. Families to feed, babies to bury, love and loss, his folks knew it. Flood or frost, ten boys to keep, hap the tattie pit with bracken, thatch the stacks with rashes, no leaks, no waste, no College course in survival by highly paid pundits.

Archie came down the yard and stared towards us, bonnet skip laughing wide, elbows poking through trails of faded blue wool. Hens sprinted to his feet. Archie looked down and thought of groceries, the hens looked up and thought of grain, it was their weekly dozens that paid Jimmy Sutherland and his travelling shop for cheese, sugar, oatcakes and the extravagance of water biscuits. Bike to Church on the Sabbath, Archie seldom went far from the croft. A small wiry man who still privately grieved for his twin brother Roderick killed at Gallipoli, poor Archie spent his life a genie at the bidding of his rather grander brother Alec. Keep the house, clean the byre, second in command to Flossy and should a stranger hove in sight, "Man Erchie, away and put in your teeth and put a stick to the fire."

Chisholm lifted a hand at Archie's shouted invitation "You'll take a strupagh." and after a little we made to the house. The warmth of Archie's welcome from the dank concrete scullery carried with it the whiff of hand milked cream waiting to become crowdie and a boiling of the hen's tattie peelings cooling on a two ring stove. He wiped his hands on a bran sack which hung behind the door, and filled a small kettle from a pail of spring water which sat on a backless chair beside the stone sink. "Go through and sit at the fire." We lifted hard backed wooden chairs from the scrub top table and sat over at the small open grate.

Archie spread the unread sports page of the Inverness Courier as a clean table cloth and took cups off the pine dresser. He was pleased to have company and a 'news'. Flossy pushed between us and lay on the bare boards, her nose poking the two pieces of coal that struggled to stay alight. 'Ardochy' as Chisholm called him, tramped in from feeding the sheep. "Ah Flossy, come out of that," he growled and in the same breath, "Erchie you let the fire down." Archie rummaged for dry sticks in the scullery. Flossy with a disgruntled eye turned three times, lay in the corner, and tucked her nose into her tail. The Councillor placed himself at one end of the living room's only hint of comfort, an ancient couch whose base made contact with the floor as he sat. Stacked at its other end a two foot pile of Council Minutes and a months Press and Journals convinced me at once that Archie, as well as incurring blame for the reluctance of his brother to buy coals, was even denied the ease of a sunken spring.

Years were to pass before the emaciated couch twanged its last and served to fuel on its own funeral pyre. After some careful bidding a grey 'moquette' replacement was secured in Fraser's secondhand furniture sale for five shillings. I provided the removal services, and with all but a green felt apron manouvered the brass studded bargain into the living room. Flossy looked pleased and for several nights she had good reason. But lying too long one morning in the arms of Morpheus she awakened with a start at The Councillor's early tread on the stair. Hearing the scuffle he entered the living room with suspicion and ran his hand over the 'new' couch. It was warm! "Ah Flossy, Flossy!" From that evening forward, in nightly ritual, the kitchen chairs were placed on the couch and Flossy wisely made her retiral on the wooden floor.

However the dog was not without guile. I passed through Ardochy one early lambing round and came on The Councillor, a bead of sweat on his brow, digging a deep hole on the edge of the burn. "Ah poor Flossy, what a useful dog, a wise, wise dog," I could see he was a shade upset, "she knew every move about the place." And read your every mood I thought to myself. "Flossy's dead?" "She didn't move when I came down this morning, she's stretched out on the floor," and after a few more spades, "not handy for the lambing without her," he continued, with a hint at the dog's lack of consideration for matters temporal. We walked up to the house. "Woof, woof," out rushed the dead dog to challenge my old Nancy. "Ah Flossy," Ardochy shouted, "be quiet, be quiet." Not to be tricked again and as a warning to Flossy, the hole was left open. Perhaps a couple of years passed and I filled the grave with Flossy, a great character, at the bottom.

Pigs and planners have something in common. Both are in the business of redesigning their surroundings, the one by nose, the other by bulldozer. The effects are not always dissimilar. Erchless now sold, Nicky and Phyllis Stackelberg decided Teanassie Lodge, one of their remaining properties, would make them an idyllic bijou residence with the 'attraction' of us as friendly neighbours. The climbing road to Cluanie looked down on this little white cottage, damp and sunless under the lea of the weeping rock and birch woodland of the Druim.

Early in June my power saw and I ripped into its jungle garden. Hedgehogs panicked, nesting blackbirds screeched, horn beam and holly joined a plume of smoke that cleared away the natural effect to lawn and rosebush. An architect who produced accounts to match his pomposity arrived on the scene accompanied by a bulldozer. "Do please retain the cottage's character," I heard the Baroness instruct the architect. A word to the 'dozer' driver might have been wiser. Within half a day, a white dust settled to reveal the remaining character, half the back wall, a precariously leaning gable and the musty stench of galloping wet rot. Cement block and steel girder soon blended the old style abode into something not unlike an army barracks. The name was upgraded to 'House' but strangely the aroma never quite departed.

Up at Cluanie we thought of pigs. Much like 'pyramid selling' they appeared to be a route into regular income, though their attitude towards antique structures had yet to be appreciated. I guessed there were pigs about the 'Braes' for each time the wind turned easterly an indescribable aroma wafted its way up to Cluanie. I suspected Willie John 'Balavulich' or rather his enterprise to be the culprit, and duly called. Contented grunts greeted me, pens full of snoozing pound notes, and smell apart, nothing more offensive than the odd trump of well fed flatulence. Willie, or Bill as his wife preferred, directed me to his neighbours Simon and Maureen MacKenzie who, as well as breeding pigs were concentrating on having a large family in the old crofting home of Caulternich above Kilmorack burying ground.

Reduced from the distinction of delivering buns round Beauly a secondhand bread van ground out the bends up to Cluanie. On its steaming radiator I read the name Trojan, a classic warning. Warriors? hardly, I allowed out six shining virgin white gilts into the contentment of a deeply strawed shed. The nubile darlings, "I'll need to get them a suitor, the sooner they're inpig the better," Simon Caulternich shut the trap door of the Trojan and grinned, he knew about these things. I leaned on the gate and smiled at them, tufty little tails curling and uncurling, heads buried in straw, ears up flapping, ah the beauties. The first stone surfaced from the bottom of the shed followed by a black nose, then another stone, more black noses. Surely not an escape tunnel? The old Trojan van rattled down the brae before I could stop it.

--

Lengths of binder twine firmly lashed to the seats secured the hastily built wooden frame which separated Simon and myself from the straw in a back of my Austin 35 van as we motored a few mornings later o'er the Glens o' Foundland down into Doricdom and the 'nae doot ava' lingo in search of a 'hunkie' sausage maker to humour the gilts.

Robert Lawsons of Dyce were famous throughout Aberdeenshire and beyond in the realms of civilisation, for their pork pies and the pedigree of the ingredients. Where better to inspect this alluring process from its satisfied grunt of procreation to the crackle and sigh of a sizzling sausage? We parked our modest conveyance round the back and knocked on the front door. The owner of the 'bacon for breakfast' factory, Mr.Robert,jnr. appeared, white coat, black bowler and pig stick, ready to reveal the trick.

Reflecting upon the 'burach' left behind in the Cluanie steading I could see at once as Mr. Lawson conducted us around his penthouse piggery that half the magic lay in containing the potential product within a given space, the other half in separating sound and smell from the finished article. We progressed towards his office down aisles of scrubbed concrete, scrubbed pigs and scrubbing pig men, it was immaculate in all but conception. And therein the point of our visit. We sat gingerly in the office, Landrace pigs stretched round the walls, Robert rolled out pedigrees. Three hundred, a really long one, I fingered my wallet, er, um, thirty pounds? A little shorter Robert smiled, but still a list of ancestors which any aspiring aristocrat might paste on the front page of his autobiography.

"Man ye hev fairly picket a quid yin," the pig man drew my eye, "fitten a gran pair o' ba's," he observed, and indeed Robert's, the name sprang to mind instantly, Robert's protruding testicles did extend, by some six inches, a body already resembling a four foot sausage on castors. A couple of tweeks of his 'ba's' and Robert lunged into the back of the van to stand cramped in a semi circle, the aforementioned appendages pressed flat in unseemly display against the back window.

We drove away. The day was young as they say, Robert slobbered down Simon's neck as boars will do, and I suggested a diversionary route home as fools are wont. Oblivious to the 'face' beaming from our rear window and the stares of overtaking traffic we swung off and climbed the high roads of Strathdon until a farm sign reading Mains of Towie brought a 'dropper' on Hugh Beattie my pal of orraloon days. Barely hello and handshake before Hugh spotted the armorial bearings emblazoned on the back window, "Fit a pair o' ba's," he whistled. A great welcome and a double toast followed.

My, my, the hospitality, the sun set early that evening. We searched the yard for the van, had Robert moved it? No, but wearying of being a window display, he now sprawled in comfort across our front seats, and being by nature a gentleman had excused himself in Simon's glove pocket. Such a jolly journey home, I know pigs don't really fly but Robert did seem a bit wild on the bends and by midnight, judging from the squeals, m'laddo was boasting to the gilts about the length of his pedigree.

Marriage was in the air, but first things first, the crofthouse needed at least ablution facilities to tempt a bride over the threshold. Alec, not exactly flushed with youth or funds, pondered the matter. His intended, a bonnie curly haired local girl, full of laughter and much his junior, sailed on a sunset trip to New Zealand. Would she return? Ah me, the pangs of parting, and what use a bathroom without a bride? Alec took a chance, not a regular feature of his lifestyle. Plumbing and proposal were put in motion.

Whitewashed old stone built 'but and ben' with its red tin roof, Alec's crofthouse and his gently worked fields, fell immediately under my eye from the heights of Cluanie. Cross the doorstep and my 'glass' could read Alec's mind. Note the smoke and I knew what time he rose. A chink of light on a moonlight night and I'd cross the tree trunk bridge over the Breakachy burn with something in the hip pocket. Alec would stretch slippered feet to the range and the tales could catch the dawn. On such a night the talk turned to septic tanks.

Where heather tracks lead paths to the west, where bending birch take the sting from westerly gale and winter snow, there snuggles the croft of Cul na Cleithe. A single line of stone walls, gable to the weather, a barefoot beaten porch to gather sunshine and gaze across silver curls of river smiling below the cushion green woodlands that buried a life of buzz and bustle on the Lovat Estates. Long empty, yet still a haunt of happy feelings, a home of souls at peace. I looked to the old croft's sunny slopes from Cluanie and sometimes of a Sunday I crossed the craggie burn that lay between us to live a little within its power.

Alec's father Sandy was a mild mannered man who worked his croft content with the soil of Cul na Cleidh, the chatter of stone voices on the mould board of his plough, the smell of a sweating horse, the cry of squabbling gulls at his heel. But to live on its few acres with a wife and family, five boys and five girls, meant work away to provide the extras demanded by an awakening generation. The hills of Braulin in the heart of Strathfarrar could be seen from his door, the distance by heather track, twenty miles, but Sandy loved the freedom of the high ground and for many years ghillied the stalking season in the glen. Walk home on a Saturday night when the stags were skinned, often in the dark. Sunday, as a good Catholic, walk the five miles to Beauly Mass and back for his dinner. An evening with the family before taking the track twenty miles to another six days of hill work dragging and carrying, a few shillings a week and the hope of a good tip from the 'toff' at the season's end.

By contrast to her gentle spouse both in manner and faith, Alec's Protestant mother was said to possess a distinctly acerbic turn of phrase. On occasion words flew about the crofthouse, assorted faults were raised, including her man's apparent lack of ambition. The full catalogue of poor Sandy's shortcomings pouring into a neighbour's ear one evening, drew the impatient remark, "Well Mary you managed ten children whatever." "Ach aye," snapped the peevish wife, "it was alright when we were at that."

To add a dash of romance to Alec's amorous designs I offered to build the septic tank. "When?" his eye glinted, a hint of lust? "Next Sunday? I'm clear if the weather's in it." He looked furtive, "Only if you're quiet about it." The chief snag to work on the Sabbath was James, his fire eating lay preaching Free Church neighbour. A man of rigid puritanical persuasion who's forthright views on wickedness, and most especially labouring on The Lord's Day, sent a tremble through the district. Even 'The Councillor', not a man to flaunt conventional beliefs, was driven to comment of James, "Isn't it lucky it's to the religion he went."

The following Sunday I looked down into a digger hole full of water. Pail after pail emptied the site for a tank. Cement by the shovel mix, sweat by the wipe, a welcome 'can', and block upon block, by six o'clock the tank was built. Only the plastering remained. Alec spent the afternoon passing the odd block, drawing deeply on 'fags' and watching the skyline for James.

I sneaked across the following Sunday. Water brimmed over the tank but mercifully the block work seemed sound. More swishing pails flew until I scraped the bottom. The site could not be described as ideal, water squirted between the blocks with a force that would have made the crew of the Hesperus feel safe. Alec seeing the problem retired to the house to make tea. Work fast. I plastered in a fury, head bent, six feet down in the bowels of his blessed tank.

Keeping a foot on the worst leak, I had the flood beaten. The plaster held. Great. Wheesht, what was that? Voices drifted down the hole. On tip toe I inched a look over the edge. Oh my Sunday hat, or less suitable words, horror of horrors, Alec, hands in pockets, leant on the gable engrossed in conversation with James. I sank back. Had my head shown? I waited. Detection? The voices droned on.

Plop, the first dollop of plaster fell into rising water. Plop, plop, hard won finish slurped off the wall, the water rose halfway up my wellies. No hint of relief, I could hear James's high pitched delivery. Icy water trickled down the wellies, my knees went under. The race was on. Long conversation, life jacket, or black exposure.

Alec's face appeared, still pale with fright, "All clear, he's got a cow for the insemination, but she'll have to wait, not the day for pandering to carnal pleasure, I'll give him a hand tomorrow," and he took a swig before passing down a bottle to help warm my feet.

So under the influence of an inoculation of 'moonshine' I plastered on. The septic tank rose to the caress of heartache moonbeams, a monument to undying affection. Under the blink of a new moon Alec made a wish. Would such abluent dedication find a flush of favour on the cheeks of his beloved? If not, romance was down the drain.

No such plebeian exertions detracted from the halcyon days which descended upon 'Teanassie House' once the fume belching bulldozer finished levelling the court-yard and skewed its way down the drive. Phyllis and Nicky Stackelberg with the help of the landscaping skill of my tractor loader, laboured in a garden of love. A plethora of patriotically named roses lined gravel walkways or sat in kaleidoscopic beds of scentless blooms. Alpine rockeries trailed flowers of exquisite minutia, instant hedges grew handsomely towards clipping, and a lightly clad nymph, standing decorously in the shade, balanced a sundial on her head without a thought of time. Most gorgeous of all courtesans of the garden, in sweeping curtsy before the bay window, the rustling tresses of a weeping willow waltzed to the breeze in a dreamland of Vienna nights, reminding the retired couple of tiara ballrooms and their gay youth in the glamourous 'Twenties.'

Never more fittingly could Goldsmith have penned, 'Sweet bower of indolence and ease', the happy pair rested from the travails of keeping up a castle, appearances, and the cost of capricious dairy cattle. The Baroness donning a frayed head square and tweed skirt could always be found, wicker basket on her arm, pruning the roses. The Baron pulling on a paint stained smock over his 'plus-fours' applied himself with equal attention to whitening the new window frames and Miss Bell's welcome trays of 'drinkie poos.'

So days dawdled by, contented hours with scarce a sigh, till yellow lilac, hard by the gate, each hanging candle bloomed, and crimson blush beside the path, each romaunt rosebush loomed. Hushed evening light, impressionistic haze, the rosebud garden and the painter were ablaze.

Up at Cluanie the gilts had wantonly sacrificed their maidenheads, some of them several times, just to be certain. Robert was resting. Not so the sows to be. In the ways of approaching sowhood their thoughts turned to bottom drawers and house building. The steading seemed unsuitable, they had already dug up the floor of the midden, the byre, and were excavating the fold. There appeared little need to enlist the destructive enthusiasm of architects and planners as they contemplated modifications to walls and doorways. I could see their efforts deserved concrete, if only to allow me some say in the design.

Electric fencing, an invention beyond even procine intellect, offered an impregnable means of containing the navvies whilst I constructed a maternity unit in the old stable. A large area of dense head high bracken covered the steep slope between the hairpin bends of Cluanie road. An ideal playpen for the gilts and their suitor I thought, knocking in foot high stakes to carry a perimeter wire charged with a waspish twelve volt sting at wet nose level. Gun turrets had crossed my mind.

'Um pah, um pah', the gilts disappeared into a green jungle of ffonds with the eagerness of grass skirted hula girls making for an initiation ceremony. In no time they were digging dens and building bracken huts, captivated and content. As weeks went by the scenery changed. Bracken, that scrunge of the Highlands, gave way to heaps of black ground and faces that lined up to be fed like a chorus of Kentucky minstrels.

Home building finished, their favourite kick now became bury the electric fence. Just inches from a sting, explosions of earth flew into the air and fell on the wire. Constant vigilance was required, Faraday's theory had been rumbled.

To stroll down Cluanie road always gave pleasure, a view across the river, the rooftops of the school, children scampering and shouting at playtime. Just a field away, in contrast the tranquillity of Teanassie House bloomed with colour in the glory of its newly laid garden.

No sight of the girls or Robert, I was always watchful, snoozing in their latest dugout perhaps? The day had turned warm and still. Rounding the second bend a view of Teanassie House filtered through drowsing birch leaves, how charming. I stopped short.

Down in the middle of the courtyard I could clearly see the Baron leaping up and down. Was he practising the Highland Fling? Arms were definitely flailing. A bit early in the day it struck me. Miss Bell stood beside the prancing figure waving a tea towel. Or was she fanning the dancer? After all, it was warm.

"Que,eek, E'een, you come queek," an anguished shout rather than the strains of Jimmy Shand floated up to me. An emergency. I cut the bends, galloped down, breathless.

Nostrils flaring, face contorted in Rasputin rage, the Baron held open the gate, "The pee'gs E'an, the pee'gs." I raced round the corner of the House. "Oh my Sainted Sows." The garden had suffered sustained attack, bomb holes littered rose beds, delicate bushes, roots in the air were stretcher cases, petals strewed the battlefield like propaganda leaflets.

The Baroness, 999 on the way, hung at the bay window sobbing in unrestrained grief. Miss Bell, no stranger to the 'blitz', though without time on this occasion to look out her siren suit, stood on the garden seat, bravely but unwisely, attempting to draw enemy firepower by flapping a tea towel.

"Struth," even the bashful sundial maiden, toppled on her back, could have been ravaged. I eyed Robert. His girls, shameless as debutantes at a Flower Power party, heads down, hips waggling, tails curling, tossed garlands of blooms behind their ears. Robert, the romantic gentleman, carried over a bunch of red roses. I didn't count, it could have been twelve.

I counter attacked. A trail of pig nuts drew the assailants back to Cluanie. The sun sets early in the hollow of Teanassie House. As I reset the sundial maiden that evening she registered an eclipse.

Succumbing to the pleasures of neighbour watching was easy from Cluanie and one of my favourite spies down the Braes was upon Alec. As a young man the 'call of the outback' had got to him and he left for 'down under.' A few years later though, recalled by his mother to run the croft, he still carried on his colonial connection, minus corks, by sporting a floppy bush hat.

Alec, the hat and his overfed collie caught on the end of my telescope, would saunter about the fields attending to the chores of the day in what appeared to be a distinctly lugubrious manner. Money spent, flushing loo, no bride, even the waddling Glen caught the mood and lay most of the day under what passed in Alec's mind for a Koolabah tree.

But the girl of his dreams did return from her Antipodean adventure. Alec and a comfy crofthouse were awaiting. All in order domestically, they plotted a secret marriage. No easy accomplishment in Dingwall Registry Office on a Saturday afternoon. Sure enough 'Jimmy the Van' raced up to Cluanie, "Guess what." "What?" "Alec's married." "Away, never." "Aye." "Where are they?" "Back at the croft." "Get the bottles, Sandy and the rest, ten o'clock, see you at the road end."

'Clink, clink', a well armed troupe, we crept to the croft door. No light, not even a sound. A soft tap, no move, a hard rap, no move, a concupiscent snigger. Hammer, hammer, long wait, last resort, an accordion blast, the Wedding March. Enough strained music, a strained Alec opened the door, six inches too far. No invitation, 'carry oot's, carry in's', we steamed past a feeble protest.

Roll out the glasses. A toast, the Bride. Roll up the rugs, the sleeves, roll out the band, a waltz. Warm up schottischa? The wall clock took the hint, a slant. Hit those tempo chimes. 'Yee'ow', Sandy's elastic legs. Mantleshelf a sweepin', rollin' an' a reelin', swingin' on the ceilin', bouncin' af the wa, ten foot square, ye could'na fa. Whoopin' an a loupin', trampin' an a stampin', 'free style' eightsome, sweatin' pile. Glen below the bed, hens off the lay, swing that girl, watch her birl. Hootin' an a 'tootin', mind y'r footin', levels fell an' spirits rose, slainte a' mhath, the plumbing goes.

Out of kindness, we propped Alec by the door, danced past him, round him, and by dawn, over him. Clandestine nuptials be damned, Alec vowed next day he would never marry again.

Glen didn't recover from the matrimonial celebrations and soon the old dog's mortal remains ended in a hole not too far from the septic tank, catalyst of his final woe. From the end of my telescope, man and hat seemed not to convey the same impression of haste without Glen's wheezing pant at his master's heel. A replacement dog which might speed, but not out pace, Alec's pensive ambles would be a neighbourly gesture. The question of a wedding present also pressed on my mind. I gave matters a little thought and eureka, a capital solution to both problems, a three legged dog.

It so happened I had just such an animal. This young dog, keen to work, sadly met with an accident under the tractor wheel, and its broken hind leg though pinned by the vet, gradually withered away. A kinder home no dog could hope for than the newly weds fireside, and one evening, having allowed an interval sufficient to deaden memories of the interrupted wedding night, I arrived on the doorstep with their present.

One lick, a couple of 'woofs' and 'Hop a Long' had a new home. To ensure a smooth transfer of ownership and perhaps round off any rough edges lingering from our previous visit, I took along a bottle of 'Oh be Joyful' for the grown ups and a few worm tablets for the dog. A reflective evening with mellow tinges measurably brightened as 'Oh be Joyfuls' rose to the incantation, 'Let us give Thanks', and Alec beamed with beatific affection upon his fireside, his friends, his fellow man and, I was glad to note, his new dog. A parting benediction, 'For what we have received we shall be sorry in the morning', and Hop a long and his Master stretched out, firm friends.

Out of concern for Alec's well being I looked in late the following afternoon. His wife quietly offered me tea. The Master slouched deep in a chair, the Hat over his eyes keeping away light, thought, and idle enquiry. "How are you feeling Alec?" a question which on closer inspection of the Calamity, I saw would have been wiser left unasked. The Hat stirred a fraction, the word, "Hellish," rumbled from below its brim. A marked silence, I glanced at his wife. True Catholic, she looked concerned. Alec spoke, "I wakened at four this morning," his faint voice a cross between groan and growl, "the head, ar-r-r-r," his hand flickered, " I came through and got three Aspirins," His head sank further into his chest. "Iain, in half an hour I really believed this was it, she gave me the crucifix to hold." He sighed with a rattle, "I could still be dying," and fell silent to allow this sombre thought sink in. I pictured the wake, it could be jollier than his wedding.

Hop a Long dragged his bottom across the carpet. The atmosphere was charged enough without reference to minor canine afflictions. I said nothing. The croak resurfaced, "Iain, through there," meaning the bedroom, "not sweating, just pouring. Oh boy, the heart. Racing a minute mile in ten seconds, an' sick." I visualised a groaning Alec lying clutching at his head, his chest, the 'chanty.' "She wanted to go for the priest." I now realised the gravity of the night's drama. It was not the time for facetious comment.

Hop a Long clearly had worms and the chair bound Calamity might yet live. I changed the subject. "Where's those worming tablets I gave you?" His wife opened the press, this shelf, that shelf, "Er," her hand flew to her mouth, "Help Alec, in the dark, you must have," sob, "by mistake," sob, "by mistake. Oh Alec, are you alright?" "What!" screamed the apprentice corpse leaping to its feet and throwing its hat on the chair.

From that day on Alec didn't look behind, his cheeks bloomed and the step in my telescope visibly quickened.

The maternity wing of Cluanie steading was in full swing. Following College advice, that founderous rock of many a farming enterprise, I concreted out the stable and built wooden farrowing crates to accommodate each of the gilts' confinements; a word which I found only be applied in one sense to the regime. As each gilt approached farrowing I moved them into the 'crate' to await their time. Bounded by side rails and a back bar, they stood or lay, head to wall in a restricted space designed to prevent them lying carelessly on the piggies they had laboured to produce.

Left to nature, a sow near her time will build a nest from whatever material is at hand, as Simon MacKenzie, my companion in numerous dubious escapades, was to discover. Missing a sow from his not entirely pig proof system, he raked the farm to eventually come on half an acre of his ripe barley crop chewed into small lengths and piled into a sizeable mound. Completely out of sight, at home in her straw house, the sow with an udder full of milk, lay on her side grunting gently to nine guzzling babies. Simon blew the house down, gathered the piggies in his jersey and the sow trotted alongside the squeaks back to her farrowing crate.

Not all sows are so quiet or accommodating. A crofter many years ago up on Kilmorack's Braes at Farley, ran gleefully to his wife one night, "Woman, woman the sow has eleven coolen, the croft will pay yet." A little later, unable to resist a peep at the treasure, he disturbed the sow. Back into the house crestfallen he lamented, " Ah Dhia, she ate the lot."

Cannibalism did not feature in the Cluanie system although the gilts chewed fractiously at the wooden barriers of their crates, and I could see it needed either tubular steel to curb their feelings or back to nature common sense to make them happy. However we persevered with the plan in which

Alison and Hector played an integral part. Before and after school it was the children's job to feed and water the mob. Slopping pails up from the well, scoops of nuts from the barn, they hurried about amongst the squeals of greed and the slobbering 'chops' of gluttony. Hector only six and under training at the dinner table, observed with a look at me, "Dad they always eat with their mouths open." Fortunately in those days most of the scholars had crofting backgrounds and the clothes clinging smell of pigs would not have been foreign to them.

Watching a farrowing fascinated the children. By Tilley lamp they followed me out to the stable. "Now no talking children." We stood quietly. I hung the hissing light on an old harness peg. Its friendly circle caught the cobwebs on sagging rafters, betrayed the dust of a century on dingy stone ledges but fell brightest on two intent young faces that watched out of huddled little duffle coats.

The gilt, flat on her side, seeming asleep, large and red behind would grunt deeply, press heavily and in a squish of slippery fluid squeeze out a miniature of mother. Sometimes they popped out in quick succession like shelling peas. Squirming and scrabbling together on the wet floor, a sharp little sneeze to clear the nose, and away round they snuffled, dragging their navel cord between mothers hind legs to nuzzle along the swollen udder until they found a stiff pink nipple dripping with milk. If all went well in a few hours a line up of perhaps eight or ten fat, full, pinky sausages would be asleep still hooked to a favourite nipple and giving it a little suck in their dreams. Mothering grunts came soft and content. With a final few pushes out flopped the afterbirth, a mystery bag of slimy skin, veins, bobbles and dark blood.

The gilts bred well and a proud Robert now had upwards of fifty sons and daughters but it was late of the year, frost and snow coated the yard and for the sake of warmth, instead of isolating the families I joined them all together in the fold. Would it work? Using wooden flakes I made a central pen, left gateways, gave it a straw bale roof, plenty of bedding and in they piled. Ten to a bed roll over, all grunts and grumbles wriggling into comfort against mother's milk bar.

Given ample straw, wood chewing stopped, one corner featured as the latrine and the remainder they kept clean for feeding and playing. A routine quickly developed. Milk shake time for the curly tails became synchronised. At some given signal all the mothers stopped rooting, flopped down to order and in one squealing stampede the spoilt kids rushed to find their appointed teat. Should any sneaky brat try to pinch another nipple a biting screaming fight broke out. The sow would jump up and shake them off until they behaved. Once settled with a round of drinks the sound of snuffly sucks filled the fold and their cold beady eyes could look quite happy.

When not sleeping in their straw hut the whole community concentrated on turning straw in a businesslike manner. Alison and Hector peeping through the door and finding the 'howkers' absorbed in their daily toil would stay hidden and make a strange squeak. In a split second every animal froze. Stock still statues, ears up, no breathing, no tails twitching, a full scale alert. Minutes passed, not a tremor. The children giggled. One shrill snort, pandemonium. Snort, snort, snort, ears flapping, tails twizzing, round and round the fold, into the straw shed, under the straw. Five seconds, not a pig in sight, the children loved it. Might have made the pig's day too but it was easy to see how the Ganderyne swine came to grief.

The children were excited. A new baby was expected any day. Already they had plans that suggested it might prove a more interesting plaything than the pigs. Towards midnight on a December night of bright moon and biting frost we told the wondering pair I was taking their Mother to Dingwall to have the baby. Betty gathered her bag and we left them in bed whispering into the dark.

Cluanie road shone, two moonlit ribbons of ice. Deep frost all day, the tractor grumbled over starting. Walk? Betty might slip, she was heavy, her pains were starting. Another turn of the key. Battery failing. A third and the engine slowly churned into life. Betty stood on the buckrake. A tortuous descent, I crawled down the steepest parts. Would we slide? I held the buckrake near the ground. Children left in bed. One slip, and ....

Slowly we wound down to where the van lay parked at the school. More pains. Hurry. Into Dingwall, the Ross Memorial Hospital. I left Betty in a safer situation. A few hours and the happy birth of our third child Elspeth.

It must have been two o'clock when I crept back upstairs. Hector had snuggled into Alison's bed and tired of waiting for 'news' they were fast asleep. For a last look round outside I lit a Hurricane lantern and made for the stable. The moon had set. A sparkling night held its breath. A silence that only the dead can hear, only the dead can touch, came close. A silence, filled with the breath of space.

I opened the stable door. Intruding light fluttered into shadows, over sturdy stall posts, a rotting head collar, untouched these years, the horses names, crude letters above once their stalls. Tom and Gentle, the last pair.

Light shivered down the side of the fold. A hook, I'd left it, above the place of Chisholm's death, an old black coat, holed, hanging, limp. It moved. A breath. Without a hand, the stable door swung.

The cycle of life had turned.

Birth, death, spirit.

HIS HOUR IS COME

'The Monarch of the Glen' painted by Sir Edwin Landseer in the 1870's was for many, and may still be for some, the quintessential spirit of Highland grandeur. Free, wild, and challenging, the lifting mists in a lofty corrie reveal the finest 'Royal' stag which might ever claim the honour of filling the sights of a 'sporting gentleman's' rifle. Such appealing work made Landseer a most fashionable Victorian artist superbly able to wring as much sentiment as can possibly be squeezed from a tube of paint. He tapped a vein of human emotion stretching from the Psalmist who lifts his eyes to the hills in the hope of salvation to the present carpet slippered age casting an envious eye over 'T.V.' documentaries. A nostalgia, verging on the reverential, lurks in the brief cases of many 'nouveux sapiens' strap hanging to a city office. The sublime longing for the far corrie and distant perspective still kindles the soul, and the wind sings of freedom in the hills of the heart's romance. Those at the raw edge of nature's freedom live amongst the hills of reality.

In his masterly painting 'Flood in the Highlands' Landseer captures the terror and calamity which befell so many during the several monumental inundations that swept the great straths of the North during the eighteen hundreds. In this expressive canvas a crofting family huddle on the thatched roof of their threatened home. Hope all but lost, the swirling deluge must surely undermine the rough foundations of the house. Bare footed and frightened, the children cling to their mother. Cat and kittens, hens and collie, the souls that make up a crofting homestead gather under the plaid of a Highland patriarch who, with stoic eye, beholds drowning livestock and the ruination of a subsistence livelihood. Artist's fancy, an extravagant canvas? Not so, a scene enacted last century by many miserable victims of nature's unpredictable extremes.

The coast of Moray is long noted for the equable nature of its climate and for the rich diversity of its wide rolling farmlands. Since the earliest days of man's agrarian heritage the area has been one of favoured settlement. It became the ordered domain of lordly Earl and humble cottar. The roots of an age old society reached deep into broad fertile acres which yielded their crops so willingly to generations of caring husbandrymen. This idyllic expression of human endeavour could be felt in the leisurely days of August 1829 when yellowing fields of grain bore heavy with the promise of a bounteous harvest, and herds of fattening cattle lay long and content in the droning summer heat.

From May through to the August of that year the Laigh of Moray shimmered. Day followed day of searing heat and drought. Trees or plants without deep root scorched and died. The land baked and cracked. Through July the Aurora Borealis danced on the northern horizon with uncommon brilliance and, though the weather varied little, the barometer showed remarkable fluctuations. The Holy wise bowed their heads at such portent and gravely waited. The carefree, in their wisdom, lived for the day. By the end of the first week of August, the prophets of Armageddon could at least justify the need for an Ark.

To the south of the favoured Laigh lie the Monadhliath. The Grey Mountains, whose height and extent, whilst sheltering the sweep of the Morayshire plains from the wet South Westerlies, give rise to lively sporting rivers, the Spey, Findhorn and the Nairn. Look north, the elements sweep unchecked from the Arctic. On the 3rd of August 1829, with barely a warning, the languor of honeysuckle day and sunset evening was shattered by a storm of unprecedented savagery.

Driven on the back of a howling northeaster, rain sluiced from the Heavens. Droplets merged to solid mass. Nothing could withstand its weight and fury. Windows were smashed, roofs torn off, blizzards swept the high tops. Small animals and birds perished in great numbers. Panicking livestock fled to byre and stable, nobody outside but was drenched in moments.

Four inches fell in the first twenty-four hours on the Cairngorm hills. A remorseless avalanche of water bore down the rivers. A tidal wave of destruction. The rain deluged for three days in Biblical dimension.

Tragedy followed, though strangely the storm's first victims were taken by the sea. By the middle day of the 3rd a violent rain filled gale beat across the Moray Firth. Below a louring sky, riven cloud and smoking crests were one. A schooner in sore distress staggered before the tempest towards Nairn's shelving beaches. Her last valiant attempt to claw off the fast shoaling waters ripped the mainsail to flying shreds. To launch a rescue boat would add death to death. A crowded beach could but watch. Powerless, aghast at the pitiless engulfing of fellow seamen, they knelt in beseeching prayer. The wind tore at coat and throat.

Opposite the mouth of the Nairn ran a strong tidal current which, combined with the outpouring of flood waters, caught the doomed vessel in a maelstrom of rearing waves. An eye witness wrote, 'notwithstanding the furious northern blast, she was hurried rapidly on like the floating carcass of some drowned creature devoid of voluntary action; and after being carried for a time as if towards Cromarty, she was seen to sink almost instantaneously, leaving only a few feet of one of her masts above the water as a frail and transient monument to mark the spot where the last despairing shriek of the crew had been stifled by the waves. A subdued exclamation of horror burst from the tender seafaring hearts who witnessed the spectacle.'

At the harbour by late evening the force and power of a surging flood was abundantly evident. 'I ventured out', reported the Pier master, 'and had the mortification to see my new pier mouldering away piecemeal, a square yard disappearing every few minutes, and whilst I watched a sizeable brig of eighty-three tons was torn from her moorings and washed into wreckage at the river mouth.' The demolition of Nairn harbour was to be completed when, a mere three weeks later, the elements struck again. On the 27th of August, an even more severe flooding befell a district already grimly facing the devastation of crop, farmland and homes. By then for many there was little left to ravage.

The Findhorn in common with other Scottish rivers boasts a historic jump of Olympic dimension. These daunting feats one suspects were preformed more out of desperation than daring and at Randolph's Leap perhaps the lad who gave the frightening gap its name discovered his athletic aptitude at the prod of a sword.

Here at 'The Leap', no great distance above Forres, the river coils through a gorge of sculptured rock and hanging cliff. Deep in this emerald ravine, heavy with leaning trees, the stealthy air is dank, the sinuous flow narrows to a few yards and plunges in a black muscled curve between wet treacherous rocks. Nature's constriction of the river virtually creates a dam.

Under the welter of unparalleled rainfall, on the morning of August 4th in the 1829 flood, the Findhorn rose fifty feet above its normal level. Witness to the immense havoc wrought by the surging current was Sir Thomas Dick

Lauder, local landowner and gifted man in the world of science and botany. During the height of the deluge he visited the Randolph Bridge at the foot of his estate and subsequently erected an inscribed stone to mark the river's peak.

Lauder was moved to write, 'Never did the unsubstantiality of all earthly things come so perfectly home to my conviction. The hand of God appeared to be at work, and I felt He had only to pronounce the dread fiat, and millions of such worlds as we inhabit would cease to exist.' Of this incomprehensible curve of fifty feet of spewing water, he penned, 'I found it in its greatest grandeur, flooding over the whole Haugh of Rannoch, and carrying large trees with their roots and branches triumphantly around it. The turmoil of the surges was so tremendous that the primitive rocks shook. No word-painting could convey an adequate idea of the violence and velocity of the water that shot away from the whirling sea above the cliffs. The force was more than that of a raging ocean.'

Before leaving the spot, the Baronet, not blindly overawed by 'its greatest grandeur', noted one of his under gardeners wade into the edge of the flood, and with the aid of an umbrella, deftly but unsportingly, drive ashore and grass a fine salmon. Sir Thomas frowned. Even such 'extremis' did not allow the taking of liberties by the lower orders. Next morning, in turn, the gardener was duly grassed on his Laird's carpet.

The Findhorn careered seawards, wild as the storm that spawned such living fury. Untamed by the backwater from Randolph's Leap, it filled the glen from side to side, tearing away crops, trees and homesteads. Running two hundred yards wide and seventeen feet high the torrent caught the Freeburn Bridge, a substantial three arch structure on the old south road, and lifting it bodily with ease, hurled the masonry into the river bed. Only the abutments remained, gaping and ragged. This was the first of numerous bridges to be dashed away, roads washed out, and embankments levelled from Nairn through to Banff.

The simple homestead of Easter Tighnafogrein, the house hid from the sun, stood a comfortable 12 feet and 80 yards from the bank of the Findhorn which had been rising swiftly since middle day on the 3rd. By evening the approaching roar of water terrified the family and they made haste to drive their cattle to the safety of higher ground.

Darkness came. Gaining waters swilled through the house. Waist deep, the current snatching at struggling legs, the two brothers carried out their ailing old mother, and wrapped in sodden blankets laid her beside a dyke on a overlooking hillside. Nothing saved but the clothes on their backs, wet and huddled, the glare of water lit the gloom of the night. A black satanic maw swallowed house, steading and sheds. At first light through grey lances of rain the only vestige remaining in sight was the gable of their byre. All the season's crop had gone.

Nor were the experiences of this family of Frasers yet finished. Further east at the farm of Knockandhu they were given refuge in a house which stood on a bank high above the Findhorn. Here at least they seemed secure enough to consider their recent loss. But the night of August 27th saw even greater ravaging of Morayshire. Down came the torrent a second time, and undercutting the high bank avalanched it without warning into the swirling river. Their short lived sanctuary teetered precariously on the brink of a newly carved red raw precipice, and poor Fraser lamented as they fled the floods again, "I believe Providence has doomed us to destruction." Indeed she ended their livelihood. When the croft reappeared, six acres of precious arable land had vanished and the remainder was ruined by a deep deposit of sand and gravel.

In Fraser's native parish of Edinkillie which followed the wide bends of the Findhorn ten miles south of Forres, twenty-six families were rendered destitute, in an age when help, rather than through the letter box, came largely from the neighbourly compassion of those equally poor.

The houses of the wealthy and influential invariably occupied eminent sites which were well clear of any danger. Local estates did however suffer heavy financial losses. The Cothall Mills on the haugh lands of the lower Findhorn were the property of Sir William Gordon-Cumming and comprised an extensive range of splendid three storey buildings which were used for flour, meal and barley milling. Lying a good eighty yards from a sound river bank they had never been considered a vulnerable site, but as the peregrinating Dick Lauder recorded, 'by three o' clock on the 4th the Findhorn flood covered the whole of the Forres haugh land. The water made its way into the barley mill loft and soon drove out the lower gable. Having opened a passage through the upper storey it poured in picturesque cascades over the north wall and fractured the end of it, until the whole building gradually gave way. Such was the strength of the current that much of the debris was deposited two miles further down river.' Moreover 'picturesque cascade' might not be the description springing most agreeably to the owner's mind.

Along successive stretches of the lower Findhorn embankments crumbled with little warning. Fresh outpourings spread great sheets of water across the easy conquest of wide flat countryside. Most of the poor, who inhabited little better than clay hovels, put ladder to wall and scrambled aloft to huddle out the night astride their thatch. Bellowing cattle plunging about in stalls were loosed with difficulty to swim where panic took them. Squawking poultry flew to the trees or sailed off on wobbling hen sheds.

Ungainly pigs struggled amongst tumbling walls, squealing until they drowned. Darkness eclipsed all. No lights, no hint of safety, only the ominous swish of water scouring through the rough hewn rafters of threatened homes. Through the blackness neighbour called to neighbour. Clutching at the reassurance of another voice, they sat out the night.

Shivering families peering through the rain laden dawn of August the 4th believed the tide had come inland. The reluctant light revealed houses as islands dotted in a sea of desolation. Some homes had lost their thatch. Wretched survivors perched on chimney head and quivering gable. Other hovels had rumbled away and the people clung in trees. No greeting curls of morning peat smoke. Destruction to crop and chattel lay beneath the flow. Manfully rowed boats pulled out through the current at first light.

At the shieling of Widow Speedman, an old bed ridden woman had been unstintingly cared for over many years by Isabella Morrison her elderly niece. The rescuer's boat bumped along the back wall of the tiny cottar house. Its front wall had gone but the thatch mercifully remained, resting on the head of a wooden braided bed. The men forced their boat under the roof. At the foot of the bed, up to the neck in water sat the niece, her arms supporting the dead body of her aunt. Scarcely sensible she stared fixedly at the livid and distorted countenance of the drowned old woman. "Bell's state of exhaustion was so great it was difficult for us to tell which was the living and which was the dead." Niece and corpse were lifted into the boat. Isabella had fought the waters for over seventeen hours. She lived on many years, the face in her mind.

Rescuing the marooned was a hazardous undertaking even for those accustomed to boat work. Three such experienced men set out early on the 4th amidst the fast spreading floods around the lower Findhorn, bent on relieving those in desperate plight. Strong the call of mercy in their hearts, a noble resolve quickly dampened as their small boat shot the rapids of a bursting embankment, swirled round like a leaf and flung them without ceremony into the water. Undeterred the spluttering rescue party waded neck deep to a second larger boat which, by virtue of his height above water level, the tallest of the trio had spotted trapped against the remains of a half demolished byre. From this stage their endeavours moved to a series of coincidences, the improbability of which would be happily seized upon by any author filling the pages of a 'Boys Own' novel.

Clambering aboard this floating donation from Providence, they were promptly underway, propelling the dinghy with lengths of floorboards in true Mohican style, and making obliquely across the current towards the occupants of a marooned farmhouse. From their rooftop perch the shivering family viewed this approaching means of rescue with some apprehension. A justified concern degenerated to horror. Some hidden obstacle, a violent lurch, a capsizing boat, and their would be saviours were jettisoned back into the element from which they had so recently emerged.

Providence is rarely partial but at the moment of their second immersion, timely help for the gurgling trio floated by in the shape of a large merrily twirling haycock. With scant debate as to its suitability as a form of water transport, they commandeered the craft, and clinging like bees to a swarm, were borne swiftly out of sight of the poor wretches left crouching on the comparative safety of their thatched roof.

Into the view of incredulous watchers on dry land sped three men on a haystack. Aware that this unorthodox mode of progress towards the firth could not long be considered seaworthy, great was the relief ashore, and not least afloat, when the craft lodged in the top branches of an alder tree. The crew were seen to disembark upon the upper boughs and allow the bobbing haystack to continue its uncharted voyage. There the trio hung for several hours endeavouring to support themselves amongst the weak and brittle branches.

Meanwhile ashore, a Dr. Banks and Sergeant Grant, having secured sufficient rope were preparing the equally dangerous task of swimming out to save the rescuers, when to the astonishment of the gathered crowd, as the swimmers were about to take to the water, one of the tree bound castaways was seen to be baling a boat with a straw hat. William Smith, no longer able to hang onto the branches, had in despair, let himself down into the water only to find his foot standing on the gunnel of a boat. The very boat which had lately created their predicament.

As became the disposition of that era, faith in an Almighty God and in his absolute control over individual and collective destiny, ensured, for the most part, the wretchedness and travail inflicted by loss, bereavement or dispossession was carried with little complaint. The will of God, as indicated by the Bible, and emphatically underlined by his ordained ministry, made for a largely compliant and supplicating people who suffered hardship and deprivation with stoic resignation.

The father of a family, Cumin to name, who spent a night in the water and lost everything, told the boatmen who came to their rescue, "I prayed long and strong and more fervently than I ever did in my life before; for it was an awful' thing to be expecting every minute to be swept into eternity in such an unprepared state, and our ears driven deaf with the roaring of the waters, and the crashing of the great trees that went booming past every minute and nothing to be seen but the glimmer of a few candles but their light was some little comfort. It seemed as if the Lord had not altogether forsaken us." His wife, less of an importuner than her man and with a pragmatism that matched her Doric, lamented to the rescuers over the loss of a tubful of clothes, "It jist sailed oot at the door an wis whalmed afore ma very een."

Something over twenty square miles of the Forres plains alone were inundated and damage to property was estimated at £20,000. One hundred and eighty-eight families were rendered destitute. Misery and death has no price.

The glinting Spey, loops, flats and rapids, takes ninety-six miles to join the tideway from its headwaters on the rolling sub-arctic plateau of the Cairngorm hills. Unsurpassable country, 1,300 square miles rising to over 4,000ft drain into this fine, fast flowing salmon river. At once a landowner's pride, a poacher's delight and the penniless fisherman's fantasy. But such scale of hill and strath has a severity of climate respected by the experienced and a life claimer of the careless. The noted flood years of 1768 and 1799 wrought havoc along the Spey from source to sea, but of the 1829 inundation not even the oldest hill men could recall a storm so swift and vicious. Strathspey suffered.

On August 3rd the fury of an arctic blizzard swept the wide shelterless tops. Horizontal snow driven on a screaming gale killed fledgling and fawn alike. Grey cascading curtains of rain draped the lower slopes, whitening every trickle to a frothing torrent, rolling boulders like pebbles, gouging burn beds to boiling cauldrons.

The crofters and cottars of Glenfeshie, a faraway strath tucked high in the hill country of the Cairngorm, watched the warring elements from below dripping thatch. Without warning, in the last glimmer of daylight, feet of water bore down on them from the heights. Foaming and tumbling in a wave through dyke and croft, it burst open doors and brimmed to the windows.

The men caught up the infirm, the women folk their children and terrified families ran for their lives. From the teeming slopes of higher ground in numbing rain they turned to watch houses torn down, hard won hay washed away, the despoiling of the few possessions that made life possible at the edge of human endurance. Within hours, close by at the old bridge of Inverfeshie, the torrent rising twenty-five feet had formed a loch five miles long and a mile in breadth. The surface rose in spiralling sheets with each gust of the gale. Without food, huddled in unceasing rain the families made shelter for the night below the flexing limbs of wrestling Caledonian pines.

Through the starless dark of a rain cursed night the surging waters spread their hill born tide of destruction over hearth and chimney piece, meal kist and larder, over the curtained box beds of moss chinked 'but and ben.' Having little choice, over the years the poor had perforce built where it least interfered with the economic or aesthetic ordains of the sporting estate. To survive the vicissitudes of wind and weather, each hard won dwelling might depend more on the fickle mercy of the elements than upon the clemency of many landowners of that era.

On an isolated green hillock amidst the alluvial Strathspey flats to the east of Boat of Garten stood a hamlet of the poorest sod houses, home to vagrant families whose menfolk were away harvesting. After the flood the enquires of Dick Lauder took him into this area. Eyeing the flotsam level as he looked down to the people rebuilding their huts it seemed incredible to him that any could have survived. At the door of a widow Cameron he got the reason in the forthright dialect of the times.

"You see the Spey wis jist in wan sea a' the way frae Tullochgorm yonder, on the ither side o' the strath, to they muiry hillocks oot by there, ayont the King's road in front o' us; Aye we kent fa' we where, the water wis a' in aboot us, an' destroyed a' oor meal an' floated off wer' peat stacks. I wis fe'ert oot o' my judgement for ma bairns, an' sal I but to oot o' this wi' them."

"And how did you escape?" queried Sir Thomas, following the account with no small difficulty. "Oh troth, jist upon a brander," replied the widow smiling up at him "A brander!" the Baronet exclaimed, in ignorance the old Scots word could be applied to other than a gridiron for the fire, and thinking it a feat bordering on the improbability of reaching the moon by broomstick, he pressed the point, "What do you mean by a brander?" "Och jist a bit float," explained the widow, "a bit raft I made o' bits o' pailins an' bitties o' moss-fir that were lyin' aboot." "What! and, and your children too?" "What else?" she laughed, amused by her interrogator's surprise, "what could I hae done wi them else? Nae horse could hae come near us, it was deep enough ta' droon twa horses."

"And how did you feather your good self over?" was the next query. "Troth Sir, I hae na feathers," came the reproving response, "I'm nae a duck tae soom. But ye see, I sat on my hunkers in the middle o' the brander, wi' ma bairns gert a' aboot me in a k'not, an the wund, that wis blawin strong enough frae the north, jist gart us safe ore' tae the land," "My word, how intrepid Mrs. Cameron, what about your neighbours?" "Fit'way would they get oot bit a'thegither upon branders," was Mrs. Cameron's triumphant reply.

The verification of this vast stretch of water, upon which had sailed the fleet of 'branders', came from a Captain 'Home from the Sea' MacDonald who farmed two hundred acres at Coulnakyle in the Abernethy district. Perhaps thrilled by an extent of water which might tug the heart strings of any land sick matelot the Captain boasted impressively, "I am satisfied that I could have sailed a fifty gun ship from Boat of Belliforth to the Boat of Garten without leaving the bridge."

On descending the bridge he must have been less impressed to find his shore base reduced to a mere fifty acres of land worth cultivating.

The 'floaters' of the Spey were men strong and able in the tough business of guiding rafts of cut logs down the length of the river from the great forest of Caledonian pine which flanked its upper reaches to the sawmills and shipyards of Garmouth at it's mouth.

Charles Cruickshank, the Aberlour innkeeper, as an experienced 'floater' well knew the moods of his river. Perhaps the nature of this hardy man relished a challenge, for as the flood rose he spotted a quantity of useful timber become lodged near the mouth of a swirling tributary. Two neighbours helped him. In minutes they had a light raft lashed together. "What about a hand on the river boys?" "Nae use getting oor' feet wet an' pullin' logs in tae dry them oot" The floater, laughing at their fears, pushed his craft onto the dark silky water, and lacking neither in skill nor strength, secured a good haul of logs.

Emboldened by this success, he set out again to secure some haycocks belonging to the minister which one by one bobbed away from the stackyard at the Glebe. Whilst the 'floater' lassoed 'holy' haycocks, racing coils of foam ridden water surged to a fresh height startling even the dauntless Cruickshank. "A horse, a horse," he called loudly across to his anxious neighbours. "Run for one of the Minister's horses and ride in with a rope or I must go with the stream."

Danger added wings, they dashed for a horse and galloped back. Cruickshank held off the swelling force of water that tore at the raft with his iron shod rafting pole. The horse refused the water, shying, rearing. The men cursed. Cruickshank fought, his full strength, the pole but a bent reed to stem such flow. A fresh surge of flood. Suddenly the struggling man lost his grip. One twist, the raft shot like an arrow, carrying the man of the river towards curling whirlpools. His loosely tied raft must break, the 'floater' coolly waited for his craft to pass close to a substantial tree. Poised, balanced, gathering his strength, unhurried he sprang. A one chance, one leap and he was amongst its solid branches. The raft cavorted into Stygian chaos and disappeared.

Frantic efforts were now made to rescue the brave man. A boat hurried to the visibly widening gap was foiled by the sheer rapidity of the current. Evening darkened, the 'floater' watched. Still no rope reached the clinging man.

"His hour is come, our struggles are in vain." Would be rescuers spoke in sepulchral whispers. The spirits of preordination writhed within the spiralling vapours of the river. The dismal evening light faded. A night of black sinister water, hissing and snaking at the feet of the silent crowd, hungered for a drowning.

Poor Cruickshank's hour had come. He wound his watch to indicate the time the watery grave would take him. Between lulls in the storm, his piteous shouts for help were borne across to his waiting friends. His distraught wife called back.

Gradually, in the depth of the night, his cries became fainter. At last only a few shrill whistles were heard. Silence, save the river. They continued to listen till all but his sobbing wife knew they could not hope to see their friend again.

In the slow light of morning it was seen that the tree had gone. Next afternoon as the flood began to wane, the body of the 'floater' was found, stark and muddy, on the haugh of Dandaleith.

The Bridge of Spey at Fochabers crossed the river in four splendid arches which gave it a span of over a hundred yards. By eight o' clock on the Wednesday morning of the great 1829 flood, the powerful bastions of masonry which carried its graceful lines were under pressure. Flooding 17ft. over normal, the river, as it shot through the pillars, cleaved into curving vortices that rivalled the bow wave of an ocean liner under power. A large fascinated crowd, confident of their safety, idled on the bridge counting the bloated carcasses, cows, sheep and horses, that swooped beneath their feet on the crests of the impeded torrent.

Amongst the onlookers at the threatened bridge were the Duke of Gordon and Lord Saltoun. Concern rather than curiosity quickly took Their Eminences up river to observe a pile driving operation which it was hoped might protect the beleaguered bridge. In the nature of many people, overawed by presence of nobility, the bulk of the crowd, regarding the two 'Gentlemen' more worthy of interest than the succession of dead cattle that squeezed below the arches, followed the pair at a respectful distance.

Only eight remained on the bridge when a crack no wider than the split of an axe zig-zagged across the roadway barely three yards from their feet. "Good God the bridge is going, run for your lives," In seconds the yawning crack almost trapped them, yelling in alarm they leapt across to safety. The two massive arches crashed with a drum rolling roar and fountains of spray into the boiling river. John Anderson, a lame young man, lacking agility went down in the flight, crushed amongst the tumbling masonry.

His companion, horror struck at Anderson's plight, lingered almost a fraction too late. He was thrown against the parapet as the falling roadway opened below his feet, but clutched at the gravel on a remaining portion and scrambled up to safety in the moments it held. "When I made the jump," he told the sombre crowd, "John made a grab at my coat tail, missed it and fell on his back, the parapet wall tumbled about him." With a scream the poor boy had disappeared amongst the shattering debris to a violent death.

His body was found that evening about a quarter of a mile downstream where his greatcoat had entangled in some brushwood. He lay on his back, his arms covering his face in a last attempt to protect himself.

Throughout the lower reaches of the Spey the wreckage of property ran into tens of thousands of pounds. Lord Seafield sustained damage estimated at £30,000 and the Duke of Gordon to the extent of £17,000. What tenant farmers, crofters and the poor lost is impossible to calculate, but few would have means to offset the calamity.

A fund was at once set up for the temporary relief of those rendered destitute and the £1,470 quickly donated was distributed amongst 671 cases which represented over 3,000 individuals. The Central Committee for managing the Flood Fund met in Elgin and decided 'the great exertions of many who at risk to personal safety took out salmon cobbles and dinghies in the spontaneous and selfless operations that saved so many lives should be rewarded.'

The Convener of the Committee, a Mr.J. Forsyth droned on, "although my members are deeply impressed with the merits of these brave men and the propriety of some reward, we should not deviate from the principle laid down in this matter and instead of money, soon dissipated and forgotten, an honourary reward, in the form of an engraved silver medal, should be given so that in honest pride on festive or solemn occasion it could be displayed by himself or his descendants as proof of his merits."

Mr. Forsyth finished with a flourish, "not one person of these truly deserving men has ever made even the most distant application to the Committee for reward."

In due course a London artist was commissioned at a cost of £60 and a suitable silver medal depicting the Bridge of Spey after its destruction was struck and sanctimoniously presented. Any tendency towards 'dissipation' on the part of 'these brave men' was thus admirably circumvented.

KEEP AN EYE ON THE BOY

Inverness has always been the hub of Highland interests for obvious topographical reasons. Sheltered harbour, spacious level pastures, a meeting point of communications 'frae a' the airts' and a handy place for keeping your feet dry when crossing the rippling river Ness.

The first bridge of any consequence to cross the Ness was said of its day to be the finest in the Kingdom. So also thought Donald of the Isles in 1410, who by way of keeping his hand in at a popular pastime of the age, had the pleasure of burning it down. The last oak bridge crossing the Ness fell ignominiously on the 28th of September 1664. A crash which created as much story and myth as it did inconvenience.

'A good story is worth telling well', alludes to that charming Celtic predilection for embellishing the facts. One version of the bridge's fall tells of a concourse of two hundred people traipsing across its tottering timbers in the equivalent of a London Bridge rush hour. Another, at considerable variance, details an old wife toiling over the shaky structure late one winter's night, bent double under a bundle of heather. A blast, snow laden of course, swept down the Great Glen and hurled the poor soul to her drowning in the swollen river. The bridge being without side railings was forthwith condemned and orders for its repair were issued. The probability is that the bridge fell whilst this work was being undertaken and a few idle bystanders, of which the Highland capital never lacked, plummeted into an unaccustomed bath.

Whatever may have been the truth, the notables of the town, MacLeod of MacLeod, the Hon. Lord Lovat and Forbes of Culloden, were anxious to see 'effectual steps be taken for putting the said bridge in good condition.' Timber suitable for the repair was not to be had in the Highlands and the Inverness Town Council of 1664 ordained that, '80 trees be bocht from Skipper Geddies to be broucht from Norway.' and further, a committee be appointed to deal with the wily skipper to check, 'anent ye length, breadth, thickness and price and sufficiency of the timber.'

This Council deliberation is an indication of the paucity of timber to be found in the Highlands at that time. Over a space of seventy years the extensive stands of native oak and pine which clothed the hillsides of Loch Ness and most other glens of the north had been cashed by the Estates to produce charcoal for the 'bloomeries' of a crude iron smelting industry organised by English entrepreneurs.

Nor was there much prospect of natural regeneration reclothing the naked hillsides. Hardly had the ring of axe on oak died away when the bleat of mutton on the move heralded the next Highland enterprise. Sheep meat from the north found a ready market to feed Highlanders, who freshly cleared from the hill, found themselves at the foundry gate or falling in the front line at 'Waterloo.' In due time the wealth produced for the industrial 'nouveau riche' found need of distraction and so the Victorian 'toff' apeing the romantic dalliances of the Royal 'We' built shooting lodges amidst empty grandeur. The term 'Forest' acquired a new meaning. Red deer ensured the hills remained bare. Families out, factories in, playground for privilege, a neat circle of human and environmental exploration.

By 1688 wood was out and for the sum of £1,300, a graceful stone bridge of seven arches straddled the swift running Ness. 'The handsomest old bridge in Great Britain.' opined the eminent Telford choosing not to draw attention to the bridge's less elegant feature, a cage of some twelve square feet incorporated in the third arch, which complete with pop hole sanitation served the purpose of a 'river loo' lock-up.

A notorious cattle reiver in 1719 found incarceration in the iron grilled apartment so oppressive he hanged himself with a birch branch. Not that this incident deterred the cell's usage. Its last occupant, Allan Cameron, a Lochaber robber, had his stay prolonged on account of the old jail being pulled down and the slow process of building a new one. The town urchins soon found ready entertainment lowering a string into the cage suitably baited with scraps of bread. Cameron 'bobbed' for these tit-bits like a hungry trout.

This novel utility of the bridge certainly did not detract from its pleasing lines in the eyes of William Turner. 'Daddy' of landscape painters he depicted the crossing in a fine watercolour not long before the bridge was washed away by the spectacular 'Inverness Flood' of 1849.

The telling feature of this deluge was the speed with which it developed. Loch Ness, at twenty-four miles long is by far the largest sheet of water in Britain and when it rose on that occasion by fourteen feet in as many hours the volume of water pouring down the short swift river onto the town must have been immense. The natural buffer to rapid 'runoff' during heavy rain provided by wooded hillsides on the catchment area had played its part in the industrial revolution. Sudden bridge 'zapping' floods became a consequence. Fortunately the 'loo' was vacant at the time.

A little over a hundred years ago the straths and glens of the Highlands experienced one of the most notable winters in recorded times. The January of 1892 was exceptional for the ferocity of its snow storms. The depth and drifting that occurred defied even the stories of the "Ah well, I remember over sixty years ago." The floods that followed as a consequence can only be compared to the monumental devastation of Morayshire in 1829.

During the first days of that January the weather swung intermittently between frost and snow but by the 7th the elements had made up their mind. Around the Beauly and Cromarty firths three feet of fluffy snow shrouded the flats. On higher ground, blizzard followed blizzard. Immense drifts, ten to twenty feet, floundered over road and rooftop moulding and smoothing the land. The wind dropped, nothing stirred, no gentle flop of snow from hunched branches, no fox in single track with skiffing tail, only deep, deep snow, smothering the world in a hollow silence.

Meantime stormbound in Stornoway, and loitering for three days on the pier were two hundred and fifty restive Lewis militiamen eastbound to their Regimental H.Q. at Fort George. Part One Orders accounted for the exodus. 'You will report for your Annual Training Exercise, etc.' Most crofter wives at their daily chores of milking the cow, cleaning the byre and emptying nappies noted a calculated reluctance towards the embarkation. No sounder reason had the women folk but to suspect yet another 'annual spree' was afoot. A manoeuvre in which many wives considered their menfolk had little need of exercise and certainly none of training.

Saturday and a lull in the gales put 'the boys' across the Minch to board a Highland Railway 'Special' which puffed out of Strome late that evening bound for Inverness. Compartments were full, men and kit, flickering carriage lights winked on a glow of emancipation within, and glared on window high snow drifts without. Once clear of possible 'informers' the soldier's spirits lifted into Gaelic song and story, some sadly, of a less than edifying nature, whilst the difficulty of performing a sword dance in the swaying confines of a third class compartment had to be seen to be appreciated. Nevertheless the mobile ceilidh, oblivious of snowflake or gale, chugged merrily towards Dingwall unaware that the engine driver could barely see the length of the funnel.

Suddenly a series of juddering snatches produced a melee of lurching soldiers and a rain of kitbags. Singing faltered half verse. Fearing attack, 'Old Sweats' shot under seats, the agile onto racks, the rotund, clutching themselves, merely went weak at the knees. The train plunged boiler deep into a gigantic drift and came smartly to a hissing, snow melting halt. Unbroken in cover from the slopes of the massive Ben Wyvis the snow field obliterated the line and enveloped the tiny Ross-shire village of Garve.

Only by stern courage and a dash of bravery was Inverness alerted that night to the serious implications for a gathering of Lewismen entombed in a stormbound train. Rumours buzzed from frost bite and breathing by snow hole, to a rapid depletion of refreshments. The latter point being taken as the likely situation, and naturally, by far the most serious.

Early on the Sunday morning, shovels at the slope, a band of muffled workmen left Dingwall. A determined relief mission. Drawn by two powerful locomotives, when still several miles short of the train load of shivering soldiers, the 'Relief Special', smoke blasting grime onto virgin white, roared into the opposite end the same impassable drift. Noble minded workers leapt out and set to with great spirit, hardy souls to a man, digging out their own train.

In the black and white conditions of a moonless Monday night shovel weary workmen finally made contact with the soldiers. Faint voices, a last frantic digging, then hugging and stamping. A meeting it was said, to rank with the moving reunions of lost explorers in the wastelands of Antarctica.

By now another relief train, laden with suitable supplies rocketed up the track on its mercy errand. Simultaneously a hand picked party of trustworthy militiamen trudged down the snow walled corridor to meet it. Sherpa style, single file, the column of soldiers, laden with victuals, wound back to their stranded comrades. Soon all pangs of hunger and even thirst were dispelled. Always a sign of spiritual uplift, singing resumed. Refreshed troops filed down the narrow cutting to the supply train which shunted them into Dingwall late that night.

Some men from the remoter parts of Lewis had been ten days on the journey and all had been six. Such were the feats that made our Empire great, although, it must be admitted, several militiamen suffering from the emotional upset of a safe deliverance had to be carried to the nearest hotel.

———————

Travelling conditions throughout the north during that storm proved chaotic. Five trains were snowed up on the Strathspey section of the Highland Line. In Sutherland, passengers spent the night in their carriages before escaping to the relative safety of Fosinard Hotel which itself was cut off.

Snow fell on snow without thaw. In Kingussie a choking blizzard left twenty inches in twelve hours. None ventured out. Such communications as could be maintained, even from farmhouse to steading, were only achieved by cutting passages and walking through icy galleries. The scene was set. Those who remembered 1849 flood dreaded what was to come, and come it did.

A spectacular rise in temperature accompanied a steady downpour. The crystal world of crunching frost dissolved. Drip by drip, the trickles grew, jostling, hurrying, each cutting a tiny valley in the yielding drifts. From high corrie and broad strath came the muted rumble of a gathering power. The snow fields were dying. On Thursday the 28th. of January 1892, a momentous thaw set in over the whole of the Highlands.

'Traveller, stop and read with gratitude the names of the Parliamentary Commission appointed in the year 1802 to direct the making of upwards of five hundred miles of roads through the Highlands of Scotland and of the numerous bridges, particularly those at Beauly, Bonar, Fleet and Helmsdale.'

An arbitrary command, doubtless justifiable, issued on behalf of a respectable list of the good and great of the North whose names, handsomely inscribed on a marble plaque, were a feature of the east abutment of Bonar Bridge, an imposing structure built to the innovative design of Thomas Telford. At a total cost of £13,971, this bold piece of engineering with a centre span of 150ft., incorporated many features calculated to improve its strength and stability. Paper theories put to the test by the afternoon of Friday the 29th of January, 1892.

Perhaps no other estuary in Scotland, excepting the Tay, discharges a greater volume of water than that of the Kyle of Sutherland at Bonar. A number of rivers, the Carron, Oykel, and Shin to name but three, carry the runoff from much of Sutherland to join the firth amidst a lattice of muddy tidal creeks and green sea washed flats.

Villagers of Bonar pulling up trousers and blinds on the morning of the 29th blinked at a monumental rearrangement of the scenery. For the faithful, digesting a devotional reading, Mount Ararat appeared on the skyline. Non believers blowing on scalding porridge rather considered their upturned rowing boats, stored for the winter, now perilously close to swishing waters which extended inland for many miles. Strathkyle and Strathoykel had joined in one vast lake. Strathcarron was under water. Debris of every description from wooden bridges to fishing boats swirled out to sea through clawing tree tops. Much flotsam and jetsam passed narrowly, very narrowly below the girders of Mr. Telford's much esteemed engineering wonder.

Such is the faith placed by common man upon the infallibility of those in society who combine inventiveness with arrogance, the locals continued to use the bridge in spite of unhealthy cracks appearing in its masonry.

During the afternoon Mr.MacPherson's grocery van clip-clopped confidently across. Trade must never be neglected. Several umbrella shielded pedestrians also sauntered over, savouring the thrill of 'wild nature' tamed by a bridge. A thrill sharply dissolving to cathartic alarm by a sudden waltzing tempo in its central girders. Strolling pace smartly quickened to respectable sprint, if not a panic-stricken dash. Bent in lung heaving breaths on the far side, the strollers watched, with some disquiet, the mighty iron trellis being toppled into the raging waters with the ease of a downpour destroying the tracery of a spider's night spun labour. Moments later the remainder of the bridge vanished into the triumphant river. Only the declamatory plaque remained.

The loss of so many substantial bridges is not surprising given the unprecedented heights to which many rivers rose. On the Ross-shire river Carron in 1892 a new steel suspension bridge, 50ft in a single girder and 32ft above average river levels, was under construction. It became an early victim. Swamped with ease the twisted framework rumbled half a mile down stream.

Another new span to cross the river Calvie was almost complete. It also joined the tangle of debris being hurled down the 12 miles to the ill-fated Bonar Bridge. No knocking off early in the 'good old days', five'o'clock and pitch dark on the evening of the 28th the workmen packed their tools. The Calvie lay frozen solid far below their scaffolding. A large herd of hinds happily crossed the ice that afternoon. Next morning the workmen returned at six on a howler of a day. Two hours before daylight, their swinging lanterns shone onto racing brown water. It brimmed through the gorge 30ft above the level of yesterday's ice bridge which the deer had found so convenient. Not a vestige of their work remained.

———————

The cloud spilling peaks of three of the grandest glens in the Highlands, Affric, Cannich, and Strathfarrar, stand against the Atlantic storms. Eastwards from watersheds lashed and cut flow anxious rivers whose pace slows only in loitering pools where salmon lie below the hazel shaded banks of Strathglass. Down centuries of settlement and cultivation ambles the river, sickle fields in the loops of its flow, shingled islands rippling its path. Alder, ash, and oak grow dark leaved with fertility, red sandy banks make ramparts where white bibbed Martins burrow, sedgy margins grow thick where glossy headed duck tend their brood, and always, from far away, look down the plover calling ridges of great hills, soft in reflection, blue in the depths of distant minds.

Only below the confluence of the Glass and the Farrar does the river become the Beauly, winding in state through an avenue of oaks. Log rafts of Caledonian pine once floated down from the glens and were hauled up the bank to a large sawmill at the mouth of the dangerous waters of the Kilmorack gorge. Into the cliff bounded gloom of this canyon slides the river. Dark, sinuous, effortless beauty, it flows below a vitrified Dun high on a crag where the peregrine nested. Down, down, to where once in days past, the thick black water tumbled from its ravine in the crowning glory of cascading falls.

My father knew the river from his boyhood and took me one day as a child to see these Kilmorack falls in their spate. I trotted the long walk from Lovat Bridge, glad we called on his friends at the mill croft. Nothing a trouble, in the old way, we enjoyed tea and scones.

"Keep an eye on the boy," the miller had warned my father and as a precaution he tied me on the end of a rope. We crossed the Beauly by a wooden bridge straddling the dimpled water on stilts of dark pine. By a path, slippery with dead leaves, we entered a cavern, hollow and booming, vibrating air dank with a misty incense. Below us the river raced and spiralled through boiling cauldrons. From above, through a cathedral window of closing branch and leaf, the sunshine day fell in long light upon a tracery of rock and sparkling water. Golden curves of sunlit power plunged into churning swirls. A dancing joy of flicking spray that romped away, leaping gaily over rock and stone, down to the waters of a favourite salmon stretch below the turrets of Beaufort Castle, the Silver Pool.

We sat awhile. I was four years old. I watched. A flash, a dark backed body leapt, glistening, flexing, quivering. It fell, a gleaming silver twist amidst the spume. Love, longing, life force, the powerhouse of nature. I wondered.

Three men down at a dangerous spot beside the fish ladder watched salmon wriggling their lithe bodies up the slimy rocks. My father signalled them for the time. It was early evening. We made back over the Black Bridge, but for some reason he was reluctant to leave and down to the river's edge we went. The sand, grains of silver in the shallows, ran through my fingers and lost its glisten. He laughed at my disappointment, his distant eyes watching the river, and turning aside, showed me the fresh tracks of an otter.

It was a tired walk back down the endless oak lined straight to the Lovat Bridge. My father told how as boys, he and his brothers would carry their trunk of belongings each dusty summer along this shaded road, away from captive school days, towards their Aunt's tiny croft and an endless playground of woods, hills, and homespun adventure.

Concern over the unprecedented depth of snow carried by the hills in the January of 1892 turned to relief for the natives of Strathglass when on the 28th, due to a mild south westerly breeze, a gentle thaw set in. Signs augured well. Happily reassured, families in croft house and village bedded cosily, blew out candles and settled down to another of the long winter nights before the coming of light at a switch.

Morning had yet to supply daylight. Risers wakened by unfamiliar gurgles, yawned and put a warm foot over the edge of the bed. Eeeeee, ankle deep icy water flowed in one door, out another. Nightshirts shot over heads, clothes grabbed from chair backs, chamber pots floated, cats scurried. Shouts of "Head for the high ground." No bidding was needed. Mothers, an arm round baby, a chain of children at heel, old and infirm on the backs of able bodied, families made onto hillsides, slipping and stumbling through a slush of vanishing snow.

Promptly at five o'clock in spite of the atrocious morning the Royal Mail gig, pair in hand, wheeled out of Tomich, a small village at the head of Strathglass. Travelling beside the driver, huddled under a canvas, were two young girls and a gamekeeper. Wavering light from the gig's oil lamps burst in yellow spray from trotting hooves and reflected a rippling flood over the road. No more than the driver expected, he pressed on. The horses bravely breasted waters soon swirling belly deep. Suddenly with a lunge the animals attempted to swim. The gig was afloat. Leaping chest deep into the current, the men pushed the gig against the bank, grabbed the frightened girls, carried them to shallow water and waded back to unloose the plunging horses. Freezing water, fumbling straps, knifeing leather traces, the men fought the horses free.

Hastily securing the gig to a tree the driver led soaked girls and shaking animals up to Fasnakyle Manse. The Rev. MacKenzie, warm and solicitous, gave them every assistance in his power, which included a stout rope. Returning to the flood as light grew, the 'Postie' saw the gig had been washed some distance away and straddled the top wires of a seven foot deer fence. Taking the strong line round his waist and balancing along the fence wires, the driver tied gig wheel to fence. Risking his life without the safety of the Minister's rope, he fought his way back against whirlpools of flood. Strung on a deer fence the Post gig remained, complete with its soggy consignment of mails, for some days.

A symbol of bravery and dedication styled in the true spirit of the Pony Express, the making of the West. 'The Mails must get through.' No arrows pierced the Postie's chest but double pneumonia must have come close.

The press of water bore down Strathglass with the force and speed of a spring tide. Embankments held the torrent until its height and weight cut a breach. The flood then uncurled across the flats faster than a man could walk, a carpet of water, rolling feet deep, froth and flotsam at its edges. Pits of turnip and tattie, their contents stirred into a curdled soup of hay, corn sheaves, trees and carcasses, were liberally distributed, jostling and sloshing, the length of the strath on a tidal wave.

Soon bridges vanished. Some such as the Kerrow trapeze of bent nail and rotting plank, an assault course even on a good day, were of little loss, but the heavy stone structure of Cannich bridge, crossing below a gorge which hid a spread of loch and mountain, was a vital link in the glen. Early that afternoon pressure built below the keystones. Proud villagers praised its strength but alas, one word too many. The structure erupted in a volcanic spray of stone and lime, scattering confidence and masonry alike without further trace.

As always the narrows below Eilean Aigas at the entrance to the Kilmorack gorge proved a bottleneck. The river damned back over four miles to the village of Struy and reached almost a mile in width. Only tree tops showed, filtering all manner of debris through a fish net of winter branches. In due time curious locals gauged the depth of the flood from the straggling sheep carcasses which hung for months amongst the upper limbs, wafting the stench of decay over a sodden strath.

At the foot of Kilmorack gorge the vision was awesome. A surge of solid water forty feet thick and a hundred yards wide spewed out, submerging the flat glacial clays of some of the finest lands in the North. The miller, below the gorge at Ballnacrask, awakened by the sudden thundering roar, ran down to his mill. The building shook. He sat to lace his boots, before they were tied water swept over his feet. It climbed the walls at a frightening rate. An ocean filling a loft, it passed the clearly marked 1849 record in minutes. The miller, pallid beyond his normal shade, feared for the wheel, the foundations, his life. At seven and a half feet into the loft the water paused, three and a half feet above the old mark, and the frightened man contended as much water passed in fifteen hours as should be spread over fifteen days.

The seething force quickly cut off the Lovat Bridge, yet another of Telford's sturdy designs. It gamely withstood the besieging flow only to succumb a fortnight later, much to the surprise of a Kiltarlity crofter Andrew MacIntosh. He cheerfully crossed it with horse and cart moments before the collapse and presumably turned to view the marvel of his achievement or bless the miracle of his escape.

The 1892 devastation had nothing to offer the villagers of Beauly other than mopping up. In 1849 it was different. Three hundred fattening hoggs cudded their way towards tastiness on a field of turnip of Groam, a level fertile farm, just a mile up river from Beauly. At first the water trickled down between the drills, quizzical sheep stood on the ridges keeping their feet dry and gazing innocently at the novelty. Suddenly a sluicing flow from the Kilmorack gorge poured over the flats. Too late to get the floundering beasts gathered onto higher ground, the unfortunate owner, a Mr. MacLennan rushed from the village in time only to wring his hands as his even less fortunate sheep were swept from view.

Two hundred reappeared as bloated, unbled carcasses swilling about the environs of Beauly. Manna to the poor, they feasted for weeks on what, to them, passed as the luxury of prime hogget. Some of this choice flotsam, though by no means all, the Beauly'ites were obliged to purchase at the stiffish price of three pence per pound. As Mr. MacLennan pointed out when sniffing around the doors, a considerable loss had been incurred and no successful business ran on philanthropy.

I'M HEADING FOR THE
HIGH GROUND

The second sight, once a feature of Highland culture, is seldom heard of today by comparison to the role it played as little as sixty years ago in the fireside conversation and day to day awareness of the indigenous people. An affinity with a less complex, but acutely more demanding world of subsistence living, kept native senses keenly attuned to the mysterious mind of the natural world. By simple extension, for folks, who with little difficulty, found credulity in a blend of superstition and religion, why not belief in the supernatural?

The village of Cannich in Strathglass is tucked comfortably at the foot of a breath catching climb which unfolds above billows of birchwood into a wide pop-up world of towering hills and shining water. Barbara MacLean, born about 1828, was a native of this village and sister to the shepherding Hugh MacLean who flitted his wife and their baby Barbara across the bealach from Kintail into the head of Glen Cannich. Aunt and niece enjoyed the same name, a feature of the once inviolable system of family nomenclature which served to bond the ethnic natives and usefully confuse an outsider.

As teenagers before the days of regular schooling 'Baab' MacLean and her friends went to village night classes of a winter's evening. Reading, writing, and who knows, perhaps the flutter of an eyelash? Commendable application of course, all to be disrupted for them in a frightening manner on a night of dangerous moonlight.

Dawdling arm in arm, the girls gossiped and giggled their way home from class. Gently swaying pines trembled moonbeams into pointing fingers. They fell pale and sinuous on the road ahead, clawing at a hollow darkness. Stealthily from the blackness of a culvert, a long, low, pink coloured creature appeared. Without legs, a stark form against the moonfingers, it scuttled noiselessly over the road to be swallowed amongst shadowy trunks, lost from the face of creation. Shrieking and sobbing the petrified girls fled for home. The classes were abandoned.

The following week after much hesitation the class resumed. The young Maclean girl walked home ahead of the crowd. In whispers, the girls hung back. At the dreaded culvert the creature rose silently before her. Barbara leapt, tackity boots flying, screaming in Gaelic, "If you belong to this world speak up," The troglodyte paused a second to long and was laid out with a badly cut face.

Next morning the Beauly doctor stitched a flapping open cheek. The Cannich trouble maker had turned his pink lined overcoat inside out to frighten the girls. "Ach, just a joke, no harm, just a ploy," he said to the practitioner, but as needle and thread pulled the wound together without anaesthetic he wished he'd thought of a less cunning frolic.

Barbara had neither fear of dark nor the supernatural. Throughout her life she would take the long climb up Glen Cannich, south wind dust or icy drift, to keep in touch with her relations. Her niece and namesake had married into the shepherding Boas of Longard and Christina the grand niece, known as 'Teenie', became a special favourite. Stops for tea and a 'news' all the way 'west the glen' in the Highland style of the time often meant it was long past the children's bedtime before the old Aunt would walk in the shepherd's door at Longard.

Little wide awake 'Teenie' peeping round the kitchen door, remembered the Aunt arriving late one night and talking in a low voice to her parents. "What a commotion, it was dark of course, I could only see the road but I had to stop. I could hear a terrible noise, back at Shalavinich, there were men working, I heard the creaking, like wheelbarrows, and what a crashing of rock against rock, pick and shovel, hammering, explosions and shouting, I heard it as plain as I'm telling you, some upheaval." Neither she nor any at the time could explain her presentiment. The year was 1895. 'Baab' was known and respected for having the 'sight', and this manifestation was remembered and retold in the glen long after her death. Proof of her revelation was to be dramatic.

Seventy years later at the bonnie hazel wooded bend of Shalavinich, dynamite and bulldozers moved in. The crashing symbols of Hydro-Electric construction blasted and built the massive Mullardoch Dam across the width of Glen Cannich. Longard, its hardships, laughter and lifestyle, a sacrifice for a picture on the screen of progress.

Dignified and reflective, the towers and cloisters of the Fort Augustus Abbey of Saint Benedict enshrine the old religion of the Highlands, and add the charm of grey mellow stone to the long sweep of hill and loch that cleave their way down Glen Mhor. Imposing yet peaceful this strategic site controlled the crossing at the head of Loch Ness, and was gifted to the monks of Beauly Priory in 1232 by Sir John Bisset of Lovat. Some of the Benedictine Brothers, never idle when it came to building, happy with their windfall, soon got busy on the foundations.

Peace reigned for three hundred years before thunder claps of religious intolerance and monastic destruction rolled down from the Edinburgh pulpit of John Knox. At Abertarff Abbey, as it was then called, deep concern, if not a knee weakening panic ensued, both theological and secular. The Prior, trusting both to avoid a strike of Calvinistic' enlightenment' and maintain a roof over his head at the same time, for 'safe keeping', in 1558 hastily assigned his monastic property to the sixth Lord Lovat.

All went quietly for some time under the cloisters until, thanks to his ill judged efforts in the failed '15' Jacobite Rebellion, Lovat's descendant, Alexander Fraser of Fraserdale when occupied in saving his skin before the English High Court, had little option but hand over the Abbey and much else besides to the English Crown.

In the eyes of this Protestant authority, Catholic Holy Water could not safeguard the consecrated status of this venerable old building and it was smartly transformed into an army barracks. The disaffected clansmen were to be overawed by military might rather than doctrinal dogma. To emphasise the point, road building General Wade, with the sycophancy worthy of an aspiring politician, complimented His Grace, William Augustus, Duke of Cumberland in 1730 by changing the Abbey's old name of Abertarff to Fort Augustus. It nicely balances Fort William and serves to this day by perpetuating the 'Butchers' name the length and breadth of the Great Glen.

One of the few, and perhaps the last lucky cannonball to be fired by Bonnie Prince Charlie's men, fell on the converted Fort Augustus Abbey. In need of practice, if not an amusing diversion, Highland Jacobites heading towards Inverness in the March of 1746 trundled their artillery, a jaded cannon, onto an eminence overlooking the barracks.

"Target, the fortress, down hill shot men. Aim, lob a cannonball down one of the chimneys." A task attainable by guided missile but somewhat beyond the known capability of a smooth bore, sightless, muzzle loading field gun. "Ready men. Fire." A warm cannonball dribbled from the barrel at their feet. "Reload, steady men. Fire." The second shot whined away, rose high, higher, lost speed, and then, guided by will power, it disappeared down a commodious 'lum.' Result, a blinding yellow flash, several minor bangs, choking blue smoke, exultant cheers from Highland soldiers and the open mouthed incredulity of their artillery officer who from that day on firmly believed the Almighty to be a Catholic.

The powder magazine had exploded. Whooping with delight the Highlanders, kilts flying, catapulted from their rock to assail the smoking pile and complete the fun of the day by dismantling what remained of this hated symbol of English rule. Still known as Battery Rock, the name may reflect national pride rather than a strict adherence to historic detail, but what a day out for the boys.

By May of that year 'Butcher' Cumberland with the slaughter of Culloden on his battle honours, camped beside the toppled stonework of Fort Augustus barracks. No less a prisoner than Simon Fraser, Lovat of the '45' hobbling to his death on the block, was paraded before the ruins to hear a triumphant Duke order their restoration.

Few families of note have known more turns of the wheel of fortune than the Lovat Frasers. 'All shall come to him that waits.' Given a suitable time lag, pride of Family, sheer vitality and not to mince words, an eye to the main chance, and the fortunes of the Lovats have always revived.

Highland troops fought over the Hills of Alma, an impecunious British Government flogged asset to fund its Crimean War and a hundred and forty years on in 1857, Thomas Fraser, Lord Lovat bought back Cumberland's restored barracks for £5,000. Twenty years later his son Lord Simon, maybe to hedge further family misfortune, presented the building to the Fathers of the Benedictine Order.

The foundation stone of the present monastery was laid in 1876 and on the Abbey's completion its fine cloisters surrounded a quadrangle opening into a library containing eighteen thousand volumes, whilst as a relaxation over frugal meals, diners weary of study may view emblazoned upon the spacious refectory windows, the Coats of Arms of the Abbey's benefactors, amongst which the Lovats are justly displayed.

'Let there be light', the omnipotent directive from Genesis. Alexandrian translators scribing the Septuagint under the spluttering flicker of reed and tallow might well have applauded the lateral thinking of the scholarly Brothers at Saint Benedict's Abbey. With eighteen thousand theological books on hand, reading in bed would be imperative. A connection between enlightenment and eye strain becomes obvious.

In 1890 the monks at Fort Augustus threw a switch that brought the first hydro electric power to the Highlands. Using the catchment area of Inchnacardoch Forest their small 18Kw water turbine not only put light in the library, it also blew out the candles for eight hundred blinking souls down in the village.

Six years later the Fort William Electric Light Company illuminated the old town and led the way towards the disfigurement of Ben Nevis and much else of the Highlands. Dingwall and Strathpeffer saw the light in 1903 from a scheme high on Ben Wyvis financed by Col. Blunt-MacKenzie husband of the Countess of Cromarty. Further south by 1910 the Duke of Atholl had his fairy castle floodlit.

The principle was proven. Initially growth remained slow due to the difficulty of transmitting electricity beyond a relatively short distance. Also there was a lack of demand, the cost of wiring and appliances being beyond the pocket or perhaps the desire of rural communities of the day. Even in this day when the street lights of Castlebay on the Hebridean Isle of Barra were extended to illuminate a single track road of croft houses, Neillie Sinclair, whose company I was wont to keep when the mood was right, remarked, "Man there's no privacy left on the island, the moon was more discreet."

Aluminium smelting from bauxite ore required vast amounts of cheap power to produce a metal that would ultimately banish the old iron pot from the kitchen. Enter British Aluminium. A clever land deal in Stratherrick on the south side of Loch Ness, neatly bypassed vociferous public objection and the need for Parliamentary powers, allowing them to set up the Falls of Foyers aluminium smelter. The site was ideal, a narrow gorge down which poured a perpendicular waterfall of spectacular beauty. Financial fortune for the Company however did not smile from the bottom of a shining pan until the escalating demands of the First World War created a market.

The success of aluminium production was the catalyst which sparked off the Hydro-electric schemes. Labour was cheap, land was cheap and work was desperately needed for a nation grovelling through soup kitchen depression and General Strike.

By the 1930's the flooding of many great glens began. Taming the wilderness, the noble sentiment of the age was glorified in promotional films of dynamite and bulldozer bashing the glens into shape. The slogan 'Power to the chimney head for £10', soon draped the Highland hills in daisy chains of pylon lines. Castles of concrete straddled the straths, and as the waters rose over croft and shieling few major lochs in the north were left without the rocky necklace of an ecologically sterile margin.

By the end of Hitler's war only two unsurpassable glens remained untouched by Hydro mania. Another exploitation of the Highlands rode triumphantly towards completion. But this time, unlike the removal of people and their cattle, unlike the damage of overgrazing by sheep and deer, unlike the stupidity of blanket afforestation, the scouring away of scores of square miles of alluvial soils at the head of many fine lochs is irreversible. The heart of the glens lay by their river banks, pulsating in a life that moved with the seasons. Harvests when there were people, nests when there were birds, winter grass for the deer, a cycle from hill top to hayfield snapped by an ignorance draped in the ermine robes of progress.

Glen Affric is regarded as one of the finest natural beauties of Scotland. Although a relatively modest dam was built at Loch Benavean the glen still retains much of its former glory. But the 1950's saw the North of Scotland Hydro-Electric Board face its final challenge. The damming of the two glens north of Affric would bring a combined catchment area of 350 square miles under control. Glen Cannich and Glen Strathfarrar were bravely harnessed. The former scheme raised Loch Mullardoch by 120ft. with the largest dam in Scotland and the latter scheme lifted the water level in Loch Monar by 80ft with the construction of the horseshoe Monar dam. The length of both lochs doubles to about thirteen miles each when the dams are full.

Glen Cannich submerged under thousands of acres of water with barely a gurgle of national notice. Strathfarrar, the last major glen in Scotland to be flooded, at least did not succumb without the ripples of a public enquiry. In the June of 1947 the Scottish Secretary of State led a bold submission to Parliament for the setting up of a Highland National Park based on the boundaries of this impressive catchment area. It would stretch fully forty miles from Kilmorack in the east to the western watersheds of these three magnificent glens. Conservation, rural development and tourism spearheaded a rallying message to the common mass-intent on playing in the countryside, and to a host of petty officials intent on days out from the office in pleasant surroundings. An imaginative paper indeed, it contained more than a hint of erosion for land owning privilege and occasioned discreet coughs of concern over the brandy and cigars.

Equally disconcerting for sporting interests, the newly formed Scottish Wild Life Conservation Committee with such radical thinkers as Frank Fraser Darling in its ranks, tagged their report onto the National Park theme. Dated Westminster, 23rd June 1947 it read with the vehemency of Jack Straw's address to the Peasant's Revolt', We are charged with conserving for posterity the wild life of our country, a wild life which has its own right to existence and survival, the urgency of the need for scientific supervision of the living natural resources of Scotland has been increasingly borne in upon us during the course of our inquiry', and ended with the inflammatory gusto of a

Communist manifesto, 'It will therefore be necessary for some land to be acquired in order that continuity of occupation and complete rights of management be secured.' Sentiments sufficient to drop a portcullis, dust down the armour and oil the man traps.

Only a Utopian dreamer could fail to guess the outcome of the enquiry. During a week of undiluted rhetoric, it ranged from 'The Rights of Man' to the Rights of Way. The two main land owning opposers of the Hydro plans, the Lovat and Fairburn Estates, quietly withdrew their objections. A flood of water versus the tramp of tourists. Water seemed the less contemptible. The Public enquiry found for the Hydro-Board who, being happy with its outcome, could certainly not be accused of parsimony in paying out compensation. Temporary disruption to the valuable river Beauly salmon fishings netted the Lovat Estate a neat hundred thousand. Sir John Stirling of Fairburn who lost the west end of Loch Monar and a pair of shooting lodges received seventy thousand.

Dynamite, bulldozers and concrete, two years construction and rising water destroyed the pristine grandeur of the last unspoilt Highland glen, the conservationists had their wings clipped, and the Nation lost an irreplaceable asset.

The three main head water dams, hold back some thirty miles of loch between them. They are built to a design which allows excess water to spill over their tops and down the face of the structures when the dams become full. Once a dam of this type begins to spill whilst running with its turbine intakes at full capacity the layman must conclude it to be out of control so far as a means of curbing a flood is concerned. At the planning stage much expert attention focused upon rainfall records and projected run-off. The Monar dam was expected to take nine months to fill, nature thought otherwise and managed it in three.

Twenty miles eastwards from these three major dams, in the middle of the Kilmorack gorge on the Beauly river, the Hydro Board built the Aigas dam. At the foot of the gorge, on the site of the falls, they built the Kilmorack dam. These two structures differ fundamentally from the three spill over dams to the west. All the runoff from 350 square miles of catchment area must pass through, and decidedly not over them.

During construction both these lower dams encountered serious problems. At Aigas, the dam rests upon a conglomerate, or 'pudding rock', which, as the name suggests, has the consistency of a dumpling and likewise is highly unstable. Finding a solid base for the dam proved as difficult as standing on a bottomless bowl of jelly. The trouble down at the Kilmorack dam was more a mixture of poor judgement and bad luck. A tunnel and coffer dam were built to channel the Beauly river during construction of the dam proper. In 1962 a 'local' with a knowledge of the river plus a little common sense remarked to the engineers, "Yon wee tube you have down there won't even take a decent spate." Idle comment or prophetic insight, that winter a flood took the lot. The shuttering wood was gathered off the beach outside Inverness. So far the Aigas 'dumpling' problem has only created mild apprehension amongst a few superstitious natives.

A gentle snowfall came to the Highlands in the early days of November 1966. No eye stinging blizzard to drive hill sheep into the entombment of snow filled gulleys. No coat clagging blast to drive red deer to the shelter of silent plantations. But it fell deeply, very deeply. A soft white quilt that rounded the countryside into the contours of a childrens painting and brought a bright light through winter morning windows. I had seen such a fall once before at this time of year when living in the remoteness of the Wester Ross hills. A feeling of unease came strongly to me. An inner sense that catches whispers from the world of nature was warning me.

From a birch covered shoulder of ground called in Gaelic the Druim, I could look down on the broad top of the Aigas dam, its side sluices and power house. The Beauly river was the southern boundary of the land I farmed and I had surveyed the dam's building with misgivings.

On the morning of November 10th a south wind lolled across the land. So warm and languid the scent of palms seemed on its breath. Already the thaw tinkled away, 'whooshes' of dull snow slid from roofs, dragging at slates, threatening sheds and panicking the hens. Mid morning opened the clouds that had denied us daylight. Each warm drop of rain released a dozen imprisoned comrades to join the merry rivulets that frolicked across the farm and rejoiced in being born again. By evening two feet of snow had vanished from the yard and was happily tearing up gravel and digging craters down the farm road. I did not join in this water borne hymn of exultation.

At nine that night I looked out, not a trace of snow remained, scooped away in half a day by a phenomenal rise in temperature. I turned in for a coat, "There'll be a fair flood tonight, I'm hearing the roar of the river, it'll be worth a look at the dam," The Land Rover picked its way gingerly down the remains of the farm road. Still it rained.

Suffused in sickly yellow light blazing from powerhouse windows, the dam, pallid faced, powerful in its impassivity, squatted in the hollow blackness of the night. A concrete Buddha below a halo of writhing vapour, astride a world in chaos. Spinning generators whined at an unearthly pitch, piercing the thunder of plunging water. The ground tremored, the atmosphere throbbed, mighty turbines rode unbridled lust with drumming beat, 'tricity' stank the air.

Blinding searchlights focused cris-cross on two curving shoots of water that spewed from emergency sluices on either side of the dam. Jets thirty feet wide and twenty feet high shot a hundred yards from the gaping sluice gates in two great arcs of solid water which collided in a translucent mass of rainbow spray on a pinnacle of rock below the dam. From under the powerhouse erupted a seething black cauldron which churned in a boiling wake to meet the cascading sluices in a turmoil of shattered waves that burst forty feet in the air.

The lower road to the front of the dam was under water, waves flung over its protecting parapet, I walked down and stood eye level with unleashed fury. A crashing force, lit from its own energy by the genius of man, burst into chandeliers of spray, bright tears of rage. Its demented roar filled the gorge, booming wall to wall, a river wild, crazed, bent on mankind's destruction and doom. And yet, above the tumult, hummed a high pitched whine, steady, distant, a million volts fizzed and crackled in magnetic menace, a surrealistic pathway to the stars. The road to outer space.

Tall pines closed over the darkened road which sloped to the top of the dam. I hurried down, taut as the tension charging the air. The two curved sluice gate gantries cocked high into the air above the railed bulwark. Hamish the dam keeper worked at emergency lifting motors, without a greeting he blurted, "Benavean and Mullardoch are both spilling, control'll know at ten o' clock if Monar is going to go."

I looked down, a giant water slide vanished through the dam, only a few feet of curved steel breasted the onslaught, the rest towered above me in an arched segment. "Hellish little safety left now, damn it I asked them in Edinburgh a week ago to let more water away, if it keeps rising the river's over the top." he hurried down the clattering passage to the generating hall. Wet and cold, I followed his last chilling sentence "If the Monar dam spills this one won't hold."

The dam shuddered violently. Water from the raging flood thundered in wild cascade through turbine and sluice. The sudden run off from three hundred and fifty square miles of the mightiest glens in the Highlands roared around me powering it's way to the sea. Transfixed I stood at its centre. The giant generating hall reverberated, brass dials and banisters tingled to the touch, needles quivered towards peaks, red alerts flashed. Were cooling filters clogging?

Blazing lights drained our faces to a sickly yellow. The atmosphere vibrated. I scented danger. A crushing dread of confinement dashed fascination into fear. Would the dam hold? Would it breach, would it swirl away in mocking slow motion, a gyrating mass of crumbling steel and concrete sweeping all in its path?

Any moment could be engulfing chaos. That tiny trickle above the pounding turbines, a fatal leak? A thin water wedge? A million tons of racing fury. What man made structure could stay this onslaught. What tenuous fixture retain its grip on the rotten rock walls of a deep narrow gorge gouged by ten thousand floods? Imagination and fear make alarming partners. Not a night for heroics. Discretion tinged with a touch of cowardice suggested the exit.

Amongst the madly throbbing turbines, Hamish the dam keeper scurried about moving numerous pot plants away from the spurting leaks which threatened to overwater his carefully nurtured blooms. His agitated activity detached me for a moment from impending doom. It seemed oddly reminiscent of my grandmother covering her 'budgie' cage with a dark cloth as wailing sirens heralded another night of Hitler's bombs.

Hamish, his plants secure, made for the top of the dam. No time to abandon a friend, I climbed fearfully back up the echoing tunnel. The rain had stopped, a colder wind caught my cheek, the clouds were lifting, I looked west and thought of the massive ice floes I'd once seen block and change the course of a thawing river. A couple whole trees and a few ice sheets could quickly plug these sluices, of that I had no doubt.

"Lucky there's no ice on the river," I shouted, the intense noise blotted out my words. Every light blazed, the phone rang, Hamish shouted into it, something about the turbines, cooling, filters, I caught words, "choking, heavy silt coming down." We dashed down steps to the base of the generators. Control lights blinked.

Suddenly, on the powerhouse forecourt, a resounding crash, a spout of water blew the height of the dam tossing a heavy iron grating aside. We dashed out to investigate. Moments later, a second blow hole, another fountain erupted. We retreated just as quickly inside. The holes blew every thirty seconds.

The pressure was on.

Phone again. Control, I glanced at the clock, ten fifteen, "Monar's holding," Hamish bawled in my ear, "but the river's still rising, lifting the sluices another foot, not much spare now." He ran.

In countless revolutions the terrified generators before me were transforming the madness of rampaging elements into a cup of bedtime cocoa, on another planet, in Glasgow. I marvelled.

I marvelled also at Hamish. In the midst of a million tons of water a minute he filled a red watering can and it seemed in a fond farewell watered any plants which had not received their daily drink via tonight's more alarming means.

That done he stepped rapidly to the office, caught up a small case and made smartly for the stairs. I was hard on his heels, up the hollow roar of the spiral staircase.

"I'm heading for the high ground," he shouted over his shoulder." "I'm not planning a night with my finger in a leak," I shouted back, and a frightened pair we fled for the hill. The dam trembled for its life.

The unblinking eye of Coinneach Odhar gazed through a carved hole in an ancient stone. Unfocused on this world, perhaps he beheld the yet to be. Saliva trickled, his voice crackled.

"A loch above Beauly will burst its banks and destroy in the rush a village in its vicinity."

Grey Kenneth, the Brahan Seer famed as a visionary far beyond his Highland homeland, made many seemingly implausible predictions, which later proved accurate down to the smallest detail. Putting aside the 'faux pas' of ending his days in a burning tar barrel, a gross oversight for a gifted visionary, there may again be good reason for acknowledging the 'old buffers' knack with prophecies.

Given today's ingenious arrangements for control of this vast catchment area it would barely require the Brahan Seer's prescient turn of mind to declare a similar prophesy. Common sense might suffice.

YOUR ISSUE WILL BE
WITHOUT ISSUE

Lord Lovat, poised, commanding and declamatory stood in the Witness Box of Edinburgh High Court addressing Judge, Jury and a gallery full of Titles, twittering Ladies and tall hats. "These men are poachers and had I been staying at Beaufort Castle I should have taken them as such."

The year was 1905. The case before the Court a curious one. The men condemned by His Lordship for 'visiting the river' were employees of his own estates and, it appeared from the evidence, had their master's best interest at heart. But more might be netted than salmon, a jail sentence could wing a brace of wealthy American sportsmen who stood trial charged with the reckless discharge of firearms in the direction of Lovat Estate fishermen. A cavalier form of deterrent which caused grievous injury to one man and delivered a light peppering to several others. In short, rights and property versus violence. Scotland's gentry were concerned.

The battlements of Beaufort Castle dominate in regal grandeur the spacious tree shaded fields which lead to a mighty sweep of the Beauly river and bountiful salmon fishings of the Silver Pool. In the stealth of a moonless July night the creak and dip of oars pulled a boat steadily across this favoured pool. The plash and swish of a net, the flap and tap of fish tails on bottom boards, six skilled men worked swiftly, silently, forty prime salmon were loaded onto a hurley :—

Bang, bang, flash. Guns barked, sparks flew in the dark. Pellets splattered across the river, rattled on leaves. Echo caught echo. A man screamed, "I am dead, I am dead." A remarkable feat of perception but not quite the most unusual happening in the case.

Unfettered by assumed pedigree or Burke's Peerage, Americans at the turn of the century bowed to but one god, the dollar. Those who entered its sanctuary sometimes nurtured a sneaking envy of the status enjoyed by the British aristocracy. The 'sportsmen' amongst these disciples happily paid handsome prices for a semblance of the grousemoor image and the position it conveyed in the social 'peck order.' Few shootings and fishings in Scotland could offer more 'tweedie' glamour than the Lovat Estate. It epitomised the scenery and society of a classic novel, the Walter Scott world, a 'movie' picture of Victorian romance. Baronial castle, cosseted ladies, guns, garrons and liveried ghillies in Lovat green, all flourished that glorious decade of summers before the stinking trenches of despair. Each year it cost the eponymous Mr. Phipps over two thousand pounds rent for three months of making myth.

The two Yankee sons of magnate Phipps, men in their twenties, were late to bed. Mr. Henry looked out on a night of starlit shadow as he drew the Castle's heavy curtains. Was that a movement? He watched. Yes. Again. Men on the river.

"John, we have poaching," an urgent shout brought his brother. A flight of grand stair, gun room, guns, cartridges, the two men reached the bank in moments. "What the hell are you doing there?" No reply, click of boot on stone, furtive figures. Cowboys and Indians, 'yippee', the Phipps opened fire.

John Fraser was guided to the witness box. His right eye had been removed, little sight remained in the left. The story was simple. Blinded Fraser was one of five employees who, along with Alex MacRae the Estate head fisherman, had netted the Silver Pool on the night which cost him his eyesight. Fraser had fished the pool with the Phipps that very day without comment on the state of the river or the health of the salmon.

But the men knew that secrecy, stealth and not a hint to the Phipps was vital. Operation 'Silver Pool' went ahead. Leader Macrae told the court, "the fish were crowded in the pool, the river was low and disease might set in. I thought it was best to remove some of the fish." Forty salmon loaded onto a 'hurley' were already trundling away to the Estate ice house when a shout carried over the river. A Phipps voice. The gang froze but made no reply. Moments passed without a breath. Crash, the night split apart. Shots found their mark. The peppered gang scattered. A man screamed in pain.

Realising a badly hit man lay in the boat, a greatly concerned Henry Phipps waded the river and carried the bleeding 'poacher' up to the castle. Fraser had been hit twice, a shoulder hung wounded, the damage to his face seemed alarming. A hastily summoned Beauly physician, Dr.Leach, appropriately pronounced 'leech', could do little for the injured eyes. A telephone call brought the foremost Edinburgh ophthalmic surgeon by the first train. No expense was spared, the Phipps were truly contrite, but no amount of cash could cure their stupidity.

From salmon netting and shooting the case drifted into a shoal of red herring. Questions to the defence dealt with the width of the river, the length of shadows, the amount of light and the weight of shot that had been fired. Lovat, called in support of his sporting tenants, roundly indicted his employees for poaching and made the point, "In any person shooting to scare assumed poachers, it is very important, of course, where there is such an invasion of rights, to get the net." He further pronounced on the difficulty of judging distance at night whether shooting at stags or men and drew at length on his experiences in the Boer War.

His Lordship's factor John Garrioch was adamant, no one had authorised or even knew of the men's poaching exploit. The testimony of MacRae, the head fisherman, "I took the salmon to the Corff House and they were added to the Wednesday's catch and sold for the benefit of Lord Lovat," was not drawn to Garrioch's attention. The factor confirmed however the magnanimous nature of the Phipps, they had spent, he said approvingly, "upwards of £6,000 on public purpose in the district and the people feel very grateful."

The final witness for the defence confirmed not all librarians to be short sighted bookworms. Dr. Morrison of Edinburgh Public Library having testified that Mr. John Phipps had a love of books and a 'remarkably fine taste in bindings', insisted it proper to shoot to scare and added with conviction, "I don't know what I might be tempted to do to a poacher." It might be assumed fortunate for all concerned that Dr. Morrison was not present at the farouche action which he bravely supported from the witness box.

The Crown Prosecution made a blunt case, "a man has no more right to fire his gun at a poacher, whether to scare or to injure him, than he has to fire at any other man. Nothing in Scottish law excuses one in discharging one's gun be it fifty or eighty yards, except when in imminent danger of one's life. To do so is a serious breach of the criminal law."

The Judge was less dogmatic. With sagely wagging wig he addressed the jury, "Unless you are satisfied that there was evil intent on the part of the prisoners to injure these men, then you cannot return a verdict of assault. The reckless discharge of fire-arms may certainly exist, although what happened was quite unexpected. You might come to the conclusion this was a mere misadventure which the accused could not foresee. In short, was it a mistake, a regrettable accident? A poacher must not be shot at any more than anyone else but it is lawful to scare away a poacher."

Hunched in the dock, the two young Phipps hung their heads. Whispers circulated the gallery, fans fluttered, the day was warm. Twenty-seven minutes later the foreman of the jury stood gravely before the court. "By a unanimous verdict my Lord, we find the prisoners," he paused for effect, "not guilty." "Bravo, bravo," loud applause and hearty congratulations. The Phipps walked from the chamber relieved by the righteousness of Scottish justice.

None of the employees was sacked, one eyed Fraser, thanks to the munificence of the Phipps, had his sixteen shilling wage raised to a thirty-two shilling a week annuity, Beauly got its spacious Phipps hall, and the poacher who suffered a posterioral blast of pellets when bending to lift the nets received a generous seventy pounds.

The latter miscreant, back at his croft and licking his wounds, metaphorically speaking that is, now considered himself a man of some means, sufficient indeed to prompt a cool cash offer for his neighbour's land. The old widowed lady, poor, proud and disdainful, met him with a scowl of refusal and later remarked to a friend, more politely expressed in the Gaelic than the English translation, "He'll need another shot in the arse before he can buy the croft."

'Just where the river issues from the cliffs overlooking the salmon leap there juts out a lofty piece of tableland. That is the burial ground of Kilmorack, and there as we approached, we beheld upwards of a thousand people collected, and conspicuous in the bright and varied hues of Highland costume.'

'Most of the people were on foot; none was barefoot. On week-days we saw scarcely a woman with shoes or stockings; but today, none was without. And, with the exception that hardly one wore a bonnet, the young women were not much to be distinguished from those of our smartest towns. They all had their hair neatly braided and adorned with a comb of tortoiseshell. Many of them had silk gowns and handsomely worked muslin collars, others were dressed in white.'

A Sunday in August 1838 and the observations of William Howitt, gentleman of the south and potted anthropologist, viewing an open air Sacrament ministered in the Gaelic to a congregation donned in their damp 'Sunday best.' Wedding, funeral or Sunday service, these handmade clothes, carefully unfolded from the 'big kist' or taken through from 'the press.' A heady scent of mothballs would waft over the worshipers. Sabbath incense, an addition to the solemnity of the service Mr. Howitt fails to mention. Equally, the writer appears unaware that the vast majority of the communicants would have carried their shoes to within a few hundred yards of the gathering. Thrift, a virtue created by the misfortune of communal poverty.

'We entered the burial ground through a dense crowd and seated ourselves on the low wall built on the edge of the precipice over the river. Beneath a spreading tree near the garden wall stood a movable booth of wood. From this booth the minister was now addressing the assembly while two other ministers occupied a seat behind him.'

'A more serious and decorous congregation never was seen. When those who had gone forward communicated, the minister again addressed them and they retired from the table, and a fresh company took their place. Another minister then came forward and there followed a new succession of psalms, prayers and addresses.'

'We left about three o'clock, but were told that not till six o'clock would the service close. Shortly after we left, the distant voice of the minister and the wild cadence of the Gaelic psalms, like the breezy music of an Aeolian harp, reminded us that it was a sacred anniversary of a grave and religious people.'

A granite pillar, grey with dignity, stands in the corner of the old Kilmorack Burying Ground and watches over the grave of Peter MacKenzie, tenant of Tighnaleac of Breakachy. During an era of doctrinal obedience which marked the Highland character with deference to the 'cloth' and a gracious manner towards mankind, MacKenzie and many of his neighbours would most certainly have taken communion in the style of Howitt's description, making observance of Sabbath and Sacrament an unbreakable ritual in the life of all but the bravest sinner.

But Peter was not a man to confuse piety and charity. He came to the district from east of Inverness, a hard working civil contractor who instilled the virtue of unremitting toil in his men with little difficulty against a backdrop of 'clearance' and potato famine. The rocky outcrop of Aigas was blasted to take the Beauly Cannich road up the Druim Pass, flood banks surrounding the arable lands of Erchless Castle were built to The Chisholm's satisfaction, and for the hefty rent of £140 a year MacKenzie took on the 'modernising' of Tighnaleac, the most agreeable tenancy on the Chisholm Estate.

Each corner and crevice of Breakachy sheltered cottar and crofthouse, the lea of a birch blessed knoll, the bank of a stepping stone burn. The Chisholms at Culour, Forbes of Millcroft, folks long scattered and dead. Forgotten today save in a name. 'Scott's wood' at the rim of the Garapol ground, 'Colin Crupach', lame Colin and his house on Spittal Street. Tailor's Turn for a bend in the road. Geordacks' peats for the man who cut the last warmth from the edge of Breakachy hill. Cruinassie, the Carnich, Teagate, they were homes. Water at the well, tatties by the door, a peat cutting share on the moor. When fires stirred to life and curled in the cold still air, feet stood on an earthen floor. Night pots to the midden, a milk pail to the byre, mother a child to her breast, father to work in shivering light, a farm by the firth, a pick for the road. Whatever to hand in a hungry land, they were glad.

MacKenzie's steading rose commodious and grand. Stone from the ruin, the disused dyke, slate by the cartfull with the best of larch. Sandstone cut to a shapely arch and, weather cock atop, it put his tenancy on the map. The cottars said, the price of the plans would have built a house.

Pride of the barn went to the threshing mill, a working sculpt. Bright red wheels with curving spokes and criss-cross belts protruded from a mighty varnished frame, mysterious trap doors opened at either end and polished metal cups on a revolving belt hid inside a long wooden tunnel waiting to pour the hard shining corn into sacks from a hole in its side. Few ventured within, only the cat and her summer kittens took the risk. A box full of secrets.

Sweating horses dragged it up from Beauly. Excited children helped heave this new age wonder round climbing bends above Teanassie school. Hand dug at sixpence a yard, a mile of deeply banked lade waited to race water down from the hill to drive the mill's splashing wheel. Ten foot diameter, three feet wide, an overshot sluice, the wheel had slosh and thump enough to 'whirr' the stripper, shak' the riddles, walk the straw, an' terrorise the men who fed its maw. But often for weeks on end at winter's whim this deposer of the flail lay still, and each night of frost on the millpond's gleam grew an inch of ice.

Glaciers of a bygone aeon swept clear the flagstone which gave site and name to the old house of Tighnaleac. Exposed, drafty and rather much in sight of neighbourhood eyes, Peter MacKenzie opted to build himself a dwelling more in keeping with his influence in the district. The width of gable denoted the presumptuous size of its ground floor apartments and a count of chimney pots told curious eyes the number of grates. Yet from a spacious high ceilinged hall, two broad flights of stairs and a tall landing window led to several surprisingly cramped little bedrooms.

However across the landing at the head of the stair a solid door opened onto the house's innovative feature, a bathroom. There below the sloping ceiling, a distinct drawback for the taller man, was installed, allegedly, the first flushing lavatory in the Braes of Kilmorack. Pump handle action and a head of five gallons, in bold Gothic lettering, it was dauntingly named 'The Niagara.' When boldly flushed, a tribute to the aesthetics of its inventor, Thomas Crapper, this porcelain edifice provided a suitable refinement for the Ministers of the Sacrament who were wont to stay with the MacKenzies at the due dates of a Sacred calender. Not for smooth ecclesiastical cheeks the chaffing winds of a dry closet, nor for such elevated minds the contemplation of a shovel in the byre and the prickle of a whisp of straw.

Naturally man's higher thoughts thrive best in comfort, and downstairs, beside the sitting room fire, the tweak of a polished handle at armchair level pushed a mechanical rod behind the lath and plaster to ring an upstairs bell in the maid's back room. Sticks up the stair, the stove would be stoked, the black boiler bubbling. Pails of hot water, carried across the landing to the vast lion footed bath, would ease the burden of prayer for the sins of the wayward poor.

Out on the land fencing and enclosure took possession. William McLeod, the previous farmer to MacKenzie, had died in 1847 leaving the community in peace, some might say backward, but Peter was progressive, kept a fine pair of horse, and his plough went wide. Broom banks and rough knolls where cottars' cows would graze were taken in. Without rights, without a cow, one by one the cottar families left.

Gable to the west, hugging the lea of a boulder broken ridge, lie the faint ruins of a cottar house, and hard by the door, too heavy to move, still the great stone of shoulder loading days. A sunshine doorstep, a slope to the burn, and away to the east, field over fields, wood upon woods, out to the firth and beyond, the finest site in Breakachy. Sweet, dry and peaceful, the home of a widow, Ann Campbell.

To the new house of Tighnaleac, MacKenzie's wife Catherine Fraser bore three sons, Hugh, Donald and John. The name was secure. Peter walked his acres. The thrush of the north wind flitted over his broad fields in the long stabs of cold October sunlight. Herald of a hard winter? He looked down from the moor. Plump cornstacks, round and thatched would feed the new mill. He smiled and turned west. In the distance, against the fading sky, a bent figure was pulling heather. He strode over, "Get home out of here woman, you'll not take your cow's bedding from my ground."

Ann Campbell straightened. Her gaze sought the long horizon, the sun's last ray glowed in failing eyes. "MacKenzie," she spoke softly in the Gaelic, "your issue will be without issue." The man looked down. A bundle of plucked heather lay between them. The widow turned for home and left the bundle to the twilight.

Peter's three boys grew to manhood and married, but of the name MacKenzie, there was none. Three wild gean trees, old and broken, bloom each spring beside the ruins of 'Ann Campbells', the sweetest site in all of Breakachy.

A night of dry frost, my 'tackets' rang on an iron road. Hugh MacKenzie and Morag his wife sat to either side of a fire, glowing in the black leaded range of Breakacky kitchen. Flames flickered over the warmth. Orange swords, a burst of green, a deep blue dance, they mimicked the merry torches in the northern sky which had lit my walk across from Cluanie to pass the

Old New Year's evening with a kindly couple from a bygone age.

Hugh and I lifted a dram. Times past drifted into our talk. Mischievous light lay behind the eyes of distant memory, his tone turned conspiratorial. Far too early one season a tup of Hugh's, intent upon ravishing his neighbours ewes, had crossed the march burn, and head in the air strode boldly over the croft of Farley, to the fury of 'Eligo' Fraser, crofting batchelor and spinner of ghostly yarns, who foresaw lambs perishing in the sleets of March. 'Leander' had his emotions duly curbed by the confines of a dark shed. A solicitor's letter followed. 'Eligo', himself no slouch with the pen, nor anything else apparently, threatened 'Breakachy' with legal redress. But Hughie, before taking on the farm after his father's death, had seen jungle warfare with the Inverness law firm of Innes and MacKay.

Only his wife and myself listened, and I saw Morag nodded with the warmth and hundredth telling. "Look here," he whispered, "I waited for a frost like tonight, not a track, the moon was high, dash it was bright but I knew the shed, I kept the wall. Lucky the burn was low, he was a devil on the halter, but he got his breakfast in the Black Isle." I laughed aloud, Morag wakened and moved to make the tea. "Well my old firm wrote 'Eligo's crowd, 'we presume you have evidence to support this accusation.' Not another word, no tup, no case," He took a cup and buttered scones on his knee and made a short Grace. Morag stood by the dresser, head bowed.

"Ach, the Home Guard spoilt the hill," mused MacKenzie, "Yes, most Sunday mornings they marched out here," Morag looked pained. The Sabbath. Hugh protested, "It was the war effort. Anyway, they threw grenades and let off bombs. Holes all over the flats." Any connection between exploding devices and ex-members of the Kilmorack Militia of my acquaintance and I realised the dangers of the 'Home Front', "The ewes were always getting drowned, no use, so I got the rent down to seventy pounds."

Crumbs fell by his chair. "Now with the new wages rates for Jimmy Ross the place doesn't pay." I sensed retirement in his thoughts. We sat quiet a little, a lifetime filled their minds. I looked at the clock, I too had thoughts. Three children, no electricity, a frozen water supply and a steep icy road. Here was a good house, more ground. Time to move?

The corner of my eye caught sight of the fattest brown field mouse come tootling around the side of Hughie's chair. Stubby tail and velvet coat, no stack yard vagrant, it sniffed his slippers and sat a second, front paws in the air. All safe, two handed, it stuffed its cheeks with the crumbs of Morag's scone. Neither of them noticed. I made for Cluanie, the mouse for the skirting board. 'The best laid schemes?' I wondered.

Next day I spoke with the Baron. Perhaps wishing a greater safety zone between our pigs and his wife's rose beds, he enthused, "Oh la. Yes Iain, when

MacKenzie speak to me you get tenancy," and though we put a new stove into Breakachy kitchen, I left the old skirting board.

The critical state of the Councillor's corns was a certain indicator that the gathering of his sheep on Erchless hill could be but days away. Even Flossy knew the signs. Extra barking greeted my call at the door of Ardochy, and Archie, flustering about the scullery with kettles of boiling water, nodded apprehensively towards the kitchen through clouds of steam.

Ensconced on the sofa behind a Ross-shire Journal, 'Long Johns' rolled to the knee and one foot in a basin of tepid water, Alec paused from reading the deaths to direct Archie as to the suitable temperature of a top up. The paramedic poured away. "Ahrrrrgh," the Journal flew to the ceiling, a lightly boiled foot shot to the couch. "Man Erchie, didn't I tell you, ahrrrgh." Flossy left for the byre, Archie hastened to feed his hens. Discretion, the hallmark of survival.

In marked contrast to the 'straight to the point, I call a spade a spade' approach of the Anglo-Saxon, the evasive manner of a Gael required the deductive power of a detective, and the patience of a priest, to fathom the circumlocutionary disclosure of any matter at the forefront of a mind so inclined. The Councillor's inferential comments, given time and attention, generally translated into 'needing a hand.' An affable approach which avoided the direct request, and left a primed 'helper' free to offer or feel niggardly.

'Ardochy' dried his foot on the length of hand towel sacking which hung behind the scullery door and applied a corn plaster with deliberation and much grunting. Neither of us remarked on feet or corns, far less gathering sheep and Archie had retrieved his position with a pot of tea when the Councillor ventured conversationally, " Rod The Trapper was down at Kate's today." The first distant clue. A roving commission about the parish over the years in pursuit of rabbits and 'good stories' rendered Rod Campbell, a messenger with portfolio and the hub of operation 'corn cure.' "Well I tell you he isn't busy just now." Time scale and a hint of work. Pause. "Wasn't he down clipping for his Chairman last week?" The reference to an important Beauly farmer who ran the local Rabbit Clearance Society almost hid the verb 'to clip.'

The topic veered towards the menace of sheep maggots, a need to get the wool off the ewes before a 'fly strike.' Even on the airy slopes of Erchless hill the situation could be bad. Mention of 'hill.' Ardochy glanced at his foot. "Ah well, umh, I should have gone down to the chiropodist with this, too late now before the gathering." The comment hung. Archie ran his tongue round crumbs on his gums, swilled tea leaves at the bottom of his cup and sought divination. I was primed. "When are you planning to clip Alec?" "Ach, it's according to the weather, there's no hurry, but Monday would do fine if you're not too busy."

"Go back, go back Duncan there's sheep above you." The Councillor's hefty bawl and a wave of his stick braced the slopes of Erchless hill and bent the ear of Dunc Chisholm striding high across it's face. The keeper turned to look upwards. Five hundred feet above and near the ridge a cut of sheep looked triumphantly down. From a spying knoll at the foot of the ground, Ardochy, telescope and voice, controlled the gathering of his flock of black face sheep. Equally intent, Flossy stood at his feet adding whines and the odd frustrated bark. Between them no sheep were to be missed.

Dawn had drawn the blinds of darkness to reveal the Councillor's troupe of 'helpers', Oldtown, the Trapper, myself and Dunc the keeper, taking the long stride to the heather grazings high on the slopes of Beinn a' Bha'ach Ard. A pack of dogs, varying in shades of colour, usefulness and degrees of obedience, romped ahead of us, terrorising grouse, putting hinds to flight and disrupting the seemly tenor of hill life with snarls and fights. The Councillor, prevented by the pain of his affliction from anything beyond a limp, remained down at the control post.

The gatherers split and made for their stations, Oldtown and Rod to the Lovat march of Farley ground, Chisholm to the shoulder of 'Hare hill.' I made out to the greens at the foot of the Beinn and sat on a boulder. A shapely stone, set in the low mound of once a dyke, for these were the lands of the cattle shieling and I would not be the first to share their vantage over the cares of a life of boundaries.

Strathglass of castle, ordered fields, of chinks of river through prison trees, hard by the folly of Fraser pride, down to the foot of a flooding tide, out to the firth and a morning sun. I turned to watch the keeper climb, of easy stride for man and hill, I lived the gift of eternal youth, the glory of its space. But 'Lassie' snuffled mice, happy in the chase, catching in her mind, storing for her dreams, and I sat alone. The summer grass of shieling days grew dotted white, the powder puffs of cotton bog, and higher than the shining Beinn, the skylark sang of freedom.

Far out, below the curved shoulder of Pollan, the clatter of grouse warning their covey to crouch carried to me on the crystal air. Presently a file of ewes and lambs bleated into sight. I turned the telescope on our commander. He sat his post, foot at rest, spying back. Flossy lay, nose on paw, awaiting action. This could be it, the signal, start of the gather. A lone figure, dogs rather than sleigh, appeared on the skyline driving the sheep, it was Santa Claus.

Hidden to the north over peat hag and ridge was the birthplace and home of Donald Ross. A far cry indeed from the suntanned face of Erchlees hill to the dark vale of Glengowrie and his croft of Tigh na Crochidher. House of the Hanging its name, though the story is never told, and Ross lived there alone, a solitary man who tended his sheep and acted as keeper on this forgotten corner of the Baron's estate.

Sometimes in the long winter nights when Festivities drew near, when a frost hung his coat on the pane and oil lamps burned low, the anchorite might feel the call of company and head for the warmth of its maw. A skin on the snow, a moon in the sky, a road and a light for the night. Cross the ice keen ridge of Pollan, a wink of sights led the way, and muffled tight against a chilling bite, tramped the man of the north, minus sleigh.

But the moon grew green and haloed, the path of its light fell wane, the first flying flakes stung a frozen face and gave Donald a snowbound mane. Yet staunch to the trail of pleasure, as the men of the '98, gamble and gold, to hell with the cold, make mine a large double measure.

Down at Struy Pub dizzy flakes danced in the beams from ill fitting curtains, made 'U's on the window sills and, with superb parabolic artistry, sealed the draught below the door. Big Sandy 'The Bun', peered into the maelstrom. "Not a night to go out, nor to go home," he opined, whereupon many of the artists within, basking below the rays of the 'optics', expressed a willful desire to be snowed up, for what the hostelry lacked in comfort it more than compensated in conviviality.

'Sandy Bun' had taken control, such as it was, behind the bar and proceeded to turn up his favourite tape of Jim Macleod.

'The Doc', leaning on the counter with pensive expression, was quoting at length, to no one in particular, from the previous week's Sunday Post. But ailments were for the 'morrow, Sandy pulled pints to the accordion beat, poured drams with the sparkle of a schottischa. In a space crowded by six, jostled half the village, and who knows what touches of surprise and delight that afforded.

'J.B.', mine host of the establishment, a fine/bass singer, but with less sense of rhythm on such an occasion, had caught the strains of a Gaelic waltz above the miscellany of song, and kitted for the state of the floor in Wellington boots, was steering Helen amongst other would be dancers, when, with a wrench and a flurry of snow, the door flew open.

Police. Help. Horror. Dancers untwined. A coarse version of Jingle Bells fell stillborn. The company fled behind each other. Exits were few. "Not me Hoff'isha" sprang to lips.

Snow avalanched into the fug. A faint outline amidst whirling flakes stood on the step blinking at the gaping crowd. The pious, of which it must be admitted there were but few, crossed themselves in the belief they beheld an avatar, whilst 'J.B.',a man of the odd ski-ing trip to Chamonix, not for the first time in association with the distilling trade, considered he viewed a Yeti.

Drip by drip the encrusted form advanced to the bar, the merest fraction of face between a 'flaps down' deer stalker bonnet and a flowing snowbound muffler. The crackling 'Greatcoat' reached to the floor, but, from below the melting mound, there peeped a pair of yellow toe capped 'wellies.' "Evening Santa, what are you for?" The cover was blown. Ah to be granted the gift of deduction. Big Sandy was ever the astute barman.

To enhance such a renowned title and not considering reindeer convenient for the summer, Donald acquired a little red Post Office van. Whereupon his occasional forays in search of lightsome company drew on a wider field, and trips to Inverness were not unknown. But hillman to the heart, no journey was undertaken except in the companionship of his two wiry terriers.

For those of the shepherd's calling returning westwards to their glens, weary of the delights of the Highland capital, the last shrine at which to unburden the soul before departing the town, was the Clachnaharry Inn. And it was to this scenic seat of solace that Donald repaired one breathless summer's evening when the length of Ben Wyvis lay on the firth and the far peak of Beinn a' Bha'ach Ard tipped the horizon, calling him home.

The Inn was no place for terriers, so with due thought for the welfare of his two friends, the penitent recluse chained them to the steering column of the little red 'Santamobile' and tiptoed inside. The sun of the summer solstice is patient in the northern latitudes and sufficient daylight elapsed for Donald to gain that perspective on life which floats above the trivia of traffic and the boundaries of human competence. The beauty of the hills, tipped upside down in a spreading sunset on the Firth, his Firth, filled the heart. Donald headed homewards down the side of it's glowing waters.

His two friends, their chains dangling from the steering column just for safety, stood on his knees, paws on the dashboard, checking the route.

Approaching at some speed, in the manner of small people driving large cars, appeared a six door Shooting Brake. Unsure of which side to pass an ambling Post Office van, its driver slowed. A cloud of burnt rubber, added further scent to the bewildering array, which at ninety miles an hour had assailed the nostrils of the biggest, tongue lolling Alsation, ever to hang a head out of a rear window.

Nothing goads a terrier more to blind fury than the sight of a large insolent dog. The enemy calmly bearing down towards Donald's guardians of the wheel could have been cocking his leg. In a blaze of eye popping rage they leapt at the wind screen. Hysterical yelps, teeth gnashing, tail quivering passion.

Small driver and large dog drew alongside. The chained terrors spiralled, savaged the side window. A derisory toot, a disdainful 'woof', the ostentatious car revved away. Loop the loop, figures of eight, the terrors flashed to the back window. Enemy escaping, bite free. Wind screen, side window, back window, hand brake, wind screen, gear lever, loops, spirals, snarls, froth, by now several turns of chain circled Donald's neck.

Those destined for greatness must have fate for a friend. Two yelping demons, chain straining length, fought at the back of a Post Office van. Donald's hands left the wheel, fought at his gasping throat. Crash barriers were yet to be, two wooden rails sufficed. With the gentleness of a sleigh alighting on a Christmas roof the little red van with barely a gurgle slid into the Beauly Firth.

Slowly the ripples smoothed away. The crimson rays of a summer night struck a perfect Yuletide glow. At water level, the matching face looking out wore a benign Santa smile. Reindeer might have to do, Donald carefully reasoned.

Erchless hill came alive. High on the Pollan ridge Ross Glengowrie alias 'Santa', waved away a dog in wide sweeping run to turn down a heft of sheep he had driven over from the north side of the ground. A shrill whistle halted his dog at just the point which offered the sheep a faint hope of escape. They poured down the face, leaps and bounces, ewes looking back, calling to lambs lost in the panic. We gatherers moved in. I still had Nancy, the great dog of my shepherding days in Strathfarrar, but gave most of the long runs to a keen young dog Lassie. Jealous of the new recruit, Nancy was hard to hold at heel when she knew from my voice that sheep were getting the better of Lassie. My eye, far out on the young dog holding a little stamping group of ewes on a knoll, would catch sight of the bonnie white collar and white tipped tail of 'experience' labouring to climb above the 'sticky bunch' and move them down. Though I knew her years felt the steepness, I hadn't the heart to call her back, it was an 'auld alliance', the hill was in old Nancy's blood.

We watched for the 'cuties' slinking into gullies, hiding in dead ground, we 'half turned' cuts of heavy coated ewes and sprightly lambs down towards the hill gate. Puffing 'dearies' to provide material for the knitting pattern, high pitched bleats to provided the tastiest Sunday roast, they filed past the 'control post' towards a bent nail and drooping net fank below the keeper's cottage, bossy Flossy in command.

The clack of shears and tongues, hazy sun and warmth, off with the shirt, the 'oldies' hung jerseys on the fence and rolled their sleeves. Much painful grinding in low gear had brought Ardochy's Morris Saloon up the steep loose track to the fank, and at middle day we gratefully watched the Councillor hobbled over to open the boot of his pride and joy. Sandwiches appeared. Ham, cheese and onion, the best that Beauly's stylish Lovat Arms Hotel could cut, but sadly, in a cardboard box since Friday, and twice at church on the Sabbath, they became enhanced with flavour of petrol to such an extent that Flossy, who journeyed to the 'gather' in their company was disinclined to pry, and Rod the Trapper, who ate and smoked, I feared might unwittingly perform the fire eating act.

Long evenings and droning midges are a Highland speciality. We'd had enough of scratching. Ardochy 'buisted' his red hirsel mark on the last creamy white side, we straightened our backs and light footed ewes streamed out to the hill. Another year's clipping past. The Struy Inn lay in sight and mind all day. Dunc the keeper hurried for a thirst quencher, Donald Ross, hardy man, headed back over the hills to Glengowrie, barely as briskly as the sheep for whom he'd worn his Santa yellow toed 'wellies' from first light. But the Councillor strode to the car with the step of a springbok, and I can now reveal with confidence to curious chiropodists that a sheep clipping cures corns.

WHERE IS THE EAGLE?

Brooding over Breakachy of the speckled fields is the old lichen grown fort of Dun Mhor. Rings of scattered stones set steep on a knoll still command the head of the rugged Teanassie gorge. Bygone ramparts, monument to the will of survival in an age over two thousand years past when Highland shoulders first bent to clear the woods and till the soil. Huts on the slopes of Craig Dhu and across the burn to the south face of Farley hill were homes to the builders of the fort. Circular houses, thirty feet wide, door to the sou'east, the banks of their walls three feet high showed clearly after a heather burning. I counted perhaps half a dozen homes in each settlement and wondered on kinship and a family life where nothing was hidden from the pangs of childbirth to the wastage of old age. Heaps of stone clearings piled on a boulder too hefty to move marked the boundaries of their loved fields. For these were the first farmers of Breakachy, men of the Bronze Age who broke the land, felt for the land, who told the weather in the sky, on their skin, who knew the power of the Moon and the Planets on the fortunes of their crops, who defended a heritage gifted by their Mother Earth. How strong their instincts, how innately resourceful in their means, how deep their respect for a natural world close to the reality of birth and death.

A spring evening, a last round of the lambing ewes and I would leave the lambs running their races on the slopes of the Carnich and climb the rocky face of Dun Mhor to sit awhile in the bowl of its ruins. About me the fallen ramparts, circles of shattered stone, hand quarried and carried, split by heat and water, fitted with skill. Aching backs and burst fingers, burns and scalds, prodigious labour amidst elemental living. And on the easterly knolls of Farley Forest lie four similar strongholds. Not a move or threat to their territory but could be spied down the length of the Beauly Firth to the great fortification above Inverness of Craig Phadrig, once the seat of Celtic King Brude, and it would appear from the careful sighting of these defenses that a signal could reach into the heart of Strathglass, to the duns that watched over the confluence of the Farrar and the Glass above the village of Struy.

I shaded my eyes. Far to the west a young May sun sank into the cleft of the Strathfarrar hills. Below me on Breakachy ground the heather tips of Loan a' Gower, the Flat of the Goats, glowed in the long spokes of orange light. Soon I knew the white collared Reed Bunting would perch on their tallest sprig chanting a croaky tune over the moor's marshy edge and the ground hugging Hen Harrier on drooping wing would float above the tussocks in search of chicks. The Golden Eagle nested high in the steep burn of Beinn a' Chlaonaidh hunting this area for the rich pickings of mountain hare and grouse. Often, as I lent my back to the old fort and quartered the hillside with my 'glass' it swept into the lens, the upturned fingers of mighty wings controlling an arrogant mastery of the air, and I would spot the rabbits scuttle under their shadow.

From my chosen eyrie I watched the shyness of spring slip across the land. I savoured her shades. Her catkin tassels, lemon tinted in the hazel gorge, hung above the emerald moss, her bravest yet humblest breath, born below the snows of a winter's tale. Against brightening skies the maroon winter brushes of silver birch burst into palest green, uncurling filigrees of nature's delight, willing the brown heather stems of frost bound nights to sprout and feed the nesting grouse. A tide of growth, gift of the lengthening day to the Maid of Spring, it swept to the ridges of crimson saxifrage, there to be crowned under the sailing clouds that dapple summer hills in the light and shade of life's fulfilment.

But that night, sweetest of all amidst the great panoply of spring's being, deep in the woodland's quivering leaf, tender, strong, filled with the passion of creation, came a spirit in song. Beyond the confines of such tiny form it rose and fell in a crystal melody that gave all a puny creature had to give, and in so doing, it touched the soul of immortality. I listened to the homecoming blessing of the little Willow Warbler. Home in an outpouring of sublime joy to the nest of its birth by the rumbling burn and swaying birch of the gorge of Dun Mhor.

And I remembered. I remembered the fox killing lambs on the field we called the Graveyard, and Johnny Fraser the keeper hunting the Teanassie burn. And I sat, rifle across my knees, on top of the old monument, waiting, watching, till the vixen, unhurried, came trotting, sniffing, listening. The yap of the terriers came, shrill ricochets on the rocks far below. Out along the track she came, through a wilderness of fallen stone, making for the safety of the open hill, and, simple, I raised a rifle to my shoulder, and she rolled. The terriers tore into her warm body, and I was sad.

And I sat. A silence fell, stealing the sun's failing light. A silence, hollow, touchable yet remote, that bade time and space fill the tomb of the dying hills. Each sound that broke their tryst with night stood alone. The quavering flute of a curlew, soft, low, then swelling, filling the flats with an exultant crescendo of wildest freedom, only to waver, to falter, to trail into the melancholy echo of an age when the turn of the stars set the pace of time in the lost corries of my mind. And in its glimmering void the throbbing snipe high above the rashy nest of a crouching mate saw another sunset, another world where veneration and wisdom went hand in hand. The ancient bond, the land and the heavens, strong in the circle of the stones was wrapped about me.

At last, in a lingering spy, my 'glass' drifted to the green ground of Urchany, heartland of Farley Forest, my thoughts to its cup stones, hollowed on flags of pagan mystery, to its tumbled shells of crofting times, falling forgotten into the long shadows. The last tenant towards the end of the century was a MacKinnon, but the sun facing slopes once carried six or eight families and the lines of dyke surrounding their scanty fields made homes for the skylark and the stubby tailed vole.

June in these croftlands was the month when crops were left to grow with little attention. They put ground to the tatties, a day at the hoe or pulled weeds in the corn, but there was all the time God made for neighbourly 'news' and a cow on the rope to the bull. The days went to the peats at the black banks of Farley moss. Communal days when the crofters of Kilmorack Braes tramped out the winding peat road beyond Cuil na Cleidhe. Men in baggy serge trousers carried long cutting spades, the women in ankle glimpsing skirts elbowed baskets of bannocks and cans of whey. They had much bending to barrow and spread the greasy peats and match the heave and grunt of their sweating menfolk. The nights were for trout on the dark hill lochans, the gloaming catch home on a stick.

At the turn of the century a freak summer storm washed out the road, and the horse and carts turned from treks to the hill for jolting loads, to queue down at Beauly pier where the 'Mary', an enterprising coaster, landed coal at ten shillings a ton. Though she was eventually wrecked in the Firth of Forth, she brought a millennium of peat cutting to a close. Except for Iain MacKay of Loch Monar, one time shepherding companion, recently retired after thirty odd years a stalker with the Red Deer Commission and now the last man of

Kilmorack to maintain the time honoured crofter's right to take fuel from the moss.

Long after the Urchany tenants left the land the fertility they built out of cattle dung and crop rotation remained. A wounded Lord Lovat home from Hitler's War saw the need to revitalise his estates and as a lover of livestock, a cattleman at heart, he was easily drawn to the romance of ranching. Highland cattle were set to graze the Urchany greens. Shaggy coats and sweeping horns maybe, but perhaps bred too long in the land of Goschen, winter took its toll and many died.

Lovat, with sound reason, judged men and bulls by their prowess on the field of action and headed for the Mecca of international cattle breeders, the auction mart of MacDonald and Fraser in Perth. Here we once met in its world renowned sale ring hemmed by the crush of Stetson hatted buyers craning their necks to buy Aberdeen Angus bulls. "Well Thomson you're far from the hills of home." "Not in spirit," I countered. He laughed and we talked of Strathfarrar, for throughout estates which straddled the Highlands from Arisaig in the west to Beauly in the east, perhaps the wildness of this glen made it his favourite. Soon it was to become the summer grazing for his noted herd of hill cows, for whilst in Perth he took the advice and shook the hand of the one armed cattle dealer Paddy O' Toole and bought cross Hereford heifers from the idolatrous County Donegal, and good Catholics, they throve.

Urchany is no longer Lovat land. Cattle, then sheep, and soon trees will cover the empty crofts, but its peoples burying ground remains untouched, simple and unmarked. And west of the flats, where the track leads to Erchless, a knoll carries the name Cnoc a Gillie Phatean, hillock of the Piper Boy. For sure of a quiet summer's evening the call of his pipes sounded across the greens. The folk at their doors would listen with pride, and in the soulful laments of their Highland race they live on.

I stirred, a faint mist rose on the flats. Lean winter stags came down to graze. In the gently changing light amidst indigo hills they stepped on a carpet of the palest pink. I turned east, the air chill, troughs of mist filled each hollow. Steady on a clear horizon shone the first star of evening, it's light steeped in memories of Dun Mhor, an eternal link with the spirit of it's people.

I looked about the old fort. A dew hinted frost, spiders had yet to spin, moonbeams sparked grains of mica, gems of an age before the defilement of knowledge. The ancients about me built again. Stone upon stone, blood upon blood, starlight and spheres. Matter and life, all exists in the endless cycle of creation and decay. Time, the mythology of man, cannot measure the soul of being. There is but change, death, and rebirth in a restless universe of immortal beauty.

I picked a way down, Nancy, my old dog of days on the high tops, tight at heel. Down through the Carnich and cudding ewes, down to a light in the kitchen and Hector and Alison feeding the orphaned lambs in boxes by the fire.

High on the keeper's list of unofficial users of Farley and Erchless Deer Forests during the 'fifties' ranked the name of Alex Murray. According to season, weather and a shrewd knowledge of the keepers whereabouts, young Murray, Captain of the clandestine Kilmorack Venison Appreciation Society, led sorties to the hill in support of the nutritional needs of a hard working crofting lifestyle. Able amongst his lieutenants on these 'sporting' sallies was Andrew Simpson, a Beauly boy, who after an inauspicious start to his farming career, a bankruptcy in Nairnshire, re-emerged as director of a Hull pet food company and a substantial Fifeshire landowner.

By no means outshone, Murray's career blossomed with equal vigour and colour. From Kilmorack orphan to Provost of the 'Fair City of Perth' is no small step on a ladder which started at fourteen on the rails of Inverness sale ring with the purchase of two pet lambs in a cardboard box for six shillings each. It stands today with the ownership of a hill farming enterprise in Perthshire spreading to thirty thousand acres, carrying seven hundred cows and five thousand ewes. Far sighted Beauly banker Kenny Morrison lent Murray his first pound in the days when a local banker's job was judging men and not merely submitting their cases to Head Office. His support did not go amiss. Whilst building this empire Murray was not idle on other fronts. He kissed enough babies to come within a nappy's whiff of going to Westminster as Scottish Nationalist M.P. for Dunbartonshire, he governed at the Agricultural colleges and the innovative Pitlochry Festival Theatre. He travelled to the Orient at the invitation of China's Ambassador, advising the Chinese on cattle projects and being feasted by the then Vice, now President of the Republic. Much other enterprise saw him in Australia, Russia and America. An extraordinary 'lad o' pairts' whose potential, one spring day on Erchless hill, might well have gone up in a puff of smoke but for the intervention of trainee venison handler Andrew Simpson.

In response to the War time 'Dig for Victory' poster, (a campaign which incidentally my grandmother took seriously, though with perhaps a variation on the slogan, by carrying the 'chanty' draped in a Union Jack down the garden each morning) a flock of Black face sheep were allowed by 'Whistling Willie MacKay' the factor, to graze Erchless hill and having done their bit for the country they remained, long after peace broke out, doing their bit for their owner Mr. Alec. MacRae of Ardochy. To cover any tracks suggesting irregular activity, Alex Murray, barely out of school, styled himself shepherd to this hirsel and strolled over the ground, in the interests of sheep welfare, with a nonchalant air not altogether shared by the 'The Councillor' as he noted the rifle which Murray boldly carried, butt below his 'oxter.'

In the month of March, a week of light easterly wind brought mornings with cat ice on the burn and days of cloudless skies that poured vitamin D on hill shepherds who, to a man, throughout the Highlands reached for their matches. Hillsides blazed, dancing flames dotted night skylines, fire fighting shepherds staggered home with singed eyebrows and young Alex felt he must join a brigade dedicated to creating tender green shoots for their sheep by this stimulating method.

A drift of smoke on the horizon was enough, the faintest tang of burning heather in the air and a shiver of excitement ran from Murray's nose to a matchbox. Summoning Simpson, "Hurry Andrew, it's a right day for a fire on the hill," and in the interests of 'Ardochy's' sheep the impulsive Alex struck but one light to a tuft of withered deer grass.

Crackle, crackle, plume of smoke, just a little fire. Puff puff, wicked wind, just a little gust. Whoosh, whoosh, licks of flame fanned out, leaping from tussock to tussock, soon a swirling inferno raced away. The great god Vulcan approved. In minutes a goodly portion of Erchless hill blazed before the startled gaze of the two boys. "It's got to stop somewhere," reasoned Andrew, a note of apprehension in his voice as a pall of smoke dimmed the sun and snow corries on Beinn a' Bha'ach Ard vanished into a purple haze.

Now wind, inside or out, plays a mischievous role in the affairs of man, and for a moment in the midst of the conflagration it held it's breath. Flames paused, clouds hung uncertain. Malice of forethought? A zestful breeze circled west, the fire wheeled about, hundreds of acres of fine young fir trees lay ahead. With the roar of an express emerging from a tunnel all smoke and sparks, it sped towards them.

Happy little Christmas trees were gleefully torched. Fireballs of red embers spurted into the dense black smoke that billowed skywards. The boys watched, horrified and helpless, stunned by the speed and ferocity of the blaze. "It's Fireworks night in daylight," whistled Simpson, "I'll tell you Alex boy, it mightn't be the Houses of Parliament but if Guy Fawkes could have seen this lot he'd burn a happy man." Mention of the master arsonist made a point. Waving arms his disciple shouted, "Help me Andrew, oh my God, we've got to turn the edge Andrew, we've got to turn it back on itself," and he ran in a gut gripping panic, jumping smouldering heaps of ash, to flail at the leaping flames with his jacket.

Feet stamping, heat searing, elbows over faces, the boys fought along the edge of a frightening, deadly advance. For every foot they killed a blaze sprang to life behind them. They were engulfed. Fire craves a victim. Alex fell.

Staggering to his knees, hands scorched, coughing and retching, acrid smoke biting his lungs, Murray stumbled again. He crawled, exhausted, trying to keep below the smoke, hot ash filling his nostrils. Flames crackled and danced about him.

Andrew, shielding his eyes, bent low and dashed in. Heat crinkled his face. Half lifting, carrying, he pulled the boy clear. Murray on his knees, gasping for breath, slowly came round. The wind dropped, the fire dulled as though disappointed. Two worried boys made for home, burnt, blackened and rancid with heather smoke.

Chisholm the keeper seeing the performance from far out on the hill ran to his house for the phone. Men appeared, fire brooms and sweat. By evening a frost closed in. The flames dwindled to a few wisps of smoke in the peat.

Old Mrs. Chisholm, the keeper's mother, whose early morning light I would see from the Erchless fields, was in her eighties. Glen Cannich saw the rearing of her own family and at Duncan's hillside cottage she had brought up his three children after the tragic drowning of his wife in the Beauly river. "Well Duncan," she said with reflection upon Murray's escape, "what's a few trees? They'll grow again."

Councillor Alec MacRae, Ardochy, strange to say, when the burning of a large area of trees came to an enquiry, barely knew the two 'irresponsible youths' involved and the issue was dropped. It was not however the last dealing the keeper was to have with the venturesome Murray.

The powerful shoulder of Pollan juts eastwards from the cairn topped peak of Beinn a' Bha'ach Ard and resting on this lonely limb of hill the deer find peace. It's broad carpet of broken stone and alpine moss is dry. Favoured little hollows are warm in the sun. A breeze is to be found, keeping summer's midges far below and bringing a timely warning of danger's scent. A dome of sky tells the weather on distant horizons to animals who know well it's moods. Ptarmigan and white hare are the hind's companions and once the sharp eyed Golden Plover kept watch. In a sense of well being and safety the deer lie content.

Peaty black gullies drain the quickening slopes that fall from the ridge. Their crumbling banks overhung by mats of green mosses, thick and juicy, are beloved of thriving stags rubbing proud new antlers clean of tattered velvet. But for man and rifle, they are the arteries of concealment into the heart of the high ground.

Hidden deep in a narrow gully which opened onto the broad back of Pollan, Alex Murray bent over the loose warm body of a newly shot hind. Sleeves rolled and a 'gully' from the sheath on his belt he worked quickly. A plump belly slit to the breast bone and the 'poch a buidhie' bulged free. Young Simpson watching Murray's expertise from the bank gently put down the rifle which moments before he had been pleased to hold, "What would you do Alex if Chisholm appeared just now?" Murray, blood to the elbow, pulling heart and lungs from the steaming cavity, spoke without pausing or looking up, "I'd be over that skyline faster than a stag." Andrew quietly cleared his throat, "Well boy now's the time, he's here."

The supernal figure of Chisholm loomed over the hollow, as silent and menacing as the means by which he had appeared. From deerstalker bonnet to hill brogues, an imposing man who ruled his ground without question. The Baron could make suggestions, shooting guests, no matter title or affectation, knew their place. As a wartime trainer of commandos in the wild country about Knoydart and Achnacarry Chisholm kept a party of men on the move for three days without food or shelter and happened to pass Iain MacKay's remote home of Pait at the head of Loch Monar. Telling Iain's mother years later of their trampings, she chided him, "Surely Duncan you could have taken the poor men in." There was always plenty venison and a welcome at 'Teenie' and old Kenny's fireside. "What!" snapped Chisholm, "and make the buggers soft."

Murray straightened as he swung. The full meaning of 'caught red handed' bore home. His knife in one hand dripped blood, the ripped out heart, gripped in his other, he let drop. Nothing moved save the trickle of water down the gully, it's sound instantly as loud as the tick of a discovered time bomb. Murray's eyes fixed on the keeper's brogues, well waxed he thought, in the detached manner of a mind on a doomsday countdown. Simpson's eye took in a large black beetle already crawling towards their kill. Chisholm's withering eye roved from hind to rifle, over the boys and round again. Neither words nor movement. Ominous appraisal. The stench of entrails, the first buzz of a fly. Nothing but wait.

Suddenly the keeper vanished, quick as he appeared. The boys sank onto stones, relieved eyes met, but some time passed before they peeped from the hollow. Of the hill man there was no sight. Longer elapsed before the shaken pair resumed work upon their quarry. Darkness was on them as they each carried half of the hind, haunches and forequarters on weary shoulders, down by the nodding gables and whispering ruins of the abandoned crofts of Urchany.

One of the 'perks of the job' allowed to the Erchless stalker, in the common order of the times, was the use of a croft for the grazing of two cows. Accordingly a couple of fine Blue-greys waxed fat as they say, on the fields about his house. Hay for the animals the Baron also supplied, delivered to the keeper's byre by Ian Cumming, the farm grieve, a man who graduated from pony man on the Scatwell estates of Strathconon to one of 'Monty's' men driving a three ton Army truck in the North African rout of General Rommel. From desert sand in his tea, victorious and relieved, he drove an amphibious 'duck' to put ashore the first wave of troops at the invasion of Sicily. Only slightly more relaxing, Cumming now raced round the Erchless policies in an open topped American G.I.jeep nursing the mechanical ailments of the farm's machinery and checking the tootling progress of tractor man 'Big Ackee Fraser' who filled the cab of his little 'Grey Fergie' with a combination of an ample girth and pipe smoke. Any extra winter feed beyond the Baron's largess, such as bruised oats, Chisholm invariably purchased, for convenience, from young Murray who passed up and down Strathglass at somewhat irregular hours and, as many thought, with a suspicious frequency.

Early one January morning as scarlet banners of cloud shone on the windows of Beaufort Castle and deer grazed low on hills of Burgundy snow, Alex shot a dark coated hind by the path that followed Loch Fada, the Long Loch, down the Lovat-Erchless march. Advancing daylight didn't favour the discreet removal of a carcass and the prudent Murray dragged it off the track to a cache, safe but handy. He was back on the croft, whistling with innocence, before his cattle could bawl for their morning feed.

Late afternoon turned crisp. Alex drove over to the yard at Ardochy. "O.K. if I leave the van for a whilie Alec?" he asked the 'Councillor' without reference to the mission on hand. "Surely boy," MacRae deliberately replied without comment. The tact of a Highlander naturally precludes the blunt enquiry of other races, but this occasion also required the avoidance of any possible complicity in Murray Enterprises. A parking fee would be another matter, unquestionably accepted, all with good grace and taste.

Darkness hurried, Alex hurried. Ahead lay the Long Loch, at rest below glowing white tops, a silken thread of water in softing light. Was that the knoll? Yes, he searched a defile, noted stones. Yes, he caught the musk of deer's blood dank on chilly air. "That's the spot," he murmured, and then, "damn it's away." Eye and instinct, a large nearby stone. Deep hoof marks cut into the soft turf, "Oh boy, loaded on a pony," Alex whispered. Only one person would take it. Senses flashed, alert, strung. A grouse cackled, another rose, he spun, hemmed by the hollow, he could be jumped. 'Devil tak the hindmaist', Murray fled, feet flew, heart pounded, Loch Fada just a stride. In Alex's mind the tactics of an ex-commando and those of an irate hill stalker could have much in common. They formed into one large menace, Duncan Chisholm. A meeting at this point would be unsatisfactory.

Regained breath, an outflanking plan and a composed Murray drove down from Ardochy to Beauly to plot counter action with a 'trusty.' That night, and knowing the keeper's habits, well after 'closing', the pair happened to be passing the road end which led to the Erchless larder. Alex needed a 'pee.' The van stopped. All innocence, all quiet, Murray dropped into shadow. The van pulled away with clear instructions, "Ten minutes, don't stop unless I put a white hankie on the dyke."

Never the door once was locked in Strathglass, the larder made no exception. Would Chisholm wait inside, ready to spring. Murray trembled, his hand cold as the clouds that parted to let the moon cast his silhouette on the larder's louvred windows. Did eyes watch? The doorknob seemed stiff, the lock turned back of it's own accord. Did a hand hold the other side? Clouds slid over a watching moon, darkness moved with the stealth of a stalk. Murray hesitated. Now, quick turn and push. The door burst with a thud against wall.

Murray stood rigid. Was that breathing? Somebody pressed into shadow? Tall black pine tops behind him speared wandering clouds. Moonlight flickered into the silent chamber. Icy fingers of light played on the white marbled spine of a hanging carcass. A beauty of a hind, firm from the round haunches spread wide on the cross tree pulley down fat covered ribs to a furry eared head left to stretch the meat as it set. All meticulously skinned and cleaned by the dexterous knife of the keeper.

Knife, keeper or no, Murray stepped in, 'gully' in hand. Slash round the neck, knife point into the spine, sharp twist, head off. Two cuts below the haunches, blade between the vertebrae, the 'moonlight visitor' had forequarters on his shoulder and keeping tree cover, behind the dyke in minutes. The heavy haunches took moments. Larder door closed gently, hankie on the stone, a panting Murray crouched. Lights came, dipped, slowed, passed. Had his 'trusty' been stopped? The 'blue boys' would flag down a van after midnight. Heart, two to the second, his ear caught the approach of an engine he knew. It stopped. Lights off, load aboard, no speaking, moments only. Turn up at Kilmorack Hall, relax, admire their work. A commando trainer might offer grudging praise. Commando leader and Murray's Laird, the fighting Lord Lovat would gladly have taken his tenant to the D-Day landings. Ten years separated Alex from that glory.

Ten days only however, the spoils mostly eaten and enjoyed, and a message filtered down Strathglass. Duncan Chisholm's cows were needing fresh 'bruise.' Murray loaded the bags, if not with a bout of indigestion at least a bout of misgivings. Bruised oats and reclaimed cache were both fresh, in mind and matter. Alex hurriedly unloaded the sacks at the keeper's byre. Chisholm had been waiting. Weather, sheep prices, a fox drive next month and then to the good condition of hinds that season. All passed in comfort for Dunc, for Murray, time was pressing. For an age when hours could be spent at will on the 'internet' of local affairs, quite understandably he shuffled towards the van at the first hint of venison on the screen.

"Well man Alex," said Dunc smoothly with a deep look at the bags, "I had a grand hind for you, but you know, some bugger took it." Perhaps Murray spoke a little too vehemently, "Away, is that so !" and shaking his head, "ah boy, you don't know who's about these days." "No indeed," replied Chisholm slowly with a hard look at the boy and, more particularly, without venturing to pay for the delivery. Murray with equal sense, refrained from asking, and they remained good friends in that unspoken understanding which made Highland living a pleasure.

Commando ridge bristles out of the heave of Atlantic swell in a hog's back of sound tactile granite on the edge of Sennan Cove, just a mile or two from Land's End. In the early '50's' I trained as an Army climbing instructor and sleeping under hedges made my way from bomb blasted Plymouth across Cornwall to join a course based at the Cove. Under the eye of the hard climbing men of half inch hand holds we spangled Sennan's cliffs with ropes and belays. The sea rose to cover rocks with an insolence and fell back with a sneer, a frothing mouth below our feet as we climbed. No downward glance for the weak stomach or faint of step.

Full Army kit weighs up to seventy pounds, hang on a rifle or a 'Tommy gun', it's a fair load. Leaping from rubber dinghies rising and falling in the swish of a swell onto slippery rocks carrying your full complement of kit and weaponry, scaling a ridge at the double, sometimes under fire, and it was training for men of iron grit. After two days we thought the ridge well deserved it's Commando name and I realised the brand of men that the late Lord Lovat welded together into some of the Wartimes toughest fighters.

To live childhood years through a war and witness the passions and the sufferings of the grownups, must have far reaching effects on a growing mind. The elation for a father coming home on leave, the brave tears at departure and the daily dread of the post. The anguish brought by the official black edged letter','We regret to inform you that your...' and the simple truth, 'has been killed on active service.' The raw edge of human emotion laid bare by a few words.

I saw the last war through eight year old eyes. I followed marching soldiers down streets, drilled like them, fought mock battles with any piece of wood resembling a rifle and gloried in the excitement of pretence warfare surging through innocent blood with an atavistic lust for killing. I admired the easy dignity and military bearing of a kilt clad Lord Lovat at the outbreak of hostilities striding down Stephen's Brae in Inverness, my aunt at the door of their Eastgate shop dropping a little curtsy and calling "Good luck, Sir." I stood by my mother in an overflowing church as head high she sang the sailor's hymn knowing my father at sea carried mines out to the Mediterranean,

'Eternal Father strong to save who's arm hath bound the restless wave...... O hear us when we cry to thee, for those in peril on the sea',and she remembered the formal letter which had brought the news of her brother's death on the battlefields of Mesopotamia a generation before. The same evocative hymn, sung with feeling, united the prayers of D-Day commandos awaiting embarkation for the Normandy assault. As Lovat remarked, 'Few men are atheists going into battle, fewer still in a shell hole.'

Perhaps the first World War primed the childhood mind of Lovat of the Commando Brigade for the dashing role he was to play in defeating the second rise of Teutonic hubris. His father, the 16th Baron Lovat who raised and commanded the Lovat Scouts to fight in the Boer War saw to the mobilisation of his men in the oak wooded parklands of Beaufort Castle. The theme, the 'bashing of Kaiser Bill by Christmas.' Upwards of two thousand mounted cavalrymen, tunics, cartouche belts, putties and breeches, paraded and drilled. Many were veterans who fought beside Lovat on the Veldt of South Africa. Endless lines of horses, avenues of tents below the castle walls, pipers playing the stirring tunes that rallied a Highlander's charge in scores of illustrious battles. The spirit of war was on wing and the fantasies of a three and half year old boy born to a long pedigree of fighting men were awakened.

Young Simon Fraser had already lost three uncles when the Highland Mounted Brigade, as they became known, sailed for the Dardanelles in 1915. His father's brother, Hugh Fraser, Second-in-Command of a Scots Guards Battalion was killed leading the gut slitting carnage of an 'over the top' bayonet charge at the battle of Ypres, where three hundred and forty six out of the four hundred front line officers were lost in three weeks of slaughter. Gallipoli proved even greater misery. An estimated quarter of a million men were lost in a debacle unrivalled in British military history. The plan was the brain child and direct responsibility of Winston Churchill, a fact well buried by 1940 under his rallying rhetoric for Britain's Darkest Hour, 'We shall fight them on the beaches.'

Lovat wrote home in 1915 from the shell pitted and disease ridden beaches of the Hellespont, 'No one can have any idea of the follies committed here. I have always had a poor opinion of the soldier politician but can hardly believe some of the stories that are apparently authentic.' The British and Anzac positions were dug into a great amphitheatre, the Turks sat on the surrounding hills. Any stalker will tell who has the easier shot. After six months there was still no fuel to boil water nor chlorate of lime to sterilise it. Myriads of flies buzzed over latrines which lacked any disinfectant. Lovat returned to East Anglia, wasted with dysentery, to command a cyclist division before returning to the front in France.

A mother's instinct is to keep her boys curls and pantaloons far into childhood in the vain hope of preserving the love and security for the 'little man' of a Peter Pan world. A father's sentiments differ, the boy must show the first signs of manliness, the earlier the better, be toughened up. Home from a long spell at sea, my father took one look at his three year old progeny and, "Let's have this lot off" was his greeting. A box on the barber's chair and four old pence put curls on the floor and me on the road to manhood. My skinniness was treated to porridge, malt and cod liver oil. Father's words, like commands on his ship, were obeyed.

A generation before 'hardening off' was more rigorous. Young Simon Fraser's father, promoted to General and home on leave with the voice of complete authority, needed but one glance at his son. Stripped to the skin, shorn of ringlets, a little velvet outfit flung in the bin, the General pronounced the boy too skinny and ordered a daily glass of raw meat juice. A daunting draft for a child to swallow at breakfast, albeit sweetened with brown sugar, but it was considered by father to be the elixir responsible for his recovery from a fever contracted whilst elephant hunting in the malarial swamps of Central Africa. A novel discovery, suitable or otherwise for a child, which the General had made during a feast of raw camel flesh served by an Ethiopian Emperor. Beyond this vampire juice the fledgling was ordered into shorts and instructed to run barefoot for the summer wherever he pleased, provided he got home for tea. Not for a Fraser the foppish aristocracy of little Lord Fauntleroy but the first taste of self reliance and freedom which the boy was never to surrender.

The bounds of adventure for country 'loons' were as far as young legs would carry them, danger lay not in a sick society but in feats of daring that turned to rashness. One summer my grandparents took a house overlooking the Beauly Firth, and on a day when seals basked in the sun and the tide left drying sandbanks from shore to shore it seemed to young minds no distance across to Redcastle. My father and his three brothers set out to take their Fraser cousins by surprise. Halfway over bare feet began to sink into deep mud, tiny creeks suddenly started to widen, with the tide washing their legs they turned, ran for their lives and didn't dare tell their mother.

Best of all the Lovat lands for the Thomson boys became the wild west frontiers of childhood imagination. Their aunt's 'but and ben', with it's iron beds, tin roof and rain water barrels, bore a suitable resemblance to the primitive living of pioneer days and from pine thickets along the trail Red Indian braves wearing goose feather head bands whooped out on the horse drawn Mail Coach as it 'galloped' down Hughton Brae.

In 1901 Colonel 'Buffalo Bill' Cody pursued by Redskins had galloped the 'four in hand' Dead Wood Stage round a circus warpath in Glasgow. A pantomime finale to a fine civilisation, destroyed by Western greed and gifts of disease riddled blankets. It took the nation by storm. Live Indian chiefs, Red Cloud, Kicking Bear and Sioux warriors found their enigmatic dignity, stealth and horsemanship the emulation of every child who strove to draw a bow.

Young Lovat's father along with Baden-Powell saw the spirit of the Redman, his wood craft ways, the loyalty to his tribe and reverence for the natural order of life as a template for the Scouting movement. From boyhood influence to the end of his days, Simon Fraser admired the Red Indian ethos and when in manhood he opened the famous Calgary Stampede it was to regret such a once proud people be reduced to a tourist attraction. He recognised an affinity with the Highland people of yore in their veneration of a common heritage, in the strength of a shared ancestry, and above all in the love of their native hills, ever for them the symbolic home of freedom, independence and space for the individual. Liberties fast vanishing under the suffocating weight of an international corporate dictatorship.

Human ingenuity as it tackles the frontiers of yesteryear's fables lacks the first mark of intelligence in any organic life form, the seeking of a healthy symbiotic lifestyle within sustainable environs. For the moment common sense and wisdom seem in short supply. Our inventive activities are modifying the environment at a rate which, without care, could well be outwith the genetic capacity of our species to adapt and survive. Will the ingenious human brain keep its flow of ideas and the changes they engender in step with the survival requirements of our current genome? The race is on. Ingenuity versus wisdom. Will it take Faith, sound scientific judgement or just good old fashioned luck to see us through?

Chief Seattle's reply to the 'Great White Chief' in Washington who made an offer for a large area of Indian land in 1854 makes this point, and is possibly the most beautiful and profound statement upon mankind's ultimate dilemma, his relationship with the soil and his soul. The wisdom of a 'savage' is worth noting by those who pride themselves on an intelligent influence on our future.

'How can you buy or sell the sky, the warmth of the land? The idea is strange to us.

If we do not own the freshness of the air and the sparkle of the water, how can you buy them?

Every part of the earth is sacred to my people. Every shining pine needle, every sandy shore, every mist in the dark woods, every clearing and humming insect is holy to the memory and experience of my people. The sap which courses through the trees carries the memories of the red man.

The white man's dead forget the country of their birth when they go to walk among the stars. Our dead never forget this beautiful earth, for it is the mother of the red man.

We are part of the earth and it is part of us. The perfumed flowers are our sisters; the deer, the horse, the great eagle, these are our brothers. The rocky crests, the juices in the meadows, the body heat of the pony, and man – all belong to the same family.

So when the Great White Chief in Washington sends word that he wishes to buy our land, he asks much of us. The Great Chief sends word he will reserve us a place so we can live comfortably to ourselves. He will be our father and we will be his children. So we will consider your offer to buy our land.

But it will not be easy. For this land is sacred to us. This shining water that moves in the streams and rivers is not just water but the blood of our ancestors. If we sell you land, you must remember that it is sacred, and you must teach your children that it is sacred and that each ghostly reflection in the clear water of the lakes tells of events and memories in the life of my people. The water's murmur is the voice of my father's father.

The rivers are our brothers, they quench our thirst. The rivers carry our canoes, and feed our children. If we sell you our land, you must remember and teach your children that the rivers are our brothers, and yours, and you must henceforth give the rivers the kindness you would give any brother.

We know the White man does not understand our ways. One portion of land is the same to him as the next, for he is a stranger who comes in the night and takes from the land whatever he needs. The earth is not his brother, but his enemy, and when he has conquered it, he moves on. He leaves his fathers' graves behind, and he does not care. He kidnaps the earth from his children, and he does not care. His father's grave and his children's birthright are forgotten. He treats his mother, the earth, and his brother, the sky, as things to be bought, plundered, sold like sheep or bright beads. His appetite will devour the earth and leave behind only a desert.

I do not know. Our ways are different from your ways. The sight of your cities pains the eyes of the red man. But perhaps it is because the red man is a savage and does not understand. There is no quiet place in the white man's cities. No place to hear the unfurling of leaves in spring, or the rustle of an insect's wings.

But perhaps it is because I am a savage and do not understand. The clatter only seems to insult the ears. And what is there to life if a man cannot hear the lonely cry of the whippoorwill or the arguments of the frogs around a pond at night? I am a red man and do not understand.

The Indian prefers the soft sound of the wind darting over the face of a pond, and the smell of the wind itself, cleaned by a midday rain, or scented by the pinon pine.

The air is precious to the red man, for all things share the same breath.

The white man does not seem to notice the air he breathes. Like a man dying for many days, he is numb to the stench. But if we sell you our land, you must remember that the air is precious to us, that the air shares its spirit with all the life it supports. The wind that gave our grandfather his first breath also receives his last sigh.

And if we sell you our land, you must keep it apart and sacred, as a place where even the white man can go to taste the wind sweetened by the meadow's flowers.

So we will consider your offer to buy our land. If we decide to accept, I will make one condition: The white man must treat the beasts of this land as his brothers. I am a savage and do not understand any other way. I have seen a thousand rotting buffaloes on the prairie, left by the white man who shot them from a passing train.

I am a savage and I do not understand how the smoking iron horse can be more important than the buffalo that we kill only to stay alive. What is man without beasts? If all beasts were gone, man would die from a great loneliness of spirit. For whatever happens to beasts, soon happens to man. All things are connected.

You must teach your children that the ground beneath their feet is the ashes of your grandfathers. So that they will respect the land, tell your children that the earth is rich with the lives of our kin. Teach your children what we have taught our children, that the earth is their mother. Whatever befalls the earth befalls the sons of the earth. If men spit upon the ground, they spit upon themselves.

This we know: The earth does not belong to man; man belongs to the earth. This we know. All things are connected like the blood which unites one family. All things are connected. Whatever befalls the earth befalls the sons of the earth. Man did not weave the web of life: he is merely a strand in it. Whatever he does to the web, he does to himself.

Even the white man, whose God walks and talks with him as friend to friend, cannot be exempt from the common destiny.

We may be brothers after all. We shall see. One thing we know, which the white man may one day discover – our God is the same God.

You may think you own Him as you wish to own our land; but you cannot. He is God of man, and his compassion is equal for the red man and the white.

This earth is precious to Him, and to harm the earth is to heap contempt on its Creator.

The whites too shall pass; perhaps sooner than all other tribes. Contaminate your bed, and you will one night suffocate in your own waste.

But in your perishing you will shine brightly, fired by the strength of the

God who brought you to this land and for some special purpose gave you dominion over this land and over the red man.

That destiny is a mystery to us, for we do not understand when the buffalo are all slaughtered, the wild horses are tamed, the secret corners of the forest heavy with scent of many men, and the view of the ripe hills blotted by talking wires.

Where is the thicket? Gone.

Where is the eagle? Gone.

The end of living and the beginning of survival.'

THE HIGHLAND CLANS IN
HEADLONG SWAY

The rising tide slopped round bodies with tin hats that bobbed grotesquely in the waves. Wounded men kept afloat by life-jackets, clung to stranded impedimenta. Barely clear of the creeping tide, soldiers lay with heads down, pinned to the sand. Half way up the beach, others dug themselves into what amounted to a certain death trap. The crumpled khaki bodies of the 2nd East Yorks Light Infantry were stacked in bunches.'

The landing craft crunched onto the shallows. Ramp down, Lord Lovat stepped cautiously into knee deep water. Piper Millin struck up 'Blue Bonnets are o'er the Border.' The Commando Brigade surged ashore. Twelve hundred battle trained men followed Simon Fraser up Sword Beach. A man of Norman blood, born to lead, nine hundred years could not quench the fighting lust, his ancestors conquered England, up a Normandy D Day beach he turned the tide in blood.

––––––––––

Lovat of the Scouts maintained that four men made Scotland a nation – Wallace, Bruce, Scott and Burns, and he believed the latter perhaps the greatest Scotsman of all. A seemingly incongruous view for a laird born to privilege, power and extensive possessions, when one considers that the Bard who helped forge the Scots character along the egalitarian lines of 'we're a' Jock Tamson's bairns', openly admired the writings of Thomas Paine, author of 'The Rights of

Man', a book which attacked the British monarchy and earned Paine an indictment for treason.

But Lovat who saw hardship in the crofting economy of the estate peoples and knew at first hand the horror of the 'trenches', rose above class prejudice. He treated the people of his estates who looked to him for a vestige of security with consideration. He valued them as friends and individuals and believed in a community of mutual respect. Returning soldiers were treated as heroes, jobs were found at Beaufort. Crofting rents, always low, were left untouched. Local village businesses were supported. Squads of men, carpenters, masons, foresters, gardeners, fencers and the rest found homes and employment on the estates. Lovat's enlightened attitude sought to use the resources available, be they fishing, forestry, shooting or farming, in the interests of maintaining a rural economy and to this end he spent a deal more on the properties than they generated in revenue.

The vast estates however were much in debt. The General's father Lord Thomas, who died of a heart attack on the grouse moors of Moy in 1887 left a legacy of woodlands planted over his lifetime. A hundred acres cut and replanted annually provided ready cash but failed to fill the financial hole.

Farming was on the slide, the hey day of shooting rents bagged from industrial 'toffs' was winged, and much of the high moorlands south of the Great Glen, Stratherrick, Corriegrath, Glendoe, Inchnacardoch and Ardachy found new owners, as did the idyllic west coast forest of North Morar. Lovat lands shrank by a hundred thousand acres. In Strathglass, nearer to home and to his heart, when Lord Derby's long lease of the Struy Estate came to an end it too went off with the rest, though at an exceptional price for the time. Twenty odd years later during the depression of the 'thirties' deer forest properties fetched no more than a pound an acre and Struy changed hands again for a quarter of the original figure to Sir Robert Spencer-Nairn, a 'lino' manufacturer from Kirkcaldy.

Energy, drive and an eye to wide horizons characterised General Fraser. Soon after the South African War he became involved with the Sudan Plantation Syndicate. Seven hundred thousand acres of inhospitable desert lying between the Blue and White Nile were transformed by irrigation into fertile cropping land which grew sorghum, millet and, most profitably, cotton. The value of the latter crop alone in 1933 reached two and a half million pounds. Management of this highly lucrative venture was in the hands of D.P. MacGillivray, the son of a tenant farmer in Stratherrick and one of thirteen children. Further proof that the large Victorian family didn't stymie enterprise, his brother, Capt. MacGillivray established the world famous Calrossie herd of Beef Shorthorn cattle on one of the finest farms in Easter Ross. More recently a nephew and grand nephew of the pioneer have become pre-eminent in

Scottish piping circles and Duncan, the latter, a composer and innovative player of Celtic music with the Battlefield Band. Lovat was suitably grateful to MacGillivray. Tenancies of two of the estates most fertile farms went to relatives of the cotton grower, one of whom Donald Fraser farming at Easter Lovat became a particular friend and many's the straw bale I carted up to Breakachy off the farm's stiff, horse killing clay.

Repeating the Sudanese formula in Brazil however proved something of a disaster. Lovat invested in the ambitious speculations of the Parana Plantations Land Co. and sent the young Master of Lovat to work on bridge building over massive rivers as a railway link was driven through the dense jungle to reach expensively cleared scrub land in an attempt to grow cotton. Unexpected frosts on the higher land made this impossible and the Company mistakenly turned to coffee at a time of glut when the 'locals' burnt dry beans as cooking fuel. Nor was fear of bandits and a Latin style revolution in the State of Sao Paulo reassuring features of the programme. A Maxwell cousin of young Lovat, transferred from Sudan as manager, died of typhoid and finally the Brazilian Government expropriated railroad and property for just a nominal sum. A capital failure, except for two Fraser boys who went out from the Lovat tenancy of Balacraggan as assistants to Maxwell. Turnip hoe to jungle machete, they established their own 'fazendas' and Simon, the elder, at least became a rich man.

If South America went sour then logging redwoods to the Pacific coast in British Columbia turned sweet. General Fraser, who became the first chairman of the U.K. Forestry Commission, was, like his father, more at home amongst timber, and his holding in the Canadian Forest Investments certainly payed much needed dividends which ultimately helped towards the substantial taxes levied on his death.

Back at Beaufort, Lovat busied with many local and national issues, the last in 1932 being a far reaching statement to Government on the Scottish economy and known as the Lovat Report. But the estate still cried out for money. Along with land sales his cattle breeding expertise helped the funds. The Beaufort Beef Shorthorn herd enjoyed a reputation for the size and substance of it's stock and in 1906 at MacDonald Fraser's Perth sale the bull Broadhooks Champion sold to the Argentine for the record price of 1,500 guineas, a figure not beaten for nearly twenty years. Success peaked in 1920 when at the Beaufort sale thirty-six head of cattle brought in the staggering total of 27,000 guineas. Staggering indeed, it is reputed that rejoicing cattlemen were happily indisposed for a week. Wholly understandable, for in those days a pound took reality into realms far beyond a sip of parsnip wine.

Brigadier-General Fraser saw to the coming of age of his eldest son, Simon, Master of Lovat, in the summer of 1932. Financial worries pressed. The celebrations were confined to local friends and the peoples of the Estates. Five hundred lunched on Beaufort lawn and in the afternoon cheered the 'slamp' youth of the district at Highland sports. John MacLean as the oldest tenant at ninety-six, presented Simon with a pair of Purdey guns, and on behalf of the employees, Duncan Cameron, forty years head Stalker in Glen Strathfarrar, gifted him with a little two seater car.

Only a year was to pass before Master became Laird. On a bitter day of snow showers Lovat watched his son ride at an Oxford point to point meeting. The chilling wind drove the crowd away but the Lovats waited. They left after the last race, Simon and his mother walking a little ahead of the General. "Go on, don't wait for me, I always walk slowly uphill," he called. When his wife next looked round, it was to see her husband fall. He died in her arms.

The remains in a simple coffin draped with the Union Jack were placed on a farm wagon drawn by a single horse. The long silent procession wound away from Beaufort up the strath to the chapel built by his grandfather at Eskadale. Snow crunched under leaden feet, winter sun through the branches of the great oaks lit on faces unashamedly weeping. Lovat Scouts who fought beside him in two wars lined the route, absent comrades lived again in their minds. Pipe-Major Willie Ross, son of a favourite Strathfarrar stalker, played 'Lord Lovat's Lament.' The Highlands had lost a great man.

The year was 1933 and Simon Fraser at twenty-two became the 17th Baron Lovat, laird of the lands which had given him carefree childhood freedom and pleasure in their woodlands and burns. Companionship also with some of the quaint old characters about the estate, for the young Simon was inclined to be solitary. Willie Fraser known as 'the moon' became the boy's mentor in matters such as the names and meanings of pipe tunes, the 'Tunes of Glory', Cogath na Sith that rallied the Highlanders at Waterloo, The Heights of Alma of the Crimean War, they were all played, for Willie was a master of the bow, and each stiring history told. He taught the eager boy to fish; worms from the garden and an old 'two-piece green heart rod, the art of tickling a trout under the grass bank, the fun of pike fishing from a boat with floating wine bottles hanging a wire trace and a bait.

Bird life abounded on the wide 'policies' of the estate and the old man schooled his young friend to know their songs from a merest snatch hidden deep in spring flowering shrubs, their nests from the linings each species would use. The names he gave bore a note of affection. Titmice were 'bluebonnets', the skylark, the 'lavrock', a song thrush, the 'mavis' and amusingly the cuckoo became the 'gowk', an Aberdeenshire word for a fool. The boy learned country ways through the eyes of an old man whose reverence for the enchanted world of the 'Little People' prevented their journeying beyond the great beech wood into the Boblainy.Forest.The same beech wood frightened my father as a boy with it's mysterious 'Will o' the Wisp' light flitting over the ground when he ran home to the croft late of an evening.

Out on the farms the laird to be knew the horseman harrowing on the 'black ground' smiled as the orange billed 'Seapie' trailed her wounded wing in pretence, and would take a sweep to avoid her three speckled eggs in their scrape amongst the stones. Or the plover with a frenzied 'peewit, peewit' would swoop at his bonnet in a loud beat of wings and taking care he would spot her mottled chicks running in the young corn before his roller. The 'turn of the day' would have passed and the skylark's brood strong on the wing before honeyed hay meadows white with clover fell to the clatter of a horse mower. The stench of sprays had yet to come, a farming life and the food it produced were wholesome, and in the diversity of the land, there was room for all.

'The moon' gained his by-name from his father and like his father he polished, trimmed and lit the scores of oil lamps which gave the castle a medieval glow. Mornings were spent shining shoes and as Lovat writes in his evocative memoir 'March Past' –

'In the stately homes of England Willie Fraser – The Moon – might have been described as 'The Boots'. No such thoughts were entertained at Beaufort for a friend who bore the same name as his chief and whose forebears, two fearless brothers, had fought and died in the Highland centre when the clans charged at Culloden'.

Scotland's story in legend, folklore and poetry fired a young mind through the tales read aloud by his mother, often as they travelled up by train from England, for she was a daughter of Lord Ribblesdale and due to the war Lovat spent childhood years on his grandfather's properties in the south. Perhaps of a melancholy turn her quotations dwelt on heroic tragedies. Glencoe's Massacre, death in victory of Bonnie Dundee with the charging Highland clans at Killiecrankie, the Duke of Montrose, the Highland histories of clan rivalries and the bloody deeds of the Wolf of Badenoch or the Lords of the Isles. For good measure the doom and death prophecies of the Brahan Seer were added.

But Lady Laura, as she was known, was of the Tenant Border blood on her mother's side and, brought up in a glen above Traquair, she revelled in the poetic sagas of Scott; Marmion with it's high intrigue and death on Flodden field, or true love and the magic book of Melrose Abbey in his 'The lay of the Last Minstrel.' A vivid imagination swept her son and his sister Magdalen into her favourite Land o' Burns, Souter Johnnie she brought alive, and Tam o' Shanter in his terror led two entranced, slightly frightened children, into the world of fey. Fairy rings in the short grass of woodland glades, hollow trunks that made tunnels into the underworld, green pools where fairy women washed their clothes, the grounds of Beaufort with it's stone bridges and winding tracks was home to beliefs now sadly smiled out of existence. But for two children who loved the countryside in all it's unfolding magic, witches and warlocks, hobgoblins and wee folk made bewitching days and filled their bedtime dreams.

'And ever by the winter hearth
Old tales I heard of woe and mirth,
Of lovers' slights, of ladies' charms,
Of witches spells, and warriors's arms,
Of patriot battles won of old
By Wallace wight and Bruce the Bold;
Of later fields of feud and fight,
When pouring from their mountain height
The Highland clans in headlong sway
Had swept the scarlet ranks away'.

Betrayed in the fastness of Assynt, the Royalist Montrose whose battles and indomitable courage fed the yearnings of a clan chief, was led through Lovat lands, tied on a shelty, past Phopachy point and it's sweep of the northern hills, to ask a drink at a well above Clachnaharry. Montrose's well to which my father took me as a boy and told the tale of how the mincing Baillies of Inverness offered their sympathy for the plight of the noble prisoner, to which the proud Duke graciously replied, "And I regret to find myself the object of your pity."

Though Clan Fraser suffered greatly in Montrose's wars his epic deeds, a brilliant night march over the Corrieyarrick Pass out of Lovat country, stung the spirit of young Fraser and he was to write sixty years later, 'Scotland's proudest soldier has remained my personal hero.' Unknowingly or not, a mother's profound influence, through story and verse, shaped her boy towards the image of a destiny, which birth and blood demanded of him, in heroic action.

Ferocious lightning strikes were commando tactics and such were the passions of terror and hatred they aroused that orders direct from Hitler in 1942 demanded any commando captured be slaughtered to the last man. A reward of one hundred thousand marks was specifically offered for the proscribed heads of Simon Fraser and a fellow officer David Stirling, dead or alive. Proof, if needed, that Lovat had brought his 'green berets' to the peak of fighting fitness and cold blooded efficiency, a task which only a man of his determination could have achieved. The path was not easy and Lovat's temperament did not always help. He detested the 'double standards of gutless politicians with the clammy hand' and his contempt for the floppiness of certain of the Army 'Top

Brass' was ill disguised. The name of General Ironside, Commander in Chief at the outbreak of hostilities, rhymed suitably, Ironside, backside, fireside, and as a linguist the General spoke nine languages, but, it was remarked did not make sense in any one of them.

Attitudes of this nature quickly brought Fraser into conflict with the Colonel of the Lovat Scouts, the Yeomanry regiment raised by his father and the most natural for him to join. Both the Commander in question, a man with a 'meticulous grasp of non-essentials', and one of his second in command, happened to be bankers, a profession of which Lovat wrote, 'Bankers are men who offer you an umbrella when the sun is shining, and ask for it back as soon as it starts to rain'. Storm clouds gathered.

Nothing infuriates Army authority more than the hint of a smirk or a laughing twinkle looking an officer in the eye. On parade, kit and horse in 'The Blues', an inspecting captain queried of me, "What have you done to your cap trooper?" "I restyled it Sir," "Why?" "I thought you would like it Sir," "Corporal-Major," he screamed, "put that man under arrest." Lovat stepped much closer to the quicksands of insubordination.

The Scouts officers billeted at Beaufort, and, in spite of a ton of coal a week passing through the bowels of it's boiler system, the long passages were a mite chilly. Banker number two requested of Lovat's young wife Rosie the supply of a 'po' to save him a shivering night walk across to the landing loo. Sniggers reached a Colonel already smarting over the previous placing of his pet Sergeant-Major under close arrest for appearing drunk enough on parade to fall off his horse before a night training march which Lovat led across the Black Isle.

A bayonet fencing incident where an N.C.O. under Lovat's training regime got a neck scratch was flagged up as mutiny, men with bleeding feet complained to the Colonel over the pace set on route marches round the Braes of Kilmorack, and worse, an unfit soldier from H.Q. put on training died of heart failure. Matters came to a head. An expeditionary force was mooted to help our Norwegian allies. The Scouts, hill men, sharp shooters and fit, seemed the obvious choice to Lord Lovat and others, but Colonel Melville stepped in at War Office level declaring these men were not infantry trained.

Melville took his usual weekly meeting at Regimental level. Norway was not mentioned, instead the question of the suitability of a blue patrol uniform for N.C.O.'s headed the agenda. Asked for his opinion, Lovat exploded, "I happen to be a poor bloody soldier, not a haberdasher!" Nobody says 'bollocks' to the Colonel with impunity. The meeting broke up.

Lovat was offered a transfer or face a charge of insubordination. Virtually a mutineer, his supercilious manner and aggressive attitude to training had almost proved his undoing. It was yet to prove his strength.

At home music helped. "This is the B.B.C. nine o'clock news read by Alva Liddell." Dunkirk, the Fall of France, the Blitz, the Nation almost faltered. My mother played and sang the songs of 1914, 'Dolly Gray, Tipperary, Pack up your troubles', it seemed to help, and once going on the piano she would play Ragtime, 'Oh you beautiful Doll, Lily of Laguna.' My father would join in from Marr's Collection of Highland Airs. He carried the thickest black hair out to his fingertips, I can see his hands playing with hesitation, there were no pianos aboard ship, 'Highland Laddie' and strange to say, as I write today, he played slowly and with feeling, 'Lord Lovat's Lament'.

Trains full of troops sleeping on their kitbags in the corridors took my mother and I north. Dawn and the Grampians, clean and fresh, flickered through grimy carriage windows, the sun on their shoulders, a pureness in their torrents, and the men rubbed the stubble on worn faces and looked out. Or perhaps an air raid on Glasgow halted the train for hours in Carstairs and the men sang the songs of Harry Lauder, greatest of troopers, 'Keep right on to the end of the road'. But from her rocking chair in Inverness, old granny scowled at the wireless when it blared 'There'll always be an England', "What about Scotland?" she fumed, dropping a stitch in the square she was knitting for the troops.

Yet the tragedies of war drew the Nation together, the sorrows suffered by each family drew communities together, only the selfish few chose to profit in petty ways below a burgeoning spirit of defiance that soared with every Spitfire that banked and dived in 'dog fights' over the Channel.

Food supplies were in jeopardy by 1940/41, 'U' boats stalked the sea lanes, the German fleet held North Atlantic convoys to ransom. The battle-cruiser Bismarck harried the Western Approaches, shipping went to the bottom, she must be stopped. H.M.S. Hood engaged her south of Greenland. News came through one morning. Our radio sat on a dresser, three knobs and a yellow dial, wicker-work over the front, a speaking face to my childish imagination. "The Admiralty regret the loss of the battleship H.M.S. Hood in action today in the North Atlantic". For long my mother stared out into the garden as though watching a blackbird that hopped a pace or two, cocked it's head and listened for worms on the newly wet lawn. Turning with a start she hurried upstairs. A favourite cousin loaded shells in the Hood's magazine, the bulkhead doors would be locked as the ship went into action and she prayed he didn't suffer the horror of an incarcerated drowning. He was twenty-two, a brilliant Cambridge student, one of fourteen hundred who perished. The sinking Bismarck took two thousand souls.

From the cargo vessels that got through, my father's ship, the Northern Coast, was constantly at sea those years, shipping supplies out of Liverpool to Northern Ireland and the Scottish ports. Day and night, in on the tide, discharge, out on the next. All harbour lights, marker buoys and lighthouses were switched off, not even house lights blinked out some guidance. Navigating at night simply by compass, log and a knowledge of the skyline set against the stars was wearing on the nerve. Unless they steamed in open waters my father remained on the bridge. Gales, fog or poor visibility demanded seamanship and instinct to tackle Cape Wrath, the Pentland tide race and miss the shipwreck laden Skerries. Sometimes they led ships bound for the Americas to a convoy rendezvous with their destroyer escort off Loch Ewe in Wester Ross. Often at night, they sailed, up through the Inner Hebrides and the narrows of KyleRhea, big vessels following the faintest stern light on the 'Northern', nose to tail and no room to swing. But mostly the old cargo ship ventured alone and unprotected, hugging the coast, taking inner channels, familiar with every barnacle from Larne round to Leith, risking submarine or shipwreck.

The Minch and her blue islands, the Shiants, lay in gentle mood, sheltered from a light north westerly breeze by the hills of Harris. Strong tides surround these islands, bountiful fishing grounds for the countless seabirds whose summer home is their cliffs and salty turf. In the pellucid light of a June day, squadrons of puffins flew in formation to their nesting burrows on Garbh Eilean, bills hung with rows of sand eel. Rafts of guillemot rode a slow swell off the point of Eilean Mhuire, the sacred island of the Virgin Mary, and out where an ebb tide put it's trail on the sea, solan geese, perhaps from Saint Kilda, made plumes of spray as with folded wing they plummeted into an early shoal of herring.

The 'Northern' brought the Shiants abeam, twenty miles south of Stornoway. The Minch glistened. The cry of squabbling gulls carried over still water. A wavering drone alerted the crew. Action stations. Roaring out of a cloud stooped 'Jerry'. Cannons strafed the decks. Bullets whined, splattering the bridge. A stick of bombs, plummets of spray, a hit in the fo'ard hold. The bomber banked, a second run, the kill. The crew blazed with a Bren gun mounted behind a rigged up canvas. My father swung the helm, corkscrewed the ship. Next run a miss. The 'Northern' sinking by the bow, lost speed. The bomber pilot climbed, he had time.

A high pitched whine, a Hurrican on Atlantic patrol roared in. The Dornier weaved into slipping turns and fled. 'Our boy' hung on. The ship's crew waved and cheered. A waggle of fighter wings and the planes disappeared over the Ross-shire hills. The tide turned. Seabirds fished again on the flood. An anxious crew worked their crippled ship into Stornoway harbour and my father put her onto the beach. That night news of the action came on the midnight bulletin. Worrying days passed before my mother knew the men were safe.

———————

The fall of Norway and Sweden, both neutral countries, in the spring of

1940 gave the German Reich the 'U' boat bases it needed to tighten the Atlantic tourniquet and secure the vital Swedish iron ore required to keep the Krupp conveyer belts of the Ruhr churning out armaments. A British Expeditionary Force floundered in winter conditions. German ski troops invisible in white overalls swept down snow slopes and mauled retreating men. Remnants of the 5th Scots Guards fought to the final evacuation from Narvik. Casualties were heavy, my sister's Orcadian husband was picked up with head wounds after ten hours in the water. Heroic action on land and sea but a debacle of War Office planning and the bitter row it provoked amongst the armchair fighters of the House of Commons brought to power Winston Churchill.

Lovat chafed, 'In war it can be hell to hang around'. A phrase used in his Memoirs which perhaps hid the poignant grief felt at the sudden death of his youngest sister Rose when only a girl of fourteen. There is no death so sad as that of the young, the snuffing out of innocence and promise and all the aspirations of youth, before the cynicism of age.

Action came. Churchill understood that the spearheads of brilliantly led German Storm Troopers had achieved the defeat of France, and he wrote, 'There will be many opportunities for surprise landings by nimble forces accustomed to work like packs of hounds.... we must develop the storm troop or commando idea'. The Chiefs of Staff were reluctant, several shambolic raids had been made on the French coast and the Channel Isles by enthusiastic 'privateers' with blackened faces and Tommy guns. Churchill enraged at such tomfoolery appointed Admiral Sir Roger Keyes, Director of Combined Operations. Two thousand volunteers went into a battle training programme of assault landings, cliff scaling, small arms fire and mountain craft. The Commando became a reality. Sir Roger's master stroke? Shimi Fraser drafted into No.4 Commando to lead a barbarous training regime in which any cut throat pirate would have felt at home ('At night it is a simple matter to kill a man walking with the moon behind him') It turned his men into the toughest bunch of desperados in the British Army.

Nor was Lovat above the type of risky prank which endeared him to the men. No.4 Commando waited in Scapa Flow aboard H.M.S. Queen Emma, a hastily converted channel steamer which brought them to the Orkneys as the jump off point for a raid on the Lofoten Islands. A stiff breeze put a goodly chop on the Flow, it seemed an ideal opportunity to try out the seaworthiness of the ship's whaler. Threatening snow and a rising wind reduced willing hands for the trials to Lovat and a New Zealand Lieutenant-Commander who felt confident of his nautical skills.

Downwind they swept, wave top to wave top, exhilarating for men and boat. Only the Commander's consummate skill saved them from flying over the submarine defence boom neatly stretched across the narrows of the Flow. The wind rose to half a gale. A wet plunging return and a seamanly circle of the Emma brought somewhat premature cheers from the men, for on the run in the bungling of mast and sail wrapped the mariners in a cocoon of canvas. Feeling free the jaunty craft tore away. Swoops and dives, tumultuous cheers, she skimmed amongst the anchored fleet, a disorientated swallow on migration. A disquieting bump halted her flight, they smacked into the skyscraper side of the pride of the Royal Navy, the newly commissioned battleship King George V. The hierarchy of the Home Fleet glared down, all gold braid and furious red faces. In the lee of the grey giant the Lieutenant-Commander disentangled himself from the rigging and the pair scuttled back to the cross channel packet, prowess tattered as the sails.

North of the Arctic Circle, just off the Norwegian coast, the Lofoten Islands were principally important to the Axis war effort for their extraction and supply of cod fish oil, a product used in nitro-glycerine manufacture and the vital component of a high explosive. 'Operation Claymore' set sail. Emma and her sister ship Beatrix with their complement of commando slipped out of Scapa on the first day of March 1942 and headed north escorted by the destroyers Afridi and Somali. Aim? Gutting the enemy's fish processing plant.

Surprise was complete. The citizens of the town of Svolvaer seemed, understandably, to be in partial hibernation. Darkness and an intense frost covered a considerate eight-thirty landing. Numb with cold, No. 4 Commando, tucked into small boats, sped from Emma's side to the docks, up iron ladders onto the quay and swarmed over the wharf. Armed to the teeth, tripping and slipping on the litter of frozen cod heads, they followed a stench, some thought a gas attack, to objective one, the fish factory. Police station, post office and town hall were quickly seized. Within a hour demolition commenced. Yawning Norwegians emerged to watch, and by ten o' clock the rejoicing townsfolk had a gala reception organised. Flags were run up, refreshments appeared. The Commanding Officer of the exercise stepped out from Control H.Q. to inspect the Harbour Master's cellar and had it's contents distributed to the crowds on the street outside. Troops wandering away from roadblocks and snipers from rooftops to converge on the telephone exchange from which a flow of insulting, if not downright vulgar telegrams, were dispatched direct to Hitler.

A rumour surfaced. Suspected German garrison in the next village. The O.C. swiftly rang the sales bell in the Fish Market where some of the lads had gathered and were engaged in pumping up a primus to make tea. A strong fighting patrol, all lusting for a crack at the 'Bosch', quickly volunteered and a string of commandeered vehicles set out over the snow packed roads led by a fish lorry with a Bren gun crew perched on the cab. Lovat with a fellow officer, Michael Dunning-White at the wheel and a Norwegian toying nervously with a loaded revolver, filled the front of the command vehicle.

The column chugged round bends along the shores of the fjord. Keen eyed and knowledgeable, Lovat pointed out a flock of snow buntings feeding on seeds in the horse manure which trailed ahead on the road. The birds twittered away up the hillside. Lovat swung his knees from the dashboard to follow their flight, the driver craned his neck to see them. Round a blind bend slap into a file of marching Germans.

Instant reflexes, a Norwegian finger tightened with shock, a heavy bullet smacked into the panel where seconds previously Lovats knees had rested. Cordite fumes filled the cab. The swerving lorry crashed onto the parapet of a bridge. A curving trajectory plummeted the Bren gun crew into the snow and in a stunt man roll, Fraser, glad of his knees, was amongst the enemy. German hands shot up. One bolder than the rest threw a canvas satchel in to the river. Two steps, a left hook from Lovat and the man followed his papers over the parapet.

Friend and foe milled about the road. The Bren gunner, furious over the breaking of his dentures in the crash and egged on by the remaining Germans who indicated that the swimmer was an ardent Nazi whom they would be glad to see removed, had to be restrained from taking pot shots. Mercifully the man and satchel were hauled out and marched off with the prisoners.

In cheerful mood the regrouped patrol chugged off again to attack a signal station flying the Swastika. Short bursts of the Brens at the door and windows rapidly drew results. The occupants fled by the back exit into the arms of a reception from the rest of the patrol. The crash of crowbar on delicate transmitting equipment brought wails from the signalling boys, there was not it's equal in the British Army, 'Beautiful stuff, please don't smash it Sir, I can't keep my hands off these dials and buttons'.

'Operation Claymore' had been a swashbuckling success, factories smouldered, twenty-two thousand tons of shipping turned turtle, and over two hundred and seventy German prisoners and Norwegian quislings were crammed into the holds of returning ships. The population stood on the quayside booing and hissing the prisoners, cheering their fellow patriots who left to fight with the Allies. Re-embarking commandos slung with plunder staggered aboard. Everything from fountain pens to a barrel of aquavit, slung aboard with block and tackle. Lovat's share of the loot? A fleece lined, rawhide Luftwaffe coat was a perfect fit along with woolly flying boots.

Sadly, back in the Clyde, the chair-bourne Ministry of Economic Warfare took charge. Kit inspection. Confiscation of all trophies. The Luftwaffe coat went on the pile, but not the boots as Lovat nonchalantly strolled down the gang plank.

'Set them on fire.' he ordered, with a gesture at the surrounding buildings, 'Burn the lot.' Not the words of a commanding officer in the British Army. They were the order of a Highland Chief bent on the total destruction of the enemy. Centuries peeled back, the light of burning Castle Dounie blazed in his eyes.

Military experts have described the part played by No.4 Commando in Dieppe raid as one of the most successful operations of the war. Hard training under Lovat tuned the men to 'concert pitch.' The hills of Achnacarry and the sea inlets of Arisaig reeled to the blast of Bangalore torpedoes cutting through barbed wire entanglements, 2-inch-mortars dropping into practice squares at 200 hundred yards, the constant rattle of small arms fire drilled holes into dummy men. When the raid came, split second timing and steel nerve were added to the fray.

'We all felt Shimi Lovat had planned the attack on the battery brilliantly. In the planning stage he had to contend with those who wanted it done differently, but he was strong minded enough to get his own way. Once the operation had started, he led and controlled it perfectly. Informally attired in corduroy slacks, a rifle hung rakishly from the crook of his arm, he looked as if he were out for a pleasant day's shooting on the moors.'

'Close quarter fighting is a messy business.' The Dieppe raid suffered it's fill of gut spilling horror. Number 4. Commando had the supreme task of destroying the heavily fortified gun emplacements that covered the entrance to Dieppe harbour. Failure? The German artillery would have the ships of the main landing force for target practice. Lovat's briefing left his men in no doubt.

Down bumped the ramp of landing craft below a rock strewn gully, banks of barbed wire, a patrolling sentry. Duck. Holes to blow, now lads. Seconds counted, rifles cracked, a German toppled from the tower, heads bobbed. In a brilliant pincer assault Lovat led his men to the rear of the battery. Grenades into the gun pits, splattered remains. Fix bayonets. Charge. Screaming commando, razor steel blades made streaming blood.

A rifle shot. A wounded commando lay prone. His assailant emerged from a building, in sheer hatred his boots crashed down on the dying man's face. A commando corporal took aim. The German clutched spilling entrails. They finished the beast with bayonets.

A black pall of smoke clung to silent gun pits. On the shore Lovat yelled the Navy to come closer. "No reason why I should get my feet wet," he said.

The main frontal landing to capture the port of Dieppe was a War Office armchair experiment to test the feasibility of invading Europe from onshore facilities. Talk was loose, the date of attack was changed. 'Jerry' knew we were coming and was ready. Six thousand men, mostly action innocent Canadian boys from the prairies, were fed to the withering fire power of von Rundstedts prepared fortress defenses. Just over two thousand returned. Bickering and back stabbing at the highest level of command resulted in no loss of life, a little hurt pride perhaps. Lovat led from the front, a fighting commander who cared for his men and shared their chance of death. 'I hold the raid itself was a disaster and the changed plans nothing short of suicidal.' The Crosses prove him correct.

'Who dares wins', the fierce slogan and resolve of Number 4 Commando epitomised the spirit of all ranks. Trained to coiled spring fitness, they waited the signal 'Operation Overlord.' D Day was on lips. A tense nation hung by news broadcasts, by every street corner paper stall, "Express, Express, read all about it." Husbands and sons waited, khaki and forage caps. Smiling through tears, never were partings so deep, a last kiss so loving, the walk away from the station so heavy.

June 6th 1944 and the greatest sea bourne invasion ever mounted, 156,000 men under Montgomery, supported by 8,000 ships and 13,000 planes were to breach Hitler's Atlantic Wall. The formidable task allotted to the 6th Airborne Division and the 1st Commando Brigade under Brigadier the Lord Lovat, DSO, MC, was to hold the left flank of the Allied bridgehead.

A tall immaculate leader, dignified and decisive, addressed his four units of Commando on the morning of the 5th. Without pomp or cheap appeals to patriotism, Simon Fraser spoke simply. He congratulated them on being chosen to fight together for the first time as a Brigade, the cutting edge of a striking force. It was better to attack than defend, the break through would mean fierce fighting by direct assault. Each commando would leap frog past the one in trouble, there would be no pause to slow the speed of a thrusting attack. "The Brigade will make history, I have complete confidence in every man taking part," and, he ended with a touch of whimsy, "If you wish to live to a ripe old age - keep moving tomorrow."

At 18:00 hours the Commando sailed down the Solent, setting out to war. Twenty-two craft in line ahead. Lord Lovat's piper played from the leading bow. Clear and wild across the water, a stirring cry, down from hill and torrent, the call to battle brought the centuries close, filling men with the spirit of the fighting clans of old, the memory and pride in a forefather's glory. The crews and troops on ships began to cheer.... the cheers came faintly across the water, gradually taken up by ship after ship.

Dawn, twelve miles to the coast, the battleships of the British Navy opened fire, Warspite, Ramillies, and the old cruiser Ajax of the sinking of the Graf Spee. Yellow flashes caught morning cloud, fifteen-inch guns hurled one ton shells onto the batteries surrounding Le Harve. Fearsome salvoes whined overhead, soon joined by a roar from the horizon, formation after formation of bombers, wing tip to wing tip, Lancasters, Liberators and Flying Fortresses.

Blockbuster bombs pounded installations. Thudding, crunching earthquakes. At head ducking level in swept fighter planes, Spitfire, Mustangs, strafing the invasion beaches. Joy sticks back, a powering climb, hard over, side slipping turns, in again, cannon shells tearing lines of puffs across the dunes. Wet and sea sick Commando closing on Sword beach looked up, cheered and sang. The planes turned home, their deafening orchestra of destruction faded.

Spouts of water slashed in patterns about the landing craft. Smoke weaved, enemy shelling made direct hits, boats were burning. "Stand by with the ramps – lower away there." From the command craft Lovat led, prodding the depth with his wading stick. Piper Millin played the men up the beach, battle hardened men aghast at the carnage of dead and dying infantry, crumpled khaki forms at the water's edge. Bullets sprayed the scene. Twelve hundred kit laden Commando fanned out and covered the sands in a record sprint.

Companions fell, brave men risked their lives to help. Smashed men made light of wounds. Lance-corporal Cunningham, the smallest man in the Commando, had his legs shot from under him as he ran up the beach. Carried to the dunes by big Murdoch McDougall, he swore, "To think they could miss a big bugger like you, those f—ing Germans, and then ———— well chose to pick on me." Though shot through the knees and both trouser legs soaked with blood, the hardy little man hobbled round patching up more wounded before following the advance with the help of his Brigadier's wading stick.

A soldiers battle. Throwing down rucksacks the commando surged on, hand grenades and flame throwers took out pill-boxes, Bren guns sprayed lead into windows and doorways. The Atlantic Wall, a system of interlocking fields of firepower in citadels of reinforced concrete was cracking, Bangalore torpedoes blasting routes through the wire avoided mine fields, a dash across a road and tram-line, the assault force was through.

Rendezvous now with the paratroopers holding two vital bridges would open up the countryside. Hedgerows and trees, cover for an advance under fire. Oncoming Germans were ambushed, a whispered order, "Pick the officers and NCO's and let them come right in." Lovat, 'I may have grown careless: they say you never hear the shot that kills you, the civilian occupants of a building damaged in the mornings blitz had been badly injured; the family begged for a doctor and bandages. As I turned to point out the medical team bringing up the rear, a sniper bullet smacked the wall beside my head with a crack like a whip. A near miss that showered the relatives with chips and rubble.'

The bridges were under savage counter attacks, self-propelled guns moved in, the Airborne lads, dug into slit trenches, beat them off. The Caen canal turn-table bridge ahead, Lovat, his piper and a handful of fighting men ran across, machine-gun bullets pinged off steel struts, mortar shells 'whoomphed.' The glider boys cheered. Commandos and marines were on Lovat's heels, snipers picked off men. The marines lost their CO.

Lush water meadows divided the bridges, ahead lay the river Orne. Livestock in the fields suffered, dead swollen cattle, others trailed their innards, bellowing, a sergeant ran over, put them out of pain. The commando pressed on.

The Orne bridge, snipers covered it, bullets cracked, spat into stonework, ricochets spun away, there were casualties. Lovat stepped out, Piper Millin struck a march, 'the good music drowned the shooting and we managed to stride over in step – almost with pomp and circumstance.'

Into the shelter of leafy trees and a welcome from hard pressed parachute men. Ahead the ridge, Lovat had argued with Generals and planners it must be taken. Two miles to go and dog tired. Surprise no longer a card, German heavy weapons moving up, enemy pressure suddenly dangerous. Hand to hand fighting along the ridge, dusk highlighting gun flashes. The village of La Plein straddled the high ground. A substantial house with out buildings, set in an orchard, would provide an overnight position. Lovat called a halt. The men cleared bodies from the buildings. A long day, if not 'The Longest.'

'It is one thing to go on the warpath; quite another to stay put and take what's coming to you.' Three days of German probing attacks around the orchard. Skirmishes, infiltrations at night with bombs, the constant hiss of shells. 'Sonk, sonk', eruptions of earth thrown high fell on slit trenches. Casualties mounted. The quick and the dead. Men were drawn together, brothers in arms. The ridge must be held, at whatever cost.

Day four, German command issued. 'The commando were to be dislodged at any cost'. The fresh morning brought bird song. From the enemy, nerve grating silence. Forward patrols reported, Germans massing. Suddenly the barrage struck. Hissing shells, crashing through branches, explosions, air vibrating, ground shaking. Men hugged flimsy shields over trenches. Just as suddenly shelling ceased. On came the German infantry.

Lovat had said, "dig in, lie low, and don't shoot until you see the whites of their eyes." Into the orchard they came, puzzled, hesitant troops. The commando held their fire. Sixty yards in, "Now." The trap sprang. Bren guns cut into screaming men. Chaos amongst apple trees set with early fruit. Killed and wounded lay still. A second wave, not realising the fate of their comrades, were obliterated. The Hun now knew commando positions, intense mortar and shell fire found its mark. Slit trenches made graves. A final all out frontal assault came, a grim wave of running grey uniforms. Steady and accurate rifle shooting inflicted gruelling German casualties. The attack faltered.

The final battle raged over No.4 commando. If they gave, the ridge was lost. Of the 455 officers and men who waded ashore four days previously, only

160 remained fighting. They held firm, elusive yet solid, field reaping fire power. The Germans sustained crippling losses. They broke, the battle turned, a swath of grey uniformed bodies lay arms outstretched, hands clenched, bleeding, unattended.

––––––––––

The orchard seemed hushed after the horror of the last attack, yet there was no truce when time came to bury the dead commandos. Survivors, dog tired and weary, carried in fallen comrades with a tenderness known to those who have faced great peril and witnessed the cruelest suffering. The elation of victory washed away, humbled by death. Graves were dug below silent apple trees whose branches bore the first swelling fruits of harvest's promise. The officer read a simple lesson for young lives for whom the harvest days of fulfilment were not to be. The ground sheeted bundles were lowered. Few the lips that did not quiver.

Sergeant George Fraser, the head stalker at Braulen in Glenstrathfarrar was one of three brothers serving in the Lovat Scouts. George followed Lovat to the commando, and that day led a bayonet charge. The Military Medal was to be his in death for the act of a courageous man. Twilight stole beneath golden leaves. A handful of troops stood, bare headed and bowed. Simon Fraser stood amongst them. The priest prayed a Requiem. A fearless leader, a man of the 'Old Faith', Lovat's thoughts lifted to the great hills of Strathfarrar, to its winding pony paths climbing slowly to the high tops which held the western horizon and the ocean of the setting sun in their solitude. Home to their peace, went the friend at his feet.

––––––––––

Furious fighting continued, the shelling intense. Buildings reduced to rubble gave little shelter. Shrapnel and splinters whined and spun. Lovat stood outside, concerned about his men. Had they hot tea? Artillery opened up. Allied or Hun? It seemed a faulty barrage. A British 25-pounder firing short the previous day had already killed one man. Shells exploded all around. Brigadier Lord Lovat went down, lay motionless, given for dead. Men scattered. On a brave impulse, Private Gerald Nicols, a Nazi hating German serving under the British flag, in a wild dash, shells still bursting, lifted Lovat onto his shoulder, and staggering under the weight of the big man, got him back into the courtyard.

A large shell fragment had smashed into Lovats back. They moved him into the stable. The medical officer gave a blood transfusion. Lovat stirred and calmly sent for Derick Mills-Roberts, Commanding Officer of No.6 Commando, himself a wounded man. Lovat was emphatic. "Take over the brigade, and whatever happens – not a foot back." He repeated the order three times, and then, "Get me a priest, get me the Abbe de Naurois."

WALLACE THE HERO OF SCOTLAND

Ladies voluminous pink knickers, elastic to the knee and known as 'bloomers', or to those of a more lascivious turn of mind as 'passion killers', once represented the height of fashion for women of modesty and decorum. Nevertheless the menfolk of Breakachy were not denied a passing glimpse of this seemly form of nether apparel. Each week two pairs of these commodious garments appeared, freshly washed and pegged to dry, on the wire fence to the west side of Cruinassie croft. The fastidious Miss Chisholm was not without a twinkle of feminine mischief.

Whilst Archie milked the cow, fed hens and prepared breakfast up at Ardochy, each summer morning Councillor MacRae betook of an early constitutional down the narrow cow patted road to the croft of Teagate where three matronly Shorthorn cows suckled their calves and cudded with tail flicking contentment. Beyond the day's first captivating sensations, the agitated scolding of a bank nesting wren, the honeyed wafts of yellow broom, Alec's head high footsteps strode manfully towards a snare of womanly wiles.

Confirmed bachelor, confirmed spinster, Alec and Kate knew each other a lifetime. Greetings were ever warm, but discreet. Whatever speculation may have crossed the Councillor's mind as to the extent of Kate's supply of lingerie, his eyes remained bashfully averted from the two pairs of 'bloomers' swaying seductively in the breeze. By the same token, Kate, the finest of ladies, might just have been amused at Alec's blushes. Who would know, that was the way of the Highlands.

This moreover was not the only assault on the MacRae fortress of bachelorhood and freedom. The Councillor kept bees. Straw skips on benches and white wooden hives on stools lined the beech hedges that sheltered his front garden. Furthermore Alec was something of a specialist, frequently winning prizes in the local Honey Shows at a time when clover scented hay fields and corn poppy roadsides put a comb of honey on the supper table in the homes of Strathglass.

Guide and champion of the apiarian fraternity throughout the Highlands was Miss Logan, bee keeping advisor to the North of Scotland Agricultural College for many years after the war. Acknowledged as an expert in the world of wax and pollen, a royal approach to beehives and the wishes of their keepers earned her the respectful title of 'The Queen Bee.'

Sadly for the Councillor, who believed bees were best left to their summer toil without supervision, 'The Queen' discovered, through an unwary remark on his part, or perhaps fondly imagined, through proselytising zeal on her part, that the Ardochy strain of hymenoptera were immune to a decimating disease of infant bees known as 'foul brood.' Her delight at such hive rocking revelation was matched only by the Councillor's displeasure.

By spreading the genes of Ardochy queens, Miss Logan's crusade on behalf of the stricken hives of the Highlands appeared something of a cross between the inspirations of Gregor Mendel and Florence Nightingale, whilst Alec, a man of Calvinistic leanings, believed in the predestined principle of leave well alone.

Windless summer evenings and the faint buzz of the last of his little friends homing into their hives, tiny legs orange with pollen, gave way to the wavering drone of a Morris Ten approaching Ardochy in the erratic manner of a worker bee flitting from flower to flower. It conveyed 'The Queen Bee'.

As was my way of a summer's evening I strolled down the brae of Ann Campbell's and over the burn to Ardochy after a day which had filled the warmth of the sun with the song of skylark fields. Fields, as fragrant in their swathes of curing hay as the snuggle of a milk maid's neck, alluring in their scent as a bewitching embrace, stolen amidst the wild flowered garlands of some hidden bower. And now, in it's drowsiness, a tired orb slipped away to the rubescent west, folding the petals of daisy and dog rose alike with the hint of a caressing touch, the merest brush of moistened lips, secretly given under the mellow light of a lover's moon.

The old house sat placidly, it's grey stones softened by golden shades. Tea towels dried on the hedge. Early to bed hens, their crops paunchy with grain, sauntered towards the corner shed, and Flossy came wagging to greet me.

Archie had his teeth in, the front wheel of a Morris Ten stood poised over the midden, I sensed something untoward. An observation heightened by the strenuous, not to say, frenzied buzz of demented bees wafting round the corner of the house. Archie made despairing signs and retired with a slam of the back door. Flossy looked up and whined. Caution and curiosity I hugged the gable and peered into the front garden.

A minor earthquake might well have wrecked similar havoc. Hive lids lay upturned, hive innards stacked frame box on frame box, shallow sections dripped unsealed honey, brood frames stood on stools. The whole apiary swarmed in a dance of rage, millions of bees in for the kill, stings at the ready, every inch of air space a high pitched kamikaze death strike.

The Councillor sheltered in the front porch, a red faced pent up witness to this vortex of ferocity. High pitched screams of anger, a splatter on the glass, an insect crawled off the window ledge trailing a wing. Ardochy winced with every plop. A royal upheaval in his sacred grove was under way.

Calmly in it's midst, Miss Logan, protected only by a veil, an old raincoat tied at the wrists, and undoubtably the royal prerogative, groped amongst the brood frames seeking out young queens. At each find she reached into a raincoat pocket took out a match box and popped in the chosen princess. A swoop of her raincoat and long tweed skirt exposed a mighty pair of pink 'bloomers'. A snap of knee tight elastic and a bemused bee found itself incarcerated up the leg of Miss Logan's drawers.

Never before had such a viewing transgressed garden or thoughts, Alec was aghast. By way of precaution he locked the porch door and retired to his settee to pause and consider. At least, I assured him, queen bees didn't sting. His ruddy face took on a pallor, I could see he had some doubts.

The following evening I walked reflectively down by the Tailor's Turn towards the tree filled gorge of Teanassie burn. Whin bushes leaned over roadside banks where the tall white cow parsley and bonnie blue speedwell bloomed unhurried and unheeded, for the new world had yet to arrive and only the ceaseless falling song of the yellow hammer broke the stillness of the air.

Pausing at the bend in contemplation, my ear caught the unusual sound of an engine, and turning I leapt up the bank, not a moment too soon. Down the brae from Ardochy, free wheeling, out of gear, blithely out of control, lacking but goggles and gloves, flashed Geordie Fraser crouched over the wheel of a little grey Fergie. His safe deliverance from a corner on two wheels I could only attribute to the distance he hung over the inside mudguard.

I admired his skill, though he didn't offer to wave, and my parting salute was cut short by a reverberating crash.

'The Queen Bee' intent upon another night of experimentation amongst the Councillor's innocent brood, drove spasmodically around the blind bends that climb up by the Teanassie falls, her eye perhaps following the flight of a hastily escaping swarm.

I hurried down to the scene of the impact. Front axle lay astride bumper, two radiators were locked in a steaming embrace. Geordie had vacated his driving seat in favour of the bonnet of 'The Queen's' Morris Ten on which he sat astride clutching it's wind screen wipers with the air of a remounted jockey after a Grand National spill.

Miss Logan standing with her back to the mangled machines appeared to be checking the contents of her 'bloomers'. As I observed to Ardochy later that evening, queen bees may not sting but they probably tickle.

Tying string to a hind leg and walking behind is not the simplest method of moving a pig. We flitted the sows and weaners down from Cluanie to the steading at Tighnaleac by applying porcine principle number one, belly first. Twenty-four hours without food and a herd of swine will follow a bag of nuts any distance at a speed governed only by one's ability to remain safely in front. The slobbering bunch cantered up the Breakachy road and were settled onto an area of head high bracken with the refinements of a mud hole for 'make up' and the remains of an old building to engage their skills in demolition.

Wallace the Hero of Scotland, shortened to 'Wal' for convenience, seemed a suitable title for the lordly Large White boar who took up connubial duties with the harem when Robert the Lawson Landrace went to the home of the happy pork pie. Several weeks passed and Wal's interests veered from conjugal rights to the conquest of Kilmorack. His territorial claims grew in proportion to the length of yellow tusks curling in scimitar style from mincing jaws. Add whiskers, a tiny pair of bloodshot eyes, Breakachy found it's Braveheart.

Feeding the herd their daily ration of nuts was not for the faint of purpose. This testing encounter generally fell to Betty. All animals can tell feeding time to the minute and perhaps breakfast was late, but one morning she raced back to the yard barefoot. "Wallace has got my wellie," I noted she dropped the affectionate 'Wal' and went to look. Sure enough a wellie boot was being flung into the air and savaged. "I'll sort the gentleman," not the exact phrase, but grabbing a large stick I tore over to the pig. The wellie boot hung tattered on a tusk with several holes through it's leg not found in the original Dunlop design. Mercifully there was no leg inside. Another toss and Wallace lost interest in footwear.

Never trust the efficacy of piercing eye contact, as any one armed lion tamer will tell you. Our eyes connected. Mine, bold, resolute. Wal, evil, rapacious. His jaw opened to it's considerable width and shut with the snap of a man trap. Slobbers frothed to the ground. It was immediately obvious my offensive weapon lacked defensive capability. Claymore, elephant gun? maybe. The end of my stick vanished in one crunch. I opted for speed. So did Wallace.

Hard on the inside track I rounded the corner of the steading. Wallace pounded behind, a dead gallop, back feet passing his ears. Into the yard. Pig ark to the rescue. Inside, on top? I chose the more dignified escape and in a flying stride of Olympian grace I alighted atop of it's corrugated iron roof. Wallace squealed to a halt and vanished inside. I had made a wise choice.

The hut rocked. I did a time and distance estimate to the byre door. Braveheart burst out, looked up and began portentous siege tactics, to wit, circling my outpost with the screech of an out of tune set of bagpipes and making a masticating movement with his jaws of a most intimidating nature. This was not a job for the 'do gooder' brigade, I shouted Betty, watching from the back door, to load the 12 bore but mind me.

A car drove into the yard, oh no, not the banker or the minister. No, 'Simon Caulternich', saviour and wild pig handler. By the time his laughter subsided, Wallace reared on his hind legs for a closer look. I threw him a wellie, he seemed partial to wellies. "Let out the gilts," I bawled. Out from the steading trotted half a dozen sweet smelling maidens. The Hero of Scotland called a truce. Slobbering turned to nuzzling, and a trail of nuts led them into captivity. Greed and sex, the undoing of man and boar.

Lacking the wisdom to appreciate that nature, rather than the College of Agriculture, had worked out the most amenable relationship between a human being and the pig, that is, leave them eating acorns, I set about adapting the steading to their supposed needs with the help of a cement mixer and a colourful large scale plan drawn up by an 'expert.' The old threshing mill was dragged ignominiously to a croft in the Braes, foaling box and dividing walls fell to the crowbar, cow stalls of the toughest Erchless larch were split for the Rayburn and the spacious result treated to a layer of snout defying concrete.

Tubular steel farrowing crates, I was informed, were just what the sow ordered. The expectant mother unable to turn, faced a combined food and water trough, put her tail against a metal slide and allowed her offspring to pop out and scramble round for a milk shake under the sun bed appeal of an infra-red bulb. I installed four such aids to animal welfare and catered for privacy and warmth with chipboard partitions and a false straw roof. Moreover to give the sows a touch of homeliness I named the cubicles, the Ritz, Savoy, the Hilton and the Baroness's favoured London domiciliary, Claridges. Sadly I noted that sows awaiting the 'big event' whiled away the days chewing at the bars or wilfully splashing water into their food troughs. I put it down to base ingratitude.

Many pleasant days were spent over at Ardochy helping the MacRaes. It was no problem for me to fit in with their careful crofting ways. Listening to Alec as we worked at sheep, harvest or whatever, always paid, for he was an extremely shrewd and wise old man and I gleaned a philosophy towards farming that turned the cleverness of a degree into a hollow charade. Payment in another form came in notes. The Councillor subscribed to a cash economy and believed that those in brown envelope authority over him were the parasites of society. A view staunchly held throughout the free and unsophisticated world of crofting as it once was, and amplified by 'Dunc Oldtown' who carried in the back pouch of his wallet an early issue hundred pound note which when unfolded on a bar counter, for observation rather than consumption, was the size and colour of a large white handkerchief and drew the approval of another round of drinks.

I worked away for 'Ardochy' as the seasons demanded, a price was never mentioned nor a bill tendered. Perhaps when the last trailer load of sheaves had been led to a stack and the three of us sat in the kitchen enjoying oatcake and Archie's 'crowdie', Alec, without a word would go upstairs. Footsteps on the ceiling, the sound of a heavy chest being pulled across bare wooden floorboards, a long silence. The further scrape of a chest going back below the bed, a clump of feet on the stair and the Councillor sat back at the table asking for more tea. Only as I stepped onto the tractor to go home did he hand me an envelope, always a used one stuck down with stamp edging, "Thanks'll no pay you," he would say. Often a week passed before we needed cash and the envelope sat unopened on the mantelpiece. It's contents were always fair and sometimes generous. The system worked without a fault for nearly twenty years. A simple and stress free set of values.

––––––––––

At the turn of the century upwards of eighteen households had homes and kailyards in sheltered sites where they least encroached upon the precious arable lands of Breakachy. By the late 'fifties' only three houses remained occupied. Kate and Willie Chisholm, spinster and bachelor at Cruinassie, Alec and Archie MacRae at Ardochy, both bachelors, and Hugh and Morag MacKenzie on the main holding of Tighnaleac who had no family. These people, by that date, were all in their sixties and apart from a few years when the Baron's keeper, Angus MacDonnell lived with his wife and red haired daughter Joan at the Culours, there had been no children in these homes since the old folks themselves were young, a span of maybe fifty years. Alison and Hector, followed by Elspeth and Sheena, were the first children to arrive on the farming scene in half a century, at a time when the substitution of horses and dung by tractors and chemicals brought about a rate of change faster, and certainly more ill omened for the environment at large, than that experienced during the agricultural revolution of the late eighteen hundreds.

Jimmy Ross who cycled the four miles up from Beauly six day's a week to work for 'Hugh Breakachy', the 'postie' who cycled from Aigas Post Office, a very occasional car, often followed by telescope, and Bill'ack Fraser's cattle float several times a year, made up the flow of traffic. Yet there was a feel of life about the 'speckled fields'. Walking everywhere, stick and dog, though it took time, had more of a sense of arrival. No standing on a doorstep or worrying about boots, "hello, hello" brought "come away in". And the children of the Braes walked over the burn to hoe 'neep', lift tatties, Jim'ack Fraser's girls, the MacRae's from Teanacoil by the river, it was the natural thing in a homogeneal society which looked on the land as part of their life.

Teanassie school down in the bowl of land where the Breakachy burn meets the Beauly served the Kilmorack children within walking distance, which, for many, meant six healthy miles of fume free exercise a day. George, the son of Kenny Campbell, a much respected head of the school, was of that last generation of children drawn to the land, by it's scents, by the feel of living soil, by it's life forms, great and small, by the yearning from behind a desk for it's sunshine and freedom, by the call of it's life force. Every hour out of school he ran up to Cluanie to work with the land as his friend. Perhaps long mornings at the hoe on the Stack yard field, and Chisholm the crofter would look at the sun and say, "Way down and see if the flag's out," and the boy ran to the dyke where the croft house showed through the leaves, and if the dinner were ready Kate would put a white cloth on the hedge.

The tuppence and press button 'A' telephone box down the Breakachy road at Teagate must have taken more to pay Rita the Councillor's niece to knock down the cobwebs than it drew in a months calls. Such drain on the G.P.O.'s resources suggested its removal. Much inspecting on sunny days and consideration at head office on wet days took place. Finally the dilapidated state of the Councillor's fencing brought the matter to a head. He wrote the Postmaster General demanding the kiosk be moved approximately four feet to allow for the re-alignment of a new fence. The curt reply intimated it would cost an astounding eight hundred pounds to move the box any distance other than onto the back of a lorry, and at current usage this would take to the year 2040 to recoup, minus the expense of Rita. The kiosk was under sentence. The Councillor took action, 'as Council representative for the Parish of Kilmorack for fifty years it will be my duty, for the amenity of the locality, to oppose the removal, etc.', he penned.

Several weeks elapsed. A large grey limousine containing two grey men slid smoothly up to Ardochy one bright June afternoon. Far less would be noted, but never a word. Shortly the kiosk vanished surreptitiously and a lorry load of poles appeared. Grey men, digging men, wires, a simple connection. The wonder of the twentieth century was installed on a shelf in a dark corner under the stairs at Ardochy with a bicycle lamp beside it to read the numbers. "Oh well I had to write, or there was no phone, and you know," the Councillor reflected, "they put it in free." Which goes to prove, on occasion, the pen is mightier than the pay phone.

Turnip thudded into the trailer off the prongs of my 'graip' as I loaded and carted a 'topping crop of yellow neeps' to the shed by the Ardochy byre one late October afternoon. The homestead at Tighnaleac, under my eye as I turned the tractor at the top of the drills on the ridge seemed a peaceful haven. Silver clouds woven with strands of sunshine edged hills of fading purple, and golden headed woodlands dressed curving slopes that flowed down to fields where the redwing soon would come. The rich berried rowans, entwined for luck by generations past, arched over the garden gate and shone in their auburn tresses, the pride of an autumn tapestry. Old Nancy in the porch, her head between paws, would be asleep.

Betty was away, the children at school, sows in the steading would be snoozing, saving their 'gurns' of greed for the first scrape of pails and the rattle of pouring nuts. I glanced across. Just a puff, that's enough. A long white trail of smoke drifted away from the byre.

My God. A fire. Straw, the steading, sows and piglets. Dropping the trailer, I galloped the tractor to the new phone. Archie at the scullery door had cheese and oatcake on the table, a teapot in his hand. "May I use your phone?" I rushed past an open mouth, fumbled in the dark hall, found nine, spun it three times. "Fire brigade please." Archie swilled boiling water round the teapot, I skipped past the table. "Steading's gone up." The teapot poised, flick lid open, Archie blinked, "Och, wait your tea man." "On fire," I corrected, bolting out, hearing a bemused call, "Wait, wait," from the back door. Never a kinder man and still holding the teapot, but not one for wastage.

The yard swirled with the dense smoke of burning straw. Heating slates cracked with staccato shots, larch timbers spat and roared. Save the sows, save the sows, I opened the end door, a red wall of flame swooped at me, seering eyes and breath, out bolted one sow, screaming and burnt. Razorback. Slammed the door, no use. Slates rattled down, I dodged away. Flames poured through the roof, sparks made leaping tracers towards the rest of the steading, the house, I feared for the house. Impossible alone, I stood a moment, gasping.

Razorback, a skinny sow, probably the cause of the blaze, would have turned in her crate and burst a bulb onto straw. She ran squealing with pain back towards the byre, her litter. Down to the house, the rifle, one shot. The dogs, how could I forget? Into the long pass round the fold, running bent, barely a breath, out flew Lassie and Teenie. Close call.

Crash, crash, down went the roof, a roaring crescendo, a cascade of sparks. Now for the rest, the fire devil licked the next timbers, they smouldered.

A Land Rover bounced into the yard, Kenny MacKenzie, good neighbour. A screeching fire engine, running men, helmets, hoses out in seconds, pumping jets. Axes smashed doors, pikes through skylights, arcs of water fell onto flames, played over unlit roofs. "Where's more water?" "The mill lade." "Plenty?" "Not much." "Make a dam." Kenny ran with a spade. A second fire engine. Steady expert men moved carefully amongst the debris, raking, dousing, searching out the last trickle of life that might hide in charred timbers.

Betty fed the men tea and venison pieces as they worked. By nine o'clock the fire was beaten, men gathered under the floodlights, lent on the front of their engines and pushed back grimy helmets. It seemed safe to issue the whisky.

Every pore of the place hung with a reek of destruction, biting smoke permeated the house, our clothes, the bedroom, the pillows. Next morning I viewed the horror of trapped death. Sows lay in heat twisted crates, burnt to blackened rib cages. The odd pivelled skin under the heaps of shattered slates. Half burnt timbers at angles mimicked limbs. Crumbling walls had felt intense heat, I hoped the pigs suffocated quickly. Clearing up was a grim week.

This loss spelt the end of our pig enterprise. An Inverness pig farmer, Tom MacKay, brought along his float and we loaded the survivors, which included the infamous Wallace. True to the spirit of the men of yore, the Hero of Scotland attacked MacKay as he unloaded the wagon. Wallace went down fighting, victim of his aversion to 'wellies.'

MY GOD, IT'S HIS GHOST

Few acres of Kilmorack's braes lie better to the sun than the sloping fields of Farley croft. Below a larch sheltered croft house the land falls steeply in a smooth round face to the edge of a birch wooded burn. The working of this ground for crop in the days of the horse was slow. Only by plodding downhill with a single furrow plough could a pair of cross garron ponies turn the nine inch cuts of soil which leaned one against another across the rig. Steady work, the clump, clump of hooves, the muffled click of iron shoe on stone, the sweet jangle of chain on leather and the swish of a glistening curve of soil packed under the plough-share as it settled with a wriggle of tiny cracks beside the ploughman's stride. Swing out of the furrow, up by the trees, drag an empty plough to a headland on the crest of the field, ease the near side rein, hold the offside horse, a click of the tongue, a lift of the handles and in slid the sock of the plough. A stoop of the shoulders, weight on the handles, another round. Flannel shirt and waistcoat, the breath of spring in his lungs, 'peewit' plovers making for the hill in his ears, and the living earth in his heart. An endless furrow at his foot, stretched beyond the horizon to the myth makers of Dun Mhor and their faith in the seasons of sun and moon.

One pass of the horse harrows knocked the spine off each furrow and the ground could be sown. Silky corn fanned out through fingers at each measured step. The sower caught each handful from the sowing sheet hung at his waist. Golden arcs, scattered on the bride of freshly harrowed earth. The horse stood ready, a run of the harrows buried the seed under a blanket of soil to await swelling rains and the warming sun.

Alex MacRae, staunch Presbyterian and strict Sabbatarian, nevertheless, as was the way of the old folk, knew well the moods of the moon and her influence on seed time and harvest. Each year he hand sowed his corn crop with Good Friday's waxing moon. Together went the pagan festival of the Goddess of Spring and a sombre overlay of Christian dogma. An unwitting blend of beliefs. The ancient sagacity of the seasons are today's superstition, and the 'truths' of today surely become the superstitions of tomorrow. Doctrines mutate down the millennia. Alone remains constant, the phenomenon of Faith.

Down beside the Breakachy burn in a hollow of Archie's croft known as the Cul Ruidh, the Councillor strode the length of the field. Wide plus-fours, a silk backed waistcoat from an old suit, neck band and collar stud, a strong figure. Tall, erect, and though well in his sixties, he carried the canvas sowing sheet with obvious ease. Back and forth, a shower of grain at each toss of the wrist, and the foot marks of his steady pace, dark imprints in a soft reddish soil, fast drying in the hot blinks of an Easter sun.

Ranged at the side of the field were the sacks of seed oats I had put down in the morning. Archie stood ready. The sower's abrupt halt signalled a refill. Staggering a little under their weight, Archie carried over two pails of the precious offering, filled the sheet, and the Councillor swung into another round.

I sat on my Grey Fergie waiting to harrow over the seed. A light job, it had been a task for the horse which passed the years in semi-retirement at Ardochy, but on a February night of sleet, in the lea of the cart shed, the old 'cuddy' had died. "Ach he was old, he wasn't masticating his food properly," the Councillor told me as I put a rope to a neck, long without it's crest of pride, and pulled the gangling bones onto the roadside to await the winch of a knackery lorry. The horse had belonged to Dunc Oldtown. Doing a 'turn' for a neighbour counted more than cash in the fashion of that day and the beast had been on a permanent unpaid loan. His pound value however was duly passed. Now my tractor was hitched to the wooden 'stretcher' and a three leaf harrow.

Archie had hung the worn leather shopping bag on the branch of a tree, out of the way of Flossie's nose, and when the last handfuls were sown Ardochy sat on the remaining half sack of oats. I turned up a pail, Archie took down the bag, Flossie looked pleased. A bottle of tea wrapped in a towel, a tin of oatcakes, a bowl of 'crowdie', Flossie gave a slow wag of her tail, and we ate, lords of all we surveyed.

Sunshine in the first radiance of spring light burst through branches just in bud. The burn, secret and dark as it dabbled in and out amongst round mossy stones, suddenly shone, a bright filigree of silver bubbles prancing and dancing over green velvet gems. A pair of yellow wagtails bobbed and curtsied into the sunlight. Each year they came, jaunty tails flickering about the stones, the slashed sleeves of a courting beau. Childrens' shouts and laughter mingled with the talk of the water. Alison and Hector played in the icy shades of the Mill pool not far above us. On summer nights when the waters ran warm from the shingle banks of the Urchany flats they would swim and splash and duck under the falls which fed it.

An oatcake crumbled as Archie spread 'crowdie', Flossie, with a sideways glance at the Councillor, took her share. Great candescent clouds built towering pillars on the iron grey plinths of an April shower. It's heavy droplets drove across the horizon above Farley's sloping fields. Ardochy watched with the eyes of an old man. " I've seen, when I was young, eight men lined out on that slope, scything a grand crop of oats. There was a woman to a man tying the sheaves, two girls were at the stooking." I saw the line of swinging shoulders working up the field, angled one a step or two behind the other. I knew by heart the tying of a harvest band which would keep the women as bent as their menfolk. I heard the sandpaper rasp of a steadily cutting scythe, the rustle of gathering a fallen crop and the setting of a stook. The petty jealousies, the laughing banter. I saw the bending of shapely and buxom women, the glances, eye catching eye, the thrill of the unspoken. I knew the lust of strong sweating men.

I rose to harrow the Councillors sowing, but he still saw the braes of peat smoke and family fields. Over the burn Sandy broke the stillness with the rattle of a cultivator as he worked ground for the tatties. "I don't know why they call him Sleepy," reflected Ardochy, "there's not a harder working man in Kilmorack, he had tatties on that field when he took Dolly a bride from Glen Urquhart." He paused, the scene lived again, "Oh, a hardy woman, she made him a good wife, she was at the planting over there that spring. Busy, busy, and him that's dead and gone was watching," for some reason he never called Chisholm by name, "ah well, said him that's gone, she'll not be so slamp at the lifting," and breaking the spell with a laugh, he said a little shyly, " and neither she was. Oh, but she made a good mother."

Sandy, thoughtful neighbour that he was, worried about 'Eligo', an old man alone on the heights of Farley croft. A savage winter, blizzards and 'flu' swept the Highlands. Aching bones and to bed with a 'toddy.' Shivering in soaking sheets',Eligo' was ill. Here and there between gaps in the dyke the steep road up to Farley had blown clear of snow but the top stretch in the lea was choked. Sandy struggled, post to post, he remembered Chisholm climbing to Cluanie. Eligo's house was in darkness, the door open, he called. No answer.

The night had cleared as Sandy followed his tracks back down the brae. An ice crystal moon spread tortured branches in beseeching arms across the footsteps of his climb. In the blackness of the shadows, his eye caught a glint. Moonlight on metal, the tackets of a boot. 'Eligo', making for help, was dead in the ditch.

Long spells of settled weather made a summer of butterfly and bird song. Handsome red and black tortoiseshell filled the garden, came into the house, beat on the windows. Out on the rough grasses of the Carnich bold fritillaries drank the nectar of ox-eye daisies and opened sienna mottled wings to a day long sun. But to the edge of the moorland came the tiniest dainty sky blue butterflies. They flitted about the sedges on the slopes of Dun Mhor and settled for a moment of simple beauty on the first rich purple flowers of the bell heather.

Each evening of an endless summer the children ran barefoot to the cool of the millpool. The buzz of insect life about bush and flower grew still. The sun, harbinger of happiness and well being to the melancholy of northern climes, tipped the last light of her summer night into hidden corries. From top of the tall larch whose roots split the garden dyke, a speckle breasted thrush sang with a clarity of voice that spoke of a brood safely reared in the forks of the rowan trees twisted together for love and luck in an arch above the garden gate.

Word came late on one of those evenings that Sandy was missing. His sons, in fast fading light, searched the falls and pools below the cliffs of the treacherous Teanassie burn. Had he fallen? I hurried to the Millpool and followed the Breakachy burn to the foot of Dun Mhor. Darkness and no sign. Dolly waited for dawn without sleep.

Crimson skyline to the east and I took the old peat road winding past the foot of Dun Mhor. The deep rumble of the burn below its ramparts echoed around me. Heartbeat of the night, hollow as the voice of a stranger entering the vaults of the universe. I stood on the shoulder of Breakachy hill. In silence beyond silence, in power transcending power, awful in silence and majesty, the flames of life's furnace burnt the sky in the birth of day. Only in that moment can the eye look upon the radiance of the sun, and see to the end of the earth.

Out along the track, a little distance before me, I saw a form hunched on a stone. I put a hand on a shoulder soaked with dew. "Well Sandy, it's making for another fine day." An empty pipe lay at his feet. His eyes sunk into the horizon, he spoke in his slow way without looking, "I was thinking," and he turned, "Will there ever be another world as bonnie as this one?" The sun caught the ruins above the abandoned Urchany crofts. "Well, perhaps there will be Sandy," and I led him gently back to the house and Betty made us breakfast.

That harvest, after I 'bindered' a fine standing crop of oats at Ardochy, the weather turned 'moochie.' No sun sparkled days to put a crackle in the straw, to scent the fields with the sweet breath of ripening grain, or put that lively spring in the fork which lifted the heart to the happiness of simple work on the land. Instead, day upon day, the fingers of a clammy mist hung drips on the drooping ears of corn.

The Councillor sat glumly in the kitchen telling of harvests of his youth when hand tied sheaves were stooked beside the old Scots pine woods to the west of Ardochy on the long abandoned croft of Lon Dhuallich, and how each evening, he and his brothers concealed traps amongst the enticing heads of corn, and by dawn a plump flapping blackcock would be lifted before the keeper did his rounds. I listened, looking to the birchs of the Coille Dhu. A grey cloak of decay drained their leaves of the gayness of autumn, and for many days from an eyrie high in one of the trees the mournful screech of a hungry young buzzard drifted out of the mists. Archie stirred and turned to me with an intent, almost frightened look, "I don't like the cry of that bird," he said in a distant voice.

Blackening sheaf heads were starting to grow as we carted the limp bundles to fences which favoured the least puff of a breeze. Lines of sheaves lent on the wires, old men, bent at the knees, grey at the pow, scattering grain like dandruff to Archie's foraging hens. The crop went to the stack yard in poor condition, by which time the weather, with more mischief than a cart load of monkeys, settled itself to an early frost. Gentle spirals of steam rose from the tops of leaning stacks. A worried 'Ardochy' hurried and heaved with props and ropes. It meant heated and 'foosty' sheaves, as we were to find at the first November threshing.

The tin roofed barn at Ardochy housed a small threshing mill powered by a carefully preserved, single cylinder, flint spark and magneto Amanco engine, which, when running, was a sight to thrill both the mechanically minded and those of concupiscent imagination. It operated in the horizontal position. An enormous 'big end', hung between two muscular leg like bearings, revolved energetically back and forth, thrusting a thick exposed piston with slow thumps into the orifice of a mighty cylinder; mercifully lubricated by drips of oil from a bottle, and cooled from a watering can should steam indicate overheating.

This was the 'nerve centre' of a day at the mill, with the Councillor at the control panel. He stacked piles of straw at the back of the barn, changed over bags full of corn, and signalled to the loft, should Archie be 'feeding' the mill too hard and be in danger of throwing the belts, by a sharp rap on the ceiling with the end of his pitch fork.

Up in the loft was less sophisticated. Archie bent over the mouth of the mill cutting strings and spreading each sheaf before the whizzing teeth of the 'strippers' in as little headroom as might put his own dentition in danger. Sensibly they remained out of harm's way on a shelf in the scullery. But woe betide if any sheaf were gobbled whole, the mill's guts would rumble, the engine labour, belts fly off pulleys and from below, extreme knocking on the floorboards would result.

A November moon was on her back, small and high, a sickly jaundiced yellow, full of water as the saying had it, an omen of wild weather which sent a stab of apprehension to the guts of those who feared her malicious humour. And surely enough, by the following night, a north wind plastered the trunks of the swaying stand of pines above Ardochy with a foreboding feel of winter. The cows came bawling to the gate, and Archie, a stockman who cared for the well being of his stock, perhaps more than for his own, rose at midnight, and pulling on a jacket, tied the beasts in the byre. Soaked with sleet, in a house with little heat, he shivered and slept. The cattle were out of the storm.

Now the days fell short and hungry. Straw to the hake, turnip to the manger, dung to the midden, fertility to the croft, a cycle which came naturally across the countless centuries since farming first brought mankind into communities and built the basis of modern life. For Archie, it dictated a daily round of feeding and caring, with shy affection, for the animals upon which the subsistence living of a croft once depended. For the cow who would gently sniff his face as he teemed sliced swede from a wire basket into her trough, who would lower her head to be scratched behind the shoulder, it meant a symbiotic role within the family, a respected place, unquestioned down the aeons, from the sacred cows of Aryan ancestors and the myths of the Minotaur, to a tin roofed byre at a road end in the Highlands and its two bachelors. For the Councillor, it meant an oil can on the mill bearings, fresh cooling water in the Amanco, and looking out corn sacks without holes. For me, a summons to the stack yard at Ardochy with tractor, trailer, and pitch fork. Straw was needed.

Out in the fresh air I forked a trailer of sheaves, loaded from a stack, in through the door, to pile about Archie's feet. Soon the 'stoor' wafted around me in foggy trails, not only belching from the doorway, it wheezed out from under the corrugated iron, from holes in the ridge, every chink a jet, the barn became a stamped on puff ball. Inside the tiny loft the 'mill feeder', crouching below the rafters, was enveloped in a lung filling smog of fungus laden particles. Every so often he emerged and leant on the doorpost, instantly aged, an old man hawking up a vile black spit. The woollen muffler he wound round nose and mouth, apart from producing a banded effect on his face, it seemed, made little difference to the intake of dust.

By the first week of February there is daylight enough to plough until six in the evening and I turned the stubbles at Ardochy until a buttermilk moon smiled on the polished mould boards and Archie waved a teapot to me over the hedge. Eggs were boiling on a swivel over the fire. Archie watched the time on their 'Yankie' mantlepiece clock. His eyes seemed enormous, his cheeks, colourless, drawn together over the lines of a slender face. On frail, spidery limbs, hung the large crooked hands of a working life. "Your clock's got a awful loud tick tonight Archie." "Oh he's been at it with his feather and paraffin." The Councillor pulled his chair to the table and Archie, in a fit of wet coughing, went through to the scullery.

A little back bedroom led off the kitchen, the brown paper blind was half drawn to keep out the sharp March sunshine. Archie dosed, his face flushed. I stood by the bed, his eyes shone with fevered brightness, but he knew me and talked of his mother. "She used to take water from the well above the Culours when we were boys," and after a pause, long as though time took on an endless dimension, "maybe a cold or something." I took the jug and went over the field of last harvest's stooks, now ploughed again for another season. The wind had a searching chill.

Archie sipped a mouthful. I put the jug quietly on the table beside him. He turned his head to gaze intently. I saw the evening sun, dipping behind the Ardochy hill, glowing through the water. He held out a hand, "I'm done Iain, I'm done." and he thanked me for my friendship. In the early hours of next morning, he died, the 13th of March.

The funeral was in simple Presbyterian dignity. A notice in the Deaths of the 'Courier', the briefest. A. MacRae, Ardochy, all friends respectfully invited. Hector went over the previous afternoon, tidied the midden and swept the yard. All was ready. The drawn blinds of the back bedroom. The coffin and its remains.

Odd showers of sleet whitened the ground, only to vanish with each burst of sunshine. A penetrating north east wind turned up collars and buffeted the corner of the yard where the grumbling hens remained confined. I helped park the cars of sombre elderly gentlemen in dark coats and black hard hats whose reversing skills owed much to the days of gig and whip.

Gathered about the back porch, beside the bedroom window, were Highlanders of the Braes, of the generation before names began to change. Old men, whose lives and interest had lived with the land they crofted. Softly they talked about things that mattered, the condition of their lambing ewes, the prospect of an early sowing, what feed they had left to take cattle through to the grass, and they waited.

At the forefront of the small group, to my surprise, stood two gentlemen of prominent positions in the North of Scotland College of Agriculture. Two men whose clever preachings on nitrogen fertiliser, on silage making and the pencil and paper of production on a viable unit, had helped the evolution of farming and crofting from a way of life, in sympathy with its surroundings, to the rat race of artificial factory food. Slightly ill at ease amongst a condemned breed, they nodded to me.

In the kitchen, Church elders and prayers. Some might have touched the remains, just a finger on the forehead, it was the way, once.

I stood beside the green porch door. It opened. Out stepped the Councillor, bare white head, grey suit, his face fresh and strong. Two faces of prominent gentlemen turned ashen. Rooted and staring, they looked at each other, at me, in horror at the Councillor. Trembling lips mouthed, "My God, it's his ghost."

Sleet settled, white specks on the shoulders of black funeral coats. The hearse moved slowly down the track away from Ardochy. We walked behind. The old turned, east wind catching breath. Kate Chisholm stood at the door of the Cruinassie croft, her head bowed.

I manoeuvred cars, one of the prominent savants took my elbow. "Look here, the death notice said A.MacRae, but that's him." "Yes, that's Alec, one of your College Governors I'm sure for twenty years, it's his brother Archie we're burying." Colour returned, "Oh boy, we're at the wrong funeral," and the pair hurried away.

Ardochy was alone that night and I sat at the table with him in an empty kitchen. He poured a dram and we sat in silence. At a crackle from the fire, he looked hard at the clock, and said with difficulty, "Archie was a man without guile, without any guile in him." And then, little by little, we talked over the day. He seemed pleased, and perhaps a touch proud that the College men had honoured poor Archie's funeral. It was not the night to tell him. Nor did I ever.

Mothballs are not immediately associated with the scents of mid summer, but on an evening when the croftlands of Loan Duchillich were white with tousle headed clovers and a hint of mist held the fragrance of their sweet nectar, the sweetest of nectar, which in the times of wholesome meadows, children would suck, and diligent bees would drink until the dew caught their wings, I walked into the Ardochy kitchen to catch the gloomy smell of important clothing.

Supper dishes awaited the morning visit of Rita, his niece, as the Councillor made a cup of tea, and with few appreciative clicks of his tongue, settled himself on the couch. I sniffed, discreetly. A matter of some gravity seemed at hand. Mothballs added mystery, if not atmosphere. Behind Alec's head, on the corner of the door, dimly, in his sparing 40 watt use of 'the electric', I spotted the culprit, a coat hanger full of formal black jacket and the peeping 'turn-ups' of a pair of 'stripy' grey trousers'. Furthermore, on the mantelpiece above my head, propped against the 'Yankie' clock, lent a large gold edged card. Highland manners forbore mentioning either.

The aroma of mothballs had faded before the Councillor rose from his couch and with an indifferent air, handed me the imposing card. "Are you busy first week?" "Ach, not really," I replied, noting the Royal Coat of Arms, "if I cut hay tomorrow, it can lie for a few days." "Well, I might go to that thing, if we left early." Her Majesty Queen Elizabeth and H.R.H. Prince Philip request the pleasure of the company of Councillor Alexander M.MacRae. Holyrood Palace, the Royal Garden Party. The mothballs leapt in anticipation.

Meadow pippets, the poor mans skylark, were reviewing a bonnie sunrise as, in my capacity as official chauffeur, I walked to meet the privately elated party goer at Breakachy road end. My hay lay cut on the Letter box field, golden on top, green below, a waft of rich tobacco, it would turn nicely. More prestigious duties called. I took the wheel of Ardochy's sleek grey Singer Gazelle, a most fitting conveyance for the occasion. A battered shoe box on the back seat, carefully tied with white string, struck the only note of incongruity.

We sped south. Inverness was well behind before I discovered why the elegant vehicle seemed to scream at sixty. It had more gears than I thought and preferred ninety. The old A9, all sharp bends, in and out under a dozen railway bridges, we crossed the Grampians in as many hours as my great grandfather took days. The Councillor talked at roughly the same rate.

No roadside 'caf' for a snack. To my surprise, for Alec was not a man noted for his extravagance, we glided to a halt before the finest hotel in the Fair City of Perth. I carried in the loaded coat hanger and waited. It's smell floated up the grand stairway. A respectful cough lead us through to the chandeliered banqueting room. "Would Sir like me to take your, er, the coat hanger?" I glanced at the Councillor, "No thanks, it's quite alright," I said, hanging it on the back of my dining chair and thereby ruining the taste of an exquisite turtle soup.

Service was leisurely, Alec was anxious. Between courses he leapt up and grabbing the coat hanger vanished to the gentlemans toilet. Exit Highlander, tweedy plus-fours, five minutes pass, enter an immaculate courtier, punctiliously attired down to silk tie, white hankie and a snuggly fitting grey waistcoat. Two plates of summer salad on the arm of a swallow-tailed waiter narrowly avoided the carpet. He blinked, stared at the face but at least recognised the smell. I glanced at the Councillors feet, still in black brogues. The shoe box on the back seat retained its secret.

The 'Big Smoke' fluttered flags from battlements, pigeons from Princes Street and displayed all the hallmarks of governing gentility, a gracious frontage and crumbling backstairs. We hummed along history, the Royal Mile, with special deference to John Knox, and arrived at the gates of Holyrood two hours early. The sun, Ardochy's watch, and he, a stickler for time keeping. Presently flocks of Ascot hats sailed past on a tide of 'stripy' trousers as a swell of important people poured towards the Palace. The Councillor set off. Black brogues, had he forgotten the shoe box? I opened all the windows and dozed in a rewarding sun.

"Well Alec, how did it go?" "Ach the Queen smiled, too many hangers on, all trying to touch the hem of the garment." "What about Philip?" "Oh, I think he was bored with the stuffed shirts, he made himself as tall as the larches." "I doubt you were better in the tweeds Alec," "Aye, you're right," and we pulled into a cafe west of Dumbarton to allow the Councillor regain his reality.

Loch Lomond and it's islands played host to peaks of slender curves as the evening fell still. Shadow and blushing sunlight outdid the pomp and folly of human conceit. But ours was the 'Grand Tour', and by supper time 'The Gazelle' bounced down a farm road on the shores of the 'bonnie banks' to the headquarters of past protege, Alex. Murray. The porch stank of sheep, a relief from mothballs, it had been a day of clipping. The welcome was Highland. A dram, a supper of mutton chops and talk. Talk of the Braes of Kilmorack, of Gracie MacDairmid, the orphan girl who reared Murray, of Sleepy Sandy, of all that once made the Highlands a family of cousins and friends.

Midnight came and I drove. The winding miles, Glen Falloch of the deer, Rannoch Moor of the peat, and Fort William asleep, four in the morning and the bends of Loch Ness, still the Councillor talked.

A sandpiper sounded the alarm, daylight swam in the Beauly river, Alec bade me stop. We sat on a curve of dyke above the water. The white string of the shoe box was deliberately untied and saved. The lid opened, I watched. A wrap of newspaper revealed two slices of Christmas cake. A salute to the virtue of thrift, was eaten. A libation of whisky, confined to a tiny Aspirin bottle, was drunk. A symbol of the morality of moderation. Mothballs were forgotten, though the cake had a tinge.

A larch tree stood beyond the west gate of Ardochy. A single tree, fine and straight, auburn of autumn, the first hint of spring, it grew in the lea of ageing Scots pines which stayed a gale. The Councillor needed fencing posts, the tree was thrown and I carted the lengths to the Beauly sawmill. One evening, a little bashfully, he told me, " I had a garden there when I was a wee boy, out of the way, on the edge of the burn. I took that tree as a seedling from my mothers croft at Yellow brook, it's over eighty years old."

He worked away, needing the strength of a young man, and I lifted a heavy, heavy fencing strainer for him to a hole which he was digging. Next day it was in place, ready for the wires. Perhaps a week passed, Betty and I were away in the afternoon, the children at school, a note was pinned to the door. 'I called this afternoon, Alec.' He must have walked across, something not done before without reason.

The Councillor died that night, sitting at the table in Ardochy. Friend and mentor to me, a Highlander of vanished days.

BEYOND THE LONG HORIZON

The mildest-mannered man that ever scuttled a ship or cut a throat', was the Byronic description used by Winston Churchill in a memo to Stalin when dispatching a convalescing Lord Lovat as part of a Parliamentary delegation to meet the Soviet leader in the Kremlin. D-Day had succeeded, the advance, soon to become a race, towards Berlin and victory, was clouded by a growing distrust amongst the Allies. The early chill of the resulting East-West Cold War could be felt, it was an onerous mission.

The picture of a swashbuckling pirate apart, Churchill clearly had respect for Lovat's potential in the game of high politics, and proved it by the offer of a position on the Government Front Bench in the House of Lords. This door opening on influential office in matters of State Lovat declined, though for a short time he became an Under-Secretary for Foreign Affairs. The effeminate London life was no place for a man of the Highlands. The Lovat Estates stretched from coast to coast across the finest hill country in Scotland, perhaps quarter of a million acres, amongst the largest privately owned properties in Europe, and to the land of the hills and the glens, Lovat returned.

His love of cattle and the rugged spacious life of cattle ranching was paramount. His eye for stock and his organising ability, turned the Lovat estates of the 1950's into one of the biggest integrated farming units of its day. Hundreds of cows, after wintering on the sheltered pastures around Beaufort, made the long trek, at first light on a May morning, to their summer pastures in the glens. A mile of hooting cows and bawling calves surging up single track roads provided a rousing pageant for those racing downstairs to protect their gardens, and a testy trip to the car wash for the office bound motorist. Glen Convinth, Strathglass, and Strathfarrar became home to the calves which, twelve months on, filled the spring sales of MacDonald and Fraser in Inverness as strong growthy stirks, and Lovat, at home with his cattle, proudly saw them round the ring.

The Beef Shorthorn breed from its reputation as the 'great improver' of native cattle throughout the world, fell into decline after the war and the Beaufort herd was finally dispersed. However, one crisp November evening before that event, I cycled down from Erchless to see them. Stars and a flickering bicycle lamp and I missed the cattleman's house, but as I cleared the trees and cycled into the park land a dim outline of the castle stood against an indigo night. Just a few lights, a family home, however grand, and then, as I took my bearings, a bright beam appeared from the battlements. The handlebars grew cold, I sat the bike, one foot the ground, the other the pedal. Window lights faded. In moments the tip of a brilliant crescent moon turned turret and battlement into a black cardboard cut out. The world felt old and empty. A long way from bicycle lamps and dubious brakes.

Dairy cattleman talked to beef herdsman, I remember his name as Geordie Sinclair and he took me into the fold at the home farm to view this acme of bovine pulchritude. Broad, brown, beautifully dished faces, down curving horns and a thick curly 'dossan' of hair, wide flat noses beaded with sweat, the cows had settled for the night and lay grunting and cudding on a fluffed up bed of fresh oat straw. Heads lifted, jaws moved, the air was moist with turnip breath.

We stepped around them and Sinclair spoke their names, "Get up Broadhooks." A prod with his boot and the favourite rose reluctantly, a mighty stretch from neck to tail, a resounding 'fart' and she turned to survey the stranger. I was astounded, such an enormous body on the smallest legs brought straw up to her belly. Great girdles of fat hung from matronly thighs and hips, her back seemed so broad as we leant on it that I suggested, "Two chairs and a tablecloth Geordie, and we can take our supper off this." Broadhooks turned her head and stretched out a tongue as Geordie scratched her shoulder. At five the next morning in the Erchless milking parlour, the finicky Jerseys lost their appeal.

––––––––––

My father told me as he sat reading of travel and adventure after his first heart attack, " One thing which can strain a man's heart boy, is heavy rowing," and, seaman all his life, he would have known of cases to bear out the remark. This perhaps was true of Lovat for in the December of 1951, whilst judging the Smithfield Fatstock Show, he collapsed. The year had been hectic, a tour of

Australia and New Zealand, opening the famous Calgary Stampede, moose hunting in the Canadian north, Chieftain of the Nova Scotia Highland games, and by no means least, the expanding of his livestock ventures on the estate. Moreover, during a family break that summer on a sandy beach in the West Highlands, which looks out over the strong tides of the Sound of Sleat to the hills of Skye, his three year old daughter, Tessa, was carried out to sea on an inflatable air bed. Lovat rowed furiously, gripped by the fear of a drowning child. The pair were rescued well out in the Sound, but maybe the cost was to be payed later that year.

For a second time in his life, and he was only forty when the heart condition struck, Lord Lovat convalesced. The latest drugs were flown in from America, and there followed a recovery to many more years as a remarkably active man. However it was timeous to relieve an onerous land owning burden from his shoulders and avoid the possibility of ruinous death duties, and Lovat made over the Estates to his children, with the bulk of the land and Beaufort Castle going to his eldest son, the Master of Lovat.

Never the less, the 'old laird's' interest in stock continued, just as my confidence was growing, and as a shepherd for Sir John Stirling on the western marches of Glen Strathfarrar I'd worked with the Lovat men, and over years, watched thousands of Estate lambs flood the Inverness mart. A passion for the lofty tops of Strathfarrar and for running my own ewes on their fine grazings needed no coaxing when a rumour reached me that some of their sheep hirsels were to be sold off.

A large cut of Blackfaced lambs swarmed into the ring, satin hair on wide heads, open nostrils and sturdy jaws, a ring of red paint round each horn, they were selected, and epitomised quality. Potential buyers squeezed amongst them, feeling backs or tails for a mark of condition before turning to 'the box' and each with his own style, the merest move of a finger, the lift of an eyebrow, began a pitting of wits, wealth and sometimes wisdom, which makes the auction system second to none in fun and fair trading.

Under the hammer of auctioneer James Fraser, bidding climbed. Lovat stood a little back from the rails, impassive, looking over heads, his distinctive angular features set off by a slight tilt of the chin. Head shepherd, Jim MacLean, collar and tie and an exhaustive knowledge of sheep breeding which had taken the Lovat flocks to the top, kept his hand on the edge of the rostrum. He had no need, colour rose on the florid face of auctioneer Fraser in line with the bids. Out of eye corners bidder watched bidder, looked again at the lambs, thought of outlets, margins, and even profits. Fraser was cajoling for another sixpence, they knew his manner, the hammer would be quick at the end. Five pounds, nineteen and six, moments pause, six pounds, six pounds. Smack, and missing MacLean's hand, the lambs were sold, a record for the centre.

Young and buoyed up by the excitement of the sale, I moved round the ring and spoke to 'His Lordship'. He was no respecter of cap in hand, nor was that my demeanour, and his bearing, always debonair and friendly, made an approach the easier. A few general remarks passed between us before I asked directly if it were possible that I might achieve my desire to become a Strathfarrar flock master by taking over, at valuation, one of the hirsels. "Well Iain," he was quiet a moment, looking at the ring, "I appreciate what you're asking," and turning with a thoughtful smile, "But I'm afraid you'll have to speak to Simon. I'm just the stooge."

A man of dignity without ostentation, of bravery and distinction, of a name and lineage carried proudly through the annals of history, who but had looked down the barrel of a gun and seen of spectrum of life in that instant, who but could rise to the greatness of the common touch?

The name Fraser is world wide. If clanship means anything, it means it to those who, through name or blood, flows the love of the old homeland, it's traditions, the spiritual links of a descent down generations. From California to Nova Scotia, from Brisbane to Wellington, the name Fraser of Lovat is revered and Shimi Fraser was fittingly proud to be the chief of a Highland Clan.

Land, its ownership and sound usage, was the touchstone by which Lovat the 'old laird' judged the well being, not only of his own family affairs, but also the sustenance of the wider society of tenant farmers, shepherds, stalkers, farm workers, and a jigsaw of interlocking tradesmen and village businesses. Changing economics for agriculture followed on the boot of the 'Dig for Victory' boom, submarines and food shortages were forgotten, an obese nation began to demand ever cheaper food to enable it keep up payments on a new 'telly' and the latest kitchen. Pressure and control by proliferating Government bodies, staffed by a plethora of green wellied experts, fresh from university, ensured that inheriting and farming large estates became a burdenous patrimony. The political expediency of creating employment by increasing and enforcing regulations spread over the countryside, in company with giant hog weed. The crunch of the 'jack boot' was on the gravel.

As a result of his heart condition commando Lovat retired and the Master succeeded to the Estates, a teenager. Coming of age celebrations at the castle, marriage and family, all fell in their due season, and as Simon Fraser took his place as the 'young laird' the deployment of agrarian based capital took on new direction. The motives were no different to those of his forebears, out of success for his own family would come the greater welfare of those who looked to the Estate as a provider of jobs and security. The old bonds were strong.

A monumental task on young shoulders, but an early grounding in the City with Hambros Bank, and 'The Master' began the movement of capital out of land into commercial enterprise and overseas investment, a far-sightedness, in character with his breeding. Sheep stocks came off the hills. Cattle stayed longer but eventually went. Tenants were generously given the first chance to buy their land. Many did so, my old friend Donnie Fraser bought Easter Lovat, one of the finest clay farms in the north, at a very fair price. With the help and advice of Giles Foster, his cousin, and Malcolm Fraser, a Tomnacross farmer's son, who handled the void between office theory and the practicalities, local ventures developed. Ova-transplant cattle breeding, a salmon hatchery, one of the largest in Europe and a leader in this technology, a mineral water bottling plant which created jobs from a sustainable resource and, in his last year, a major housing and holiday complex had reached the planning stage.

Daring and dash were never absent from the Fraser pedigree. The Master of Lovat played hard to establish a modern enterprise on the base of a fast eroding tradition. He was at his most financially exposed, new skills yet to learn, new investments yet to bear. Had Simon Fraser lived, the courage and driving force of a man of vision would have added much to the fortunes and welfare of the clan he cherished. 'Je suis pres'. I am ready. It was not so.

Cattle ranching has been a lifelong romance and I admired the fine droves of Lovat cattle spread over the hill country in their summer haunts. Eventually I was able to buy a proportion of these breeding cows when the herds were dispersed. They went back to ground they knew, the riverside grazings of Strathglass, and I achieved something of a ranch.

For many years Lord Lovat lived in retirement at Balblair, a house on the ridge above the Beauly river. Down through the trees lies the ford of Ross, one of the great river crossings of the north and many's the drove that must have breasted it's current. I thought of talking with the 'old Laird' of his love of cattle, and telephoned Balblair. It was not a good day, for after a few words he remarked, "I'm just a sick old man ," and I replied I was sorry. "Don't be sorry," he said in a stronger voice, "that's the way it is."

Snow lies still in the corner of dykes but in the March sunshine the crocus blooms, and chaffinch sing in the waiting birch. Plain granite slabs read without pretence.

16th BARON LOVAT, 1871, 1933.

ROSE FRASER, 1926, 1940.

ANDREW FRASER, 1952, 15TH MARCH 1994.

MASTER OF LOVAT, 28TH AUG. 1933, 26TH MARCH 1994.

17TH BARON LOVAT, D.S.O. M.C. 9TH JULY 1911, 16TH MARCH 1995.·

Lord Lovat wrote in tribute to the hills which watch over his burying ground, 'Away to the west, and twenty miles beyond, like giants at a hunting, lie the high tops of Glenstrathfarrar, their shadows changing with the sun'.

The Frasers gathered, the grounds of Beaufort filled once more with the Clan, rallied again, as in a call to arms ringing above the clamour of battle, as in a joyful celebration marking some happening in the line of their Chiefdom. The Frasers, never the last to serve with their Chief in the honour of Scotland, never the first to leave a happy occasion, a Clan rightly believing itself second to none in carrying their Highland heritage as a badge of vigour, fairness and distinction to the corners of the globe. The Frasers came, from croft, farm and factory, from Beauly, from London, from California, frae a' the airt's, to the green swards, to brilliant sunshine and a breeze that brought in its teeth the last snows of Sgur na Lachpich from the heights of far Strathfarrar, and the skirl o' the pipes on its breath.

The young Laird, coming of age, inheritance in the face of tragedy, put all behind, and for the day joined the fun. The clash of shinty clubs, Cameron versus Fraser. Tug o' war, Black Willie, "steady now, steady, heave, heave, pull together lads". Young Fraser took his rope with the rest, kilt, Lord and all, one of his boys.

And the presentation table, Giles Foster, cousin, factor and friend, loyal man who helped the family through difficult times, Malcolm Fraser, local boy, who gave a lifetime of support, Davie Tuach who began his career in the Beauly garage mending punctures and rose to be its Director, and Johnnie Fraser, stalker and friend of the 'old Laird', as was his father Duncan.

Presents passed, gracefully received, then came a Fraser from California. A dirk of days when men lived by pride and word, was handed to Lord Lovat. It's inscription reads, 'Donnachadh, Se mi dobhea cunnich mi orm, se mi do bhea.' 'Frisealach'. 'Duncan, for the sevices the Frasers at Broalan gave to the Lovat family'. The giver, a Fraser of generations parted from his homeland, told of a memorable day of stalking on the sweeping hills of Glenstrathfarrar with Duncan Fraser. The same Duncan whose sons, led by Commando Lovat, gave their lives to the liberation of Europe. And the lasting hills of Strathfarrar looked down, and will remember.

The mantle of generations of a Fraser Highland Chiefdom lies on young shoulders, good wishes flow, a thousand years of bravery, turmoil and success, from dungeon depths, a Fraser has risen, and will rise again.

From the flapping coolness of a marquee we repaired to the Lovat Arms in Beauly. The 'Young Laird' amongst his own, piping, dancing, and 'a wee dram' in Highland fashion, what and where better!

Two dogs, three children and myself, could gather the ewes and lambs down from Breakachy hill in half a day. Heather tops and winding gullies, high with bracken, wide soft flats where the bog cotton blew, and on the sunny face of Craig Dhu, the remains of turf dykes and tiny dwellings, perhaps of shieling times. This hill ground, in common with much of the Highlands had been under sheep for well over a hundred years. No longer did young folk, with maybe a watchful granny, spend the summers herding Highland cows on pastures of fescue and bent, but the benign influence of their modest ways remained, a legacy of diverse life forms bequeathed by grazing cattle adding fertility to the poorest soil.

Wild flower and bird life abounded. Yellow tormentil held up four petite petals, spright amongst the brown tipped moorland grasses. Milkwort bloomed purple and shy, beside stone scatters, but favourite of all, on the neglected shielings, the bold little speedwell, its cheerie blue head matching the sky on a smiling day. Tussocks sheltered the nests of the passionate calling birds, curlew, snipe and plover. And by their homes the bog orchid bloomed, sometime purple, sometime white, and I would bend to catch a breath, luxurious in a bleak land of hill and lochan. Lochans by whose reed edged margins I watched the russet headed wigeon, caught its airy whistle on the evening still, watched the glossy green mallards scuttling about their nuptials, and on the waters of Loch na Gluic, Loch of the Water Lilies, I saw, one October morning, a migrating flight of the graceful Slavonian Grebe. The reeds, bowed in autumn brown, had crinkled ice about their feet, and the birds swam along its brink with little nodding movements of their heads. Just the once I saw them.

Simple sights, engraved on the memory of the molecules that make us part of the oscillating playground betwixt mass and wavelength. Part of the everlasting energy of a cosmos in spirals of destruction and creation. Part of the paradox of death amidst the beauty of a boundless melody which unfolds before a universe, template and womb to the sobbing notes it has spawned.

Less wistful than the fleeting birds, badgers dug into sandy hillocks at our west boundary where the rusting deer fence ran past a lochan full of screeching black headed gulls nesting on its soggy island. Foxes, patrolling their boundaries over the years, turned ant hill turrets green with urine messages and their dark, bone filled droppings, and the wildcat, early on my April lambing round, drinking at the Millpool and keeping his feet dry, lithe as a lynx, crossing the stones with his bushy ringed tail curved low for balance. One spring, perhaps the same beast, taking ducks from the back of our steading, laid a trail of feathers to a slab angled cairn on the shoulder of Craig Dhu. It was dry and quiet, I put aside the rifle and looked down on the spread of Breakachy, its blend of give and take survival, and I envied the freedom of the hunter, who lived, and took only his need.

Pylons traipse across the south side of the ground, crossing a ruin known as the Bochan Dhu, and Hugh MacKenzie got his disturbance money for 'caterpillar' tractors crossing the ground. He hastened to the finest tailors in the north, Campbells of Beauly, bought a splendid tweed three piece, and christened it 'my Hydro-electric suit'.

Children and dogs, a zip in the day, and we left from the back of the house with Betty watching from the kitchen window. Alison ran, Hector strode, and Elspeth dawdled. Lassie pranced, Teenie slunk, and old Nancy padded. The breeze hurried, the clouds scurried, and shadows scampered in and out of the sunshine which lit on eager faces. Shouts directed the children, whistles the dogs, ewes called hasty come on bleats to lambs, one glance over their trotting shoulders, and the gathering rolled.

Alison had the longest round, out by the Lovat march, a little running figure, flying hair and a ragged dress. Hector took the middle ground, golden headed and swinging arms. Elspeth sat on rocks. I kept the ridges, sending off dogs should fleeing sheep out pace a gatherer and attempt to turn back. A hurly-burly of bleats and stamping hooves which had the hill in turmoil. Meadow pippets fluttered from nesting knolls, curlew fled the flats, beating wings, piercing warning cries, and to my unkind amusement, the lapwing, with shrill notes and resounding flaps of their wings, dive bombed old Nancy who had reached an age when the pursuit of galloping sheep gave way to snuffling amongst the mole hillocks.

A circuit of the ground, pursuing white woolly threads which undulated along trodden paths and spun together, half a mile from the hillgate, into a ball of sweat and bleats. Darting lambs seeking mother, mothers sniffing each lamb that passed, dogs lapping water, children red faced and brown armed with health. Home by the mill lade track, down to the fank, a clipping and a count of the flock. Any shortfall in lambs was blamed on Mr. Fox's menu. It was family operation with fresh air and thriving appetites thrown in.

Every shepherding hand turned against the fox, and on a quiet September evening when mists rose from the hill burn and bracken fronds began to yellow, I walked over the springy turf of the Garrapol towards the Breakachy gorge. The lambs were sold and away. There was time. Lassie ran a pace or two ahead, I paid no heed until I saw her freeze and lift a paw. A young fox crept out of the undergrowth, whimpering, unsure, and seemingly lost. Perhaps looking for its mother? The hair rose on Lassie's neck, but she made no move. I watched, motionless. Whining and twisting, with the flattened ears of token friendship, it came over to the dog, and stood just a few feet from her, nose outstretched, shiffing. She waited my word. I made three steps, intent of eye, and slowly raising my shepherds crook, I brought its horn handle down on the head of the submissive young being. It lay dead. Lassie barely sniffed, and I threw the body under a whin bush, from where it has, ever since, troubled my reflections.

Unable to divide benefits from bombs, altruism from greed, to mistake intelligence for wisdom, to forget our dependence on a holistic environment, the race is on for mankind to survive the follies of his own ingenuity. Breakachy years were for farming and learning, realising that the clever overnight fixes for increasing food production, demand an expanding control over the natural world. In the ambitions of those who would feed the starving from a pandora's box of genes and chemicals, lie the seeds of corporate domination. A existence of bogus sympathies, denying the privilege of freedom, and the caring emotions that flowed from the pleasures and hardship of working with the natural order of the planet.

At Breakachy we built silage pits, barns and loading banks, fenced and drained the land. We reclaimed the rough out by grazings and made silage to winter a large herd of suckler cows. It was a hard working drive to modernise a farm which had changed little in generations. Several years passed emulous of 'college' ideals, before a growing realisation of the pitfalls, not only for the diversity of wildlife but for the health of family and consumer, culminated in my reading Rachel Carsons 'Silent Spring'. Instinct alone told me that the use of D.D.T. and later, the organo-phosphorous sheep dips, made mandatory by the government, was far from wise, and though I didn't apply sprays or pesticides, artificial fertilisers did feature in the system, until I discovered sunshine and clover provided a healthier result. Cattle numbers were reduced to a herd of pedigree Aberdeen-Angus which throve as a mosaic of natural grasses gradually returned to the fields. To my immense pleasure, masses of daisies, buttercups, and other 'weeds', frowned upon real farmers, took up residence, and amongst them appeared my friend, the tiny blue speedwell. I stopped poisoning the moles, there was room for them too.

Hector worked at my shoulder, a growing boy, and many days walking home up the Letter box field he would come on a four leaved clover and bring it proudly to me, and I would tell him "Hector, you'll be the luckiest boy in the world." His interest in the farm and helping at every turn could not have been bettered and I began to depend on him. One March, before the lambing, Sheena was born, a lively flaxen haired thing, and Betty was confined more to the house. Hector took on the work of a man and together we handled the place. Farming was his life.

Cattle, sheep, tractors and bustle, Old Nancy took to sleeping in the front porch or sometimes in a shady den under the garden rhubarb, if the weather turned warmish. She grew deaf, did as she pleased, and deserved her retirement.

Puppies and old dogs get in the way. At a rambling distance Nancy still liked to follow me but might arrive by a gateway in time to scatter the sheep. The ridges of the great vistas of the Highlands had seen her prime, the silent tops of Strathfarrar were known to her powers in our shepherding days together. But the years slide past, and one summer's afternoon when southerly puffs of warmth made the hollows of the hill lochans a place of the sun, we took children and picnic baskets out by the shoulder of Craig Dhu to the sandy shallows of Loch Fada.

Nancy looked out as we left and I called, "are you coming old dog?"

Clean and cold, splashes and shrieks, never was childhood more vital, more imprinted on the memory that lives beyond the confines of change. I lay and watched. Hector had taken his fishing rod, a token soon abandoned, and they played without a thought for tomorrow, as is bliss of innocence. Beinn a'Bha'ach Ard stood, a little distance, and I turned my glass, and saw in her corries the freedom days of the high tops, the melancholy of yesterday's happiness, the sadness which is the curse of memories.

Towels were wrapped, sandwiches were eaten, shivering had stopped, it was time to go. I glanced up to the heather banks and the road home. A black and white face appeared. Old Nancy looked down on the party, but it was two days before she made it back to the porch.

It was the 3rd of March, I hurt my back pulling a plough at the mouth of the shed. Hector stayed off his studies to help. A hard day for a boy, he fed the cattle, lifted heavy sacks of barley into the bruiser, he was sixteen. Above the Teanassie gorge the fence wires were cut and he fell. I ran, up the stumbling slippery burn. His broken body lay, and I put my jacket below his bonnie golden head.

Gently, I opened an eye. The blue was the blue of distant hills, of the distant hills that see beyond the long horizon.

LOST HORIZON FOUND

Cattle driven south fed industry's nascent sprawl,
Coal and steel, cotton bobbins, woollen loom.
The people forsaking sickle, flail and clay floor gloom,
Embraced silicosis thraldom and a Company 'double end.'
Puritan pupits kept them suppliant and built Empires.

Sheep driven north claimed croft and hill,
Hog and ewe to breed on cattle mouly ground,
The sweat of seaweed creel and hand dug corn.
Pulpit proclaimed ships sailed out and created Nations.

Industrial 'toffs' arrived.
Bastards, bred of self interest, born of greed.
Lamenting land and kinship, the people went,
Torrent and tide carried seeds of strength in dreams of life.

My Grandmother cried.
I watched, fascination tears on crinkled cheek.
Under burning thatch, with child at skirt,
On backs their bundled homes, her people left.

Glencalvie wept.

A spring snow shelter, the gable lea of church,
Their last claim, a name on glass,
My mother thought MacGregor.
Young, I didn't think again.

Sixty years without a thought,
Sunday drawn, I pushed the iron gate at Croick,
The stones called out MacGregor, the gable scroll the same.

The Minister preached, Absalum, my son, my son.
I knew at last, and cried on Granny's knee.